D0248888

FOOTNOTES

FOOTNOTES

HOW RUNNING MAKES US HUMAN

VYBARR CREGAN-REID

St. Martin's Press
New York

FOOTNOTES. Copyright © 2016 by Vybarr Cregan-Reid. All rights reserved. Printed in the United States of America. For information, address St. Martin's Press, 175 Fifth Avenue, New York, N.Y. 10010.

www.stmartins.com

Illustrations on pp. 1, 87, 159, and 225 copyright © David Surman

The Library of Congress Cataloging-in-Publication Data is available upon request.

ISBN 978-1-250-12724-2 (hardcover)
ISBN 978-1-250-12725-9 (ebook)

Our books may be purchased in bulk for promotional, educational, or business use. Please contact your local bookseller or the Macmillan Corporate and Premium Sales Department at 1-800-221-7945, extension 5442, or by email at MacmillanSpecialMarkets@macmillan.com.

First published in the United Kingdom by Ebury Press, an imprint of Ebury Publishing, a Penguin Random House company

First U.S. Edition: July 2017

10 9 8 7 6 5 4 3 2 1

For Adam

CONTENTS

Part IV: Roaming

Life is always worth living, if one have such responsive sensibilities. But we of the highly educated classes (so called) have most of us got far, far away from Nature.

– William James, 'On a Certain Kind of Blindness in Human Beings', 1899

We do not 'have' a body; rather, we 'are' bodily.

– Martin Heidegger, 1961

If it be possible to compress into a sentence all that a man learns between twenty and forty, it is that all things merge in one another – good into evil, generosity into justice, religion into politics, the year into the ages, the world into the universe.

– Thomas Hardy, *Journal*, 1876

INTRODUCTION

THE PRYING SPRITE OF
PECKHAM RYE

I am lost on Peckham Rye. I'm running a seven-mile lasso: a few miles out, a big circle around the common, and the same miles back. I like this distance. I can just about get away with not taking any water and I don't have to worry too much about food before, during or after the run. But I am done in. It is that awful day when the plane trees seem to give off all their pollen in one great gasp. Plane-tree pollen particles are obese compared to those of other plants and trees. Londoners have to wander round for the entire day gouging it from their eyes. It's nasty stuff. It sticks to my face and gathers in the creases of my arms and neck. What havoc it must be causing in my lungs I can only guess, because they hum and whine like a legion of wasps trapped in a bell jar. Despite this, I am enjoying the run and I love coming to Peckham Rye because it seems to possess a kind of magic that makes the pasts, both real and imaginary, present.

As a child the poet and seer William Blake had visions of angels in these trees. Today, jewels of broken glass are strewn across pavements and there are queues outside the locksmith's because there have been riots. The sun warms the earth beneath my feet, everything looks saturated with pigment, and if I can keep going long and steady enough a wave of ecstasy will soon break over me. And when that comes, the burrs, the static and the clamour of the everyday will be washed clean from me. Virginia Woolf called them 'moments of being': those few seconds when we are only ourselves, and our senses reverberate with the pleasure of the present.[1] It is when what is buried beneath the down of the everyday becomes immediate in a way that is raw and urgent and overwhelming. (Runners call it 'the high', and when it kicks in, you feel calm and invincible, super-sensitive to your surroundings, and you know that at that moment there is no one else in the world enjoying a better experience.)

It is 2011, and although I have been running badly for years, I have suddenly found myself able to access longer distances. So every day I run, and I run, and I run. Compelled to do so, but unsure why, I don't think I have paused to consider it in any detail until today and my encounter with a sprite of Peckham Rye. Yet here I am, many miles from home, with nothing on my feet, whispering along on the grass in the summer sun.

With *pizzicato* steps I continue along the worn pathway. I am now skirting the edge of the Rye – an unfenced enclosure, centuries old, that has withstood waves of suburban expansion in south London. It is ringed by estate agents, petrol stations, eighteenth-century villas, and post-war council blocks built on the bones of bombed houses. There are whitewashed walls garlanded with ribbons of razor wire and from high fences the giraffe-heads of CCTV cameras peer down from their pens, glancing side to side. Traffic and concrete and plane trees to my right; tame, trim grassland to my left.

Unlike the young William Blake, I am not expecting wraiths and angels, but as an eight-year-old in 1766, he had walked here on a summer's day from his home on Broad Street in Soho.[2] The little rogue had wandered for eight or ten miles and must have been exhausted on reaching the climb of Dulwich Hill. The vision that he saw in the trees became the core of his beliefs that ran against the grain in the high Age of Reason in the eighteenth century – it was the beginning of a life-long commitment to the ideal, to worlds above, beyond and beneath – and it formed the basis of his character as a mystic. And too, it was the beginning of a life lived on the very edges of sanity.

From angels to devils: the novelist Muriel Spark used the Rye as the stage on which her demonic antihero Dougal Douglas (a shabby, suburban Lucifer) played puppet-master to those around him; charming them into sexual liaisons, immoral behaviour and murder, before disappearing entirely.[3]

All of this is mixing in my blood: the magic, the alchemy, the feel of the place firing up through the 200,000 subcutaneous receptors in my feet; the smells and the colours seem overwhelming, and the experience feels transformative, even shamanic.

I am in the final few miles of the run. My body swings back and forth to the rhythm of its own movement. I have made it to one of the quiet side-streets off the park, where approaching me is a young preschool boy, the sprite, a few paces ahead of his mother. A credit to his parents, he moves aside to let me pass. I smile. As I do, he squints, the sun hard in his face; eyeing me, he calls out, 'Mum?', his phrasing is musical, like he is singing the square-root symbol, 'What's that man running away from?'

I splutter a laugh, and try to select from my drop-down menu of 'clever responses', but nothing comes. I'm already gone so I quickly shout over my shoulder, 'Old age!' But the question clings like chewing gum. I have heard it before. I am sure I have heard it somewhere before.

For the rest of the run, and for hours, even days, afterwards I think about that question. I manage to come up with some answers: I'm running from my asthma, emails, responsibilities, middle age, my chair, my desk, my chores – I'm pleased with the benign nature of these causes; I don't mind being their quarry because I think I understand them. I'm on the run from my genetic inheritance, too, I think.

My father was not at all active, and although he boasted that he was 'as strong as an ox' he didn't even make it close to retirement. In his early fifties he entered into a seemingly constant cycle of strokes and heart attacks. He was without speech for the last ten years of his life. He died when he was just 62, but seemed impossibly older than that the last time I saw him.

In my early life he had been either a figure of indulgence or violent and unpredictable rage, so I never got to know him then. By my teens, he was practically mute. His inability to communicate made him all the more unknowable to me, his character and personality hidden behind a gravestone facade that could express few of the nuances between joy and sadness. His most common emotion was that of abject frustration at the crossed wires between what was in his head and what came out of his mouth. A man who had written hundreds of poems, played chess for his country, reduced by his mid-fifties to someone who expressed childish wonder at the magical abilities of a TV remote control. Though I try not to think about it, this future is surely one of the things that I am running away from.

As time went on, other, darker, motivations for running began to come into focus, and I needed to understand them.

Without realising, the sprite of Peckham Rye had set me off on a journey that would occupy me for years. The writing of this book became a series of adventures to, among other places, a rain-drenched and precarious mountaintop in the Lake District, Venice's crumbling city streets, the redwood forests of California, the world's most advanced running clinic and laboratory in Boston, and to Michigan, where I met researchers at the forefront of advances into environmental psychology.

But this is not just a book about running, and it is not only for runners. If you are a cyclist or a walker you will learn, here, as I did, many of the things that you already know instinctively, but have not put words to. When people ask you why you do it (run, walk, cycle, etc.), you'll have an answer that you know in your heart is a little rehearsed and doesn't fully capture your reasons for doing what you do. You know deep down that what you do is right for you, but you can't make total sense of it. You will find many of the answers articulated here.

Or perhaps you are like many of the people whom I meet who are waiting to be persuaded to go outside a little more often; if so, this book is for you, too. There are no endurance races here; I have become a fairly average runner, who runs average-to-long distances, in quite average times. The things I've learned and the adventures I've had while running are within moderately easy grasp of anyone willing to give it a go.

I turned up an embarrassment of riches when it came to investigating the benefits and rewards of running, beyond simple 'health' and 'fitness'. But I think what deters many people from trying or persisting with running is the idea of it as a competitive sport. Some people might be surprised that 10 per cent of the UK population ran in the last year, according to research conducted by Sport England; that's about 6 million people. Recent figures suggest that gym attendance and swimming are in slow decline, while running is on the rise, but the numbers of us regularly running could still be much higher. In other categories of collected data (the 'recent inactive' and 'inactive' – i.e. those who had not run in the last three years) the words respondents used to describe why they were distancing themselves from running included: 'painful', 'hurts', 'repetitive', 'injury' and 'boring' (the list goes on, and the words do not improve). Why is this? The 10 per cent love it and the 90 per cent think them insane.

Too many of us remember too well our experiences of 'sport' from school. The idea of running as fundamentally competitive is also popularised by the media. I have to urge the many beginners to whom I talk to 'take it easy'. Their innate belief is that good running is about speed – I don't think it is: good running is about quality of experience. So I tell them that it takes guts to go slow, to ignore the other runners who pass you by, and to focus instead on having a good time and doing what's best for you. A time may come to 'push yourself' or 'train hard', but it shouldn't be part of the initial acclimatisation to movement if you are only just finding your feet. Recent research also shows that runners wishing to improve their speed should spend at least 80 per cent of their time at low intensity, so beneficial is it to heart, muscle, skeletal and neurological health. But how can we be expected to love running when the majority of adults in the West are no longer able to stand straight upright?[4]

When I started to think about running, I felt the need to find the answer to that simplest of questions, Why do I run?, and in doing so to find out why it is that we all run. I wanted to know what running was, and that is part of what *Footnotes* is about. But although the answers to that question came easily, understanding them did not, because running proved to be so many different things.

In 1950s Paris, so called psychogeographers set themselves the task of using movement to study 'the precise laws and specific effects of the geographical environment, whether consciously organised or not, on the emotions and behaviour of individuals'.[5] This is where I started with *Footnotes*, but before long, running took me in some entirely different directions. Modern psychogeography is almost entirely concerned with one kind of movement: walking. It is an activity that I love, but it is passive and reflective in comparison to running. Running cannot be psychogeography because the ways that movement alters what is happening in the body's endocrine, musculoskeletal and nervous system, in its organs and cells, on its skin and in its blood, have a richly rewarding effect that can create a psychobiological frenzy of sensual reflectivity not found in any other activity, and certainly not in walking.

For a while, I thought what I was doing was a kind of psycho*jog*raphy. But as time went on, I realised that something was out of joint with this whole model.

It's nearly 200 years since John Keats aimed his famous insult at poetry's then commander-in-chief. With the concision of a career-ending tweet, he accused Wordsworth's poetry of being an exercise in 'the egotistical sublime'.[6] In Wordsworth's best work, like the 'London' sonnets, *The Prelude* or 'Tintern Abbey', place disappears into psychology. There is a celebrated Mont Blanc sequence in his unfinished epic poem, *The Prelude*, where, arriving at the summit, Wordsworth is crushed by the disappointment of seeing the actual place, and he 'grieved/ To have a soulless image on the eye/That had usurped upon a living thought/That never more could be'.[7] The magic of Mont Blanc is only restored when Wordsworth leaves, returns to the lowlands, and is able to take mental possession of the place once again.

Psychogeography seemed a little like this. Places are more than a backdrop for our experience of them. When I was running through environments, was I right in thinking that more was going on than merely my responding to them? I was sure that something was going *back*, that the exchange went both ways, and I wanted to find out if I was right. What I discovered was that the answer lay at the very heart of the way we live now.

Steve Jones, the evolutionary biologist, wrote some time ago that he thought we had about 150 years before we blew up the world, and he recently changed this estimate to about 50. Our relationship with the natural world, to notions of ecology and biology, matters more urgently now than ever before. This is not a particularly new concern; it has been the meat and drink of literature, poetry and philosophy for centuries. And I suspected that running was about the same thing. I was convinced that it put me in touch with my own biology. But was it also a means of developing a greater understanding of the complexity and super-interconnectivity of the natural world as a whole?

I wanted to find out why it is that we seek out views, or natural environments, or try to get away from our screens and give in to the delicate seduction of the mossy path – a seduction that I could never quite escape. *Footnotes* recounts these adventures and stories, and the discoveries that I made out on my runs; it also describes where those runs took me, what running can teach us, and how we can transform ourselves through it. It is about what places and movement mean to us, about how much they matter, and how we can all too easily be lured away from them by modern life. It is, to paraphrase Wordsworth, motion recollected in tranquillity.

First I was a non-runner, then I was a bad runner. Now that I'm a better one, it makes me look back and reassess all the changes that I can see in myself in the last ten years. Did it really put my life in order? Does it help me to understand what my body needs and why it needs it? Does it raise my self-esteem? Does it make me better at my job? Does it nurture my levels of curiosity about the world? Why do I like to trespass, but only when I am running? Why does it seem to help me to focus? And why does running on treadmills feel so unbelievably strange?

This book is about the abundance of amazing things that I have learned about the body, the landscape, and the ways that we cut through it when we run. It is about how running has become a part of who I am and how it makes my life sustainable. It keeps me going, because I don't want to be without the uncluttered disorder of the natural world, and experiencing my body while I'm in it. I don't want to miss out on its transformational potential, and I cannot bear the thought of forgetting what it is that I am. Whatever it is that running and the environment continue to give back to me, it helps me to concentrate on the things that I know matter most. It also helps me to make the kinds of decisions that I want to continue to make. It has become a kind of playful overturning of the named, labelled, directed and focussed life that someone of my age ought to be leading. It allows me to step off life's pathways and into the bracken; to turn my back on the fingerpost and tumble into the weeds. Running has changed me so completely that, now, even the sight of a landscape painting instils in me a deep desire to step into the frame, and beyond it. To run toward the horizon, feeling the cool grass beneath my feet, and be gone.

PART I
SENSING

1.
FOOTNOTES TO A BODY OF KNOWLEDGE: OUR BODY'S INTELLIGENCES

THE SOUTH DOWNS AND BOSTON

My great religion is a belief in the blood, the flesh, as being wiser than the intellect. We can go wrong in our minds. But what our blood feels and believes and says, is always true.

– D.H. Lawrence,
letter to Ernest Collings, January 1913

Those who wish to forget painful thoughts, do well to absent themselves for a while from the ties and objects that recall them.
– William Hazlitt, 'On Going a Journey', 1822

Barefooted she proposed to perform her pilgrimage; and her clean shoes and change of snow-white thread stockings were to be reserved for special occasions of ceremony. She was not aware, that the English habits of comfort attach an idea of abject misery to the idea of a barefooted traveller
– Walter Scott, *The Heart of Midlothian*, 1818

FINDING OUR FEET

If our bodies know best, why are they easily injured when we do something so seemingly natural as running? On the one hand, running seems very easy, but that is only because our bodies are so very good at it. The most powerful supercomputer on the planet cannot administer the sheer number of computations it takes to run, untethered, on two legs. Wherever our running intelligence is, running is not all conscious to us and is so complicated that only the T-1000 Terminators of our imagination are able to do it. Because our running knowledge is buried so deeply within muscle fibres, cells and our DNA, we have to accept that we cannot fully articulate its complexities. That doesn't mean our bodies don't know how to do it. We may feel our way towards understanding the alchemy of running by learning how to use our senses, getting them firing, and seeing what they are capable of, and accepting that our bodies know more about running than we ever will.

Our running intelligence is unquestionably there, but it is not so easy to lay hands on, because in many of us a proportion of it has been forgotten. It's like reading a whole oeuvre of Austens or Atwoods and keeping them on your bookshelf. The details of each book may have faded in your memory. The plots don't quite make sense as you remember them. Some of the character names have gone. But in those books there will be snippets of dialogue or dramatic moments that require no effort to recall, because for whatever reason they stayed with you, adhered to some bit of knowledge you already had, or clung like burrs because the books knew some emotion of yours that you had never shared or even named. Likewise with running, once you have garnered a little experience, you won't need to remember how to push forward from toe-off, or how to counter-rotate, because these things will have stayed with you and become part of your vocabulary of daily movement. Just as with running, all the forgotten details of those books are in your library; you just have to work a little to recover them.

There are some pretty basic things about running that may have fallen from your habits of daily movement somewhere along the way between childhood and adulthood. It's not just that these are things that you will have forgotten; you may even have forgotten *how* to know them. So there are obvious things like: When you run are your gluteal muscles firing? Are your soleus muscles so atrophied that they can no longer function effectively during plantarflexed landing (with the foot tilted slightly downwards)? Because you have been mostly sat down since the age of five, there's a good chance that you also have an anterior pelvic tilt. You can look in a mirror and see some of these things – like poor posture, or that convex arch in your lower back, or the hunch in your shoulders. You can feel your soleus muscles – for some people they will be so insubstantial that they don't even know they are there. You can even feel your gluteals as you run, and see if they are firing, or just bobbing around like everything else seems to. Many of us have to train our bodies back, and it's hard and it takes time. And I don't mean a fortnight of heel-raises done while attacking the washing up, I mean *time*.

There is good news; you are already able to do most of what is required for you to run. The bad news is that everything else you will have to learn and remember. So, these first chapters are about our bodies, everything from mechanical muscle function to what D.H. Lawrence called the 'blood consciousness', his term for innate, embodied knowledge, a concept that has its roots as much in ancient Daoism as it does in modern philosophy.

Before I go on to explain some of the incredible things I discovered about running during the writing of this book, I'm going to tell you a little about how I got here.

LOSING YOURSELF ON THE SOUTH DOWNS

Most people's acquaintance with running begins at school, where some flourish at it, but most of us are taught through the brutality of cross-country runs and asthmatic sprints to steer clear of such a horrid, painful and pointless activity. And here in education, as with running and so many other aspects of my life, I proved to be a late starter, dawdling for decades after the starting pistol had been fired.

In 2003 I tied up a loose end that I had been tripping over for years. I had left school with little except pocketfuls of sticky sweet-wrappers and resentment. At the age of 16 I saw my final exams as little more than a relief from the boredom of class attendance. I hated being at school, and did my best not to attend at all in my final years. I think an E in Maths was my best result. Mostly, I got a U – the same grade I'd have got if I'd failed to show. Biology I finished early, and sat in silence while others around me seemed to be writing with such intensity that they scratched splinters of wood from their desks. In the final moments I noticed that someone next to me was writing on the back flap of their exam paper. I had stopped on the final right-hand page because that's where all the previous papers I'd sat had finished. Having idled there doing nothing for half an hour, I turned the page in horror as I saw an unlabelled diagram of the female reproductive organs. 'Pens down, please.' Thirty years later and I can still remember the injustice of being denied probably the only opportunity I had to bag some easy marks, and all for the want of three simple letters: PTO. They awarded me one letter for my efforts: U.

In English (a subject with which I am now better acquainted) I fared equally poorly. What that boy wrote about *Far from the Madding Crowd* and *To Kill a Mockingbird*, two novels which to this day I have still not read, I can only guess. U.

I segued into a number of not-so-good jobs, the low points being an attack by a drunk wielding a cheeseburger, having to gouge vomit out of an overflowing urinal, and being threatened with being put through a window for not filling out a coach ticket in a timely enough manner. A pattern began to emerge where I seemed to be staying less and less time at each job; with each new role I reached the boredom threshold sooner. By my mid-twenties, and after about ten jobs, I had had enough. I wanted to go to university.

I cracked my knuckles on some Open University courses, and I was ready to play.

I signed up to read English and began with a great deal of trepidation, but soon discovered that in the time since school something had changed in me and I was able to apply myself. Seven years later, with a BA and an MA behind me, I completed my studies when I finished my doctorate in 2003.

It was sometime during the seemingly endless days of writing my PhD thesis that I took up running. I lived in a hamlet in Sussex where I could open the back gate, cross a road, and from there could be on rural footpaths with stupendous views for miles. My then partner would go out to work in the morning and my days would vary between sitting at my desk and looking out of windows for hours, and watching reams of really loud, stupid films (there were no neighbours to disturb). Guilt would eventually wrench in my gut and I would settle into work properly sometime in the afternoon. It sounds blissful now – I had no formal job because I was on a scholarship, but it was boring, too, having no work friends and living deep in the country with no one to talk to from morning till night.

I started slow with my PhD, but I still managed to do it quite quickly. By the end of it I worked in such a sustained manner that I began to see stars, like when Jerry bashes Tom on the head with an unfeasibly weighty mallet. The way I could dim the flicker of the stars was to wash them in those long-distance views towards the South Downs.

Feeling a little time-poor in my writing-up year, I began to run so I could cover more distance in less time. I remember periodically suffering with shin splints (where the anterior tibialis tears away from the bone). I now know that this is a common complaint among beginners; I probably bought some new trainers to remedy the condition.

From the very beginning of my running career I knew in my heart that there was something lurking in the long grass other than 'exercise'. From the moment I started, I knew it was giving me more than I asked from it.

It was also around this time that I started to see physios every once in a while for minor ailments. This usually entailed me stopping running until whatever was troubling me went away. Then, a few weeks or months later, forgetting all, I would start up again and be able to keep going for eight, ten or twelve weeks before I would get injured and the cycle would begin again. This sequence went on for a few years: through a move to Brighton and a new job (a step-up to a research fellowship – and with the likelihood of fewer burger attacks).

All I knew about running biomechanics at this point was that there were different kinds of feet and that some needed more support than others. I bought new trainers in the hope that I could outsource my running mechanics to them.

The shop I went to at the time was a cavern of running garb, gels, water bottles and watches. The windows were small, the type apple-cheeked urchins look through in Dickens novels, and there was never any room to move around inside. It was basically Ollivander's (the wand shop from Harry Potter) but for runners, and the staff could be equally eccentric. On one occasion a tall, skinny dude with a crazed expression and huge hair came to help me.

'I quite like these shoes,' I told him.

'No! The shoes must be *right* for you!'

He then got me to take off a shoe and a sock.

'Now jump up and down on that leg. Let's see what you've got.'

Not at all sure of what I might have, I looked round for hidden cameras. People idled around me, fingering running vests, choosing socks. What I was being asked to do seemed like business as usual to them. So I bobbed up and down for a bit trying not to catch anyone's eye. Time slowed. Inspiration struck him and he ran off to grab a pair that probably had a phoenix's tail feather in the sole, and I was given the shoes that had chosen me, like a magic wand that had chosen its owner. I say 'given', I mean they cost me £85.

It's easy to be judgemental, but the truth is, if I had hopped instead on my other foot I would have left Diagon Alley with a completely different set of trainers, because Ollivander's first error (among many) was to assume that all runners have symmetrical feet. They don't.

I got by in them: the divination method for choosing shoes must have had something going for it. At the very least, I knew they were well suited to hopping up and down on at least 50 per cent of my legs.

Over the next couple of years, I became more committed to my running because I found I needed it even more than I had in the past. So many things seemed to be going well for me. We lived in a nice house. After a decade and a half together we got hitched with a Civil Partnership. I segued from the nice research fellowship into a good job at a good university, yet I found myself running further and further every day in an attempt to shed an ever growing weight of anxiety that seemed all the more unbearable because I couldn't make any sense of it. More than anything, the pressure that I felt building in my heart seemed to come from a sense of unbearable stasis, a feeling that concrete was being poured all around me and my body was about to be disposed of.

My response, quite naturally, was to run.

I lace up, spin the key in the lock, fold it neatly into my shorts pocket, and I'm away – following the pathways that will lead me towards the long spinal peaks of the South Downs. As soon as I start moving, and my heart starts beating, I feel a sense of relief that something real is happening at last. No longer fretting about the future, for an hour I will drift, distracted by the present as it glides by.

I climb to the brow of the hill at the end of our road and turn north onto a thickly clogged artery of cars headed for the heart of Brighton. I am moving against the stream of traffic to find air. After a mile up this road, the traffic turns hard east or west and I am suddenly alone. A couple of hundred more metres and I cannot even hear it. A network of pathways leads me towards the peaks from which, because the air is clear, I will be able to see the Isle of Wight to the west and most of Sussex and Surrey to the north.

The South Downs are an escarpment of chalk deposits, folded like dough against mid-Sussex's greensand and Weald clay. They are some 60 million years old and they are slowly shifting apart from their sibling, the North Downs. Both stretch in parallel for hundreds of miles.

Where beech forests dominate the woodland of the North Downs, there are only two forests in the eastern half of the South (in Stanmer and Friston). This lack of cover means that from certain coigns of vantage I will be able to look out upon something like a thousand square miles of the South-east.

In 1773, Gilbert White (of Selbourne) referred to the South Downs as his 'chain of majestic mountains', where he saw 'new beauty every time' he walked them,[1] and the nineteenth-century poet and naturalist W. H. Hudson wrote that 'during the whole fifty-three mile length from Beachy Head to Harting the ground never rises above a height of 850 feet, but we feel on top of the world.'[2]

The much underrated early Romantic poet Charlotte Smith devoted a sonnet to this place – although like many she could not resist the landscape's invitation to explore herself. In 'To the South Downs', she asked,

> Ah! Hills beloved – your turf, your flowers remain;
> But can they peace to this sad breast restore,
> For one poor moment soothe the sense of pain,
> And teach a breaking heart to throb no more?[3]

The syntax is rugged as Downs chalk, and the poem sees in this place an inoculation against something that cannot be borne. It ends in the bleak wish for oblivion as a liberation from pain. This desire for the heart to stop 'throbbing' is also found in Thomas Hardy's 1898 lyric to sexual frustration:

I look into my glass,
And view my wasting skin,
And say, 'Would God it came to pass
My heart had shrunk as thin!'[4]

If only we might stop feeling, both poets say.

And when I touch the first grass of the Downs I feel like I have stepped onto a web; that my movement has set it tingling; that this is tightly spun fabric, all connected; that the past is suddenly tangible; that it is a labyrinth in which I am not lost. My absorption is so complete that I feel I am no longer seeing with my eyes, but with the pores of my skin. The last thing I feel is the desire for it to end.

In mile three, I am still headed away and I arrive at Devil's Dyke. It is the longest and deepest dry valley in the UK. Legend has it that the Devil himself dug the mile-long 300-foot trench to flood the churches on the Weald. He was disturbed in the act by an old woman who tricked a rooster into crowing. Thinking morning was about to break, the Devil fled. The last shovel of earth thrown over his shoulder landed in the sea to become the Isle of Wight 50 miles away.

In the nineteenth century, it became one of Sussex's principal tourist attractions. Tens of thousands were ferried up here on the newly laid railway. The trains are long gone. The only evidence of their having been here are the few scattered balls of concrete mixed with an algebra of rusted iron protruding from the tussocky grass.

I have been here hundreds of times, but I have never once seen it looking the same. It is not one place, one view, but an anthology of them that always leaves me wanting to know more about them. At the moment, this place and seeing it this way seem the only things that stir my curiosity.

The acidity of sun-baked cow shit pinches at my nose. The smell is part of a sensory trigger which brings to mind the wildflowers I expect to see. The grass will be peppered with clumps of white clover, which bees will dodge and dash between. There will be sprays of ragwort, the sheep are fussy eaters up here so they shear everything around it, leaving it standing pert and absurd, looking like something a magician might have pulled from his sleeve. There will be dock, common sorrel, silverweed and ground elder, always gathered in a gang, swaying in the breeze – and the custard-yellow petals of gorse, with their heady almond scent, gruff enough to cut your face if you lean in too close for its aroma.

On days like today, the Downs take on a strange timpanic resonance. As my feet strike the ground it sounds empty as a drum. People have farmed the land here for many thousands of years, before the geometric hedgerows, before the cricket pitches and tennis courts that now appear on the Weald below. Others in that time will also have wondered at this same ghostly echo from within the hills, sounding weightless as pumice.

Chalk particles begin their life in the sea. They are the fossil remains of trillions upon trillions of phytoplankton, microscopic inhabitants of the ocean. They are the base of the food chain, and support all life on the planet (producing about half of the world's oxygen). And when they die, they sink to the bottom of the ocean bed, and layer upon layer, over countless millions of years, they produce the solid chalk that we see on the white cliffs of the south coast, and as I look down, beneath my feet, the particles are breaking upon the air like flour ground in a mill.

Virginia Woolf also used to escape onto these downs. In her essay 'Evening Over Sussex' she found displeasure in the impossibility of being able to capture the beauty of the place in any meaningful way.[5] In the most tremendous of views, there are numerous others around you that you will have already missed. She found herself fracturing into multiple selves in order give shape to the torrent of sensation. Finally, she learned a kind forgetfulness that gave her peace. A disappearance of self so that the journey might be 'performed', she said, 'in the delicious society of my own body'.

I am learning that this is how you experience a place, not from the single perspective of your eyes. I think lots of people get this from running. It stirs an elemental consciousness that feels responsive to other life. For there is nothing here that seems not to be living – even the fence posts are covered in reindeer lichen (*Cladonia impexa*). Larches reach with propulsive energy to the sky like giant arrow-points, and there are orchids, blackthorns (whose venomous bite I have come to respect), squinancywort, autumn ladies tresses, chalkhill blues, roe deer, holly, barbastelles, beeches, old man's beard, adders, wild clematis, bastard toadflax, coppiced hazel and crab apple, while the meadowland is smeared in the arterial spray of poppies.

I am halfway through the run: my diaphragm loose, as if my lungs fill all the way down to my hips. My breathing is tantricly slow. I believe I could do this for the rest of the day – I could continue till sunset, and may never need to go home. I can stay in perpetual motion.

I turn towards the slope and in the breeze the pinion of the tall meadow swells and ripples. It sings with bees like an airborne power line. I fan my fingers to caress the tips of the indigo grass. The wild chemical frenzy of the runner's high hits me and I am lost in its compound effects. Nothing matters but this profundity of being in the present.

A little later, on the way back, and despite the painkilling chemical cloud of the high, I feel a familiar dull ache in my knee that stiffens with each mile.

By the time I get home, I am acid bitter with anger and frustration. I enter into days of denial before booking in to see a physiotherapist.

Running was supposed to be freedom and escape. Now, through recovery, it would be measured, monitored, and rationed in little morsels – the opposite of all that I needed it to be.

Maybe it was that night, or the next, or a week later, that we were out at dinner with a couple we knew (my friend and his wife). It was one of the last things that we did together. My weight, which I have always struggled with, had been burning away. And because I had been spending so much time out running in the sun, and swimming in the River Adur, I was becoming tanned (though, if I'm honest, it was as much due to the carotenoids from a feverish bout of juicing). During dinner, the conversation weathercocked to my appearance. I am not good with compliments so I sat like a salted slug and listened. The things that were making me look like I did were happy things, but I was doing them because I unhappy. Neither were they things which I had worked to achieve. They were the indirect by-products of depression. I wasn't trying to lose weight, or get tanned, so how could I take the credit?

And then those words that would stick in my head, to be recalled for years afterwards: my friend's wife turned to him and in a stage whisper joked: 'But I don't understand, what's he running away from?'

The joke, if it was a joke, hit the ground like a safe. There was an awkward silence.

It was probably only a few days later that I went to stay with another friend for a couple of days. Like going out to run, I felt like I was evading terminal indecision. And without realising, I had left my partner, never to go back. A few days became a week, then a fortnight, and a month, and so on.

Since then I have seen similar things happen to others. They take more care of their appearance, spend a little extra on their haircut, lose a bit of the flab. They get their teeth done, start exercising. Unaware, they have set course towards an exit. Before they know it, they have been slowly drawn back, like an arrow creaking in an archer's bow. Finally, they reach the point where they are quivering, bursting with tensile energy waiting to be released. Then they are gone.

On my first night I felt like a weight had lifted. And in the coming days I kept waiting for the anxiety to return, but it never did. All I really needed was to run.

With all that was going on for me, I took rather lightly the news that I had one leg longer than the other. At the time, this was considered a high-risk factor for injury.[6] My legs had been measured before on previous visits to experts. But it was when I returned to see Ricky, a physiotherapist and part-time speed-drummer in a punk band, that he took a few minutes of video of me running. We watched the tape back in slow motion. It was horrific. From behind, and with only two legs, I had managed to create the effect of a drunken tripod evading a predator.

In the first few frames all looked normal. My right heel struck the ground, it jarred a bit, then rolled medially (towards the centre of the body) then laterally (away from the centre) through to toe-off. Fairly normal. Then the left heel struck and we both lunged back from the screen, 'Eugh!'

Ricky's hand covered his mouth in horror. 'I've not seen that before.'

'What do you mean?'

He brushed his fringe from his eyes and pointed at the screen as the stride came round again: 'Anything like . . .' he waited, '*that*.' And we chorused 'Eugh!' as the left heel landed again.

'Your heels are basically acting like brakes, taking all the momentum out of your stride and ramming it up through your joints. That means every next step is like starting from your first one.'

As the video played, he leaned in, squinting to get a closer look, trying to make sense of the weird and disrupted grammar of movement. Then he hit rewind and we watched it again, rapt.

My heels were crashing into the treadmill with each step, but lots of runners do this. What was really strange was that my body had been compensating for the leg differential by bending at the knee. But not forward or back – outwards, laterally, away from my hips, and more strangely – without pain. So I had one straight leg, one bowed. With every foot-strike, the knee would capitulate under my weight, bamboo-bending like it would never stop. While the right foot ran a little heavily onto the arch, the left landed at such an extreme angle that it did not use the arch at all. (That's why if I had hopped on my left foot in the runner's wizardry shop, rather than my right, I would have left with a completely different pair of shoes.)

I was an utterly grotesque runner.

The trainers that I had most recently bought were 'motion control'. That meant that they were fine on my right, in that they stopped my foot from rolling too far inwards, but were worse than useless on the left because their arch support was basically pushing my knee even further outwards. 'Motion control' shoes were sold to prevent over-pronation: to prevent the foot rolling too heavily into the arch. Recent research though has begun to question this.[7] Over-eating, while complex, is measurable. Once you exceed your calorific expenditure, you are 'over'. Pronation doesn't work like this. All feet pronate, but there is no point or angle which can be said to be the measurable limit, because the relationship between pronation and injury is still not understood.

I was trusting my shoes too much, so I decided to work out what sort of pressure I was trusting them with. I knew that every time each foot hit the floor my joints had to absorb around three times my body-weight. When I was beating the drums of the hills on the South Downs, I was running at about 160 steps per minute. I weighed about 80 kilos and I was out for about an hour:

80kg (body-weight)
× 3 (impact)
= 240kg (pressure going through heel, knees, hips, back, etc.)
× 160 (steps per minute)
× 60 (minutes in an hour)
= 2,304,000kg

Conservatively, that was two kilotons pounding through my joints every time I went out, cushioned only by a little bit of rubber that didn't stop it, but merely slowed it down. That figure, converted into London buses, the old double-decker kind, is the equivalent of 192 of them banging through my joints. If that's difficult to imagine, then think of London buses piled 800m high (about the height of two Empire State Buildings).

I was astonished. Remembering my exams, I naturally had to check the numbers several times, because I couldn't believe that the calculations were correct.

As I was slowly getting back on my feet in my real life, living in a friend's spare room, sorting out my debts, while trying to work out what was going on, I wasn't so successful with my running. And I needed it, terribly. I was trapped in the training equivalent of Snakes and Ladders. I would start to increase to a moderate beginner's mileage, and then would land on the board's longest snake, which would take me straight back to square one.

For the next few years, I never got any rhythm going. I tried orthotics that corrected the movement, or supported the movement, or titivated it, or attempted to bypass it. Nothing worked. I bought several pairs of new trainers that I could not afford, but I got injured at the same rate as I always had.

Years passed. I moved house. Then I moved cities. But I kept returning to running, despite it not wanting me as a friend.

What may look like idiocy to some is tenacity to others. Whichever of these kept me going, I never gave up trying new things to keep me on my feet.

A few years on, around 2009, I was living in Brockley in south-east London. My sister came to visit and her children were tootling along beside us as we walked the angular pathways on the northern lower fields of Greenwich Park on a warm sunny day.

Two runners approached us as we chatted. When they came into focus, the closest I can come to describing what I felt was that I was offended. One was shod in the standard clunky trainers, but the other was barefoot. It was an emotional reaction which mixed questions like *why would you do that?!* with a sense of public-spirited indignation – *you might give people the idea that it's OK to run without protection* – as well as vanity: *what right have you to ignore a whole body of knowledge concerning correct running technique that it has taken me years to acquire?!* I thought only in exclamation marks. My sense of offence was so concrete that it took me days before I remembered my uncle.

Throughout our childhood, he was a heroic figure to us. We rarely saw him in person, but there was a black-and-white 8×10 on our wall at home of him stepping over a finish line looking like he had been shot in the back, pain written in every deep fold of his face. His hands were raised in a gesture of either triumph or surrender, it was not possible to tell. Wearing a running vest and shorts (and nothing else) his bare feet, visible in the photo, had blisters like walnuts – they had been cooked on the hot asphalt. The finish-line tape was stretched, about to break, across his chest as he won a marathon somewhere long ago.

Going barefoot, I remembered, was not new. Not in the least. It was all tied up with our relationship with our bodies, with the environment, and the distance that we like to put between ourselves and the natural world. There is a history to this distance, and it is perhaps a briefer history than we might imagine, one that I will come back to shortly.

It didn't take me long to convince myself that here at last was the miracle cure to all my problems: I wasn't the problem; it was my shoes that were to blame. I felt as excited as a convert at an evangelist's rally. What I needed to do was get back to nature, I thought, back to where running began.

Practically on a whim, instead of lacing up to do what was then my regular several-mile circuit of Lewisham, Hither Green, Blackheath and Greenwich, I left my shoes behind.

It was high summer. I ran like a swift: light, darting, quiet – my shadow dancing on the pavements. My feet lapped hungrily at the tarmac like a dog licking its bowl. On the high street I slipped through the squall of shoppers and was past them before they even heard I was there.

I returned ecstatic – feeling I had done something real and seen all the places I had trodden anew.

The next day, I couldn't walk. For at least three days after that, I couldn't walk downstairs without gripping the banister with both hands.

I was desperate to know more.

I had switched from a heel-strike to a forefoot-strike without realising, and had abused muscles in my lower legs that had atrophied, from lack of use. I wasn't aware that I had changed anything so drastic, but there is something in your brain, body, or the sole of your foot that in most people just clicks and changes the way you run when you go barefoot. It's believed to be a simple evolutionary mechanism to get us to run correctly.

When you land on your forefoot, the soleus immediately engages to soften and slow the impact of your landing. It's the muscle that helps to make it possible for you to jump off a chair without hurting yourself (imagine landing on your heels, and that should give you some sense of the miracles the soleus can work.) For many, the soleus muscle has atrophied because it is so little used in walking and heel-running. As recent studies suggest that the shoes we wear actually change the way our foot strikes the ground, such muscular atrophy makes sense when we are brought up in shoes for most of our waking hours from the age of four.[8]

In another recent study, habitually shod heel-striking runners were stripped of their shoes and analysed as they ran barefoot on soft rubber and hard concrete. On the soft rubber, 80 per cent of the runners continued to heel-strike, with 20 per cent switching to midfoot and forefoot striking. But on the hard surface, 65 per cent of the runners automatically changed their technique to a forefoot strike to accommodate their new environment.[9]

A good runner basically needs a Palaeolithic body: one that is used to regular movement, has a strong core, excellent gluteals (from standing and getting into and out of regular squats – because there are no chairs), and with well-developed intrinsic and extrinsic muscles in the feet and lower legs. But most runners today have an Anthropocene body, being one that has been reshaped by modern life. It is a body that is less used to regular movement, with a weak core, overstretched and flimsy gluteal muscles permanently stressed from spending so much time sitting down, lower-leg muscles which are papery thin, and feet which are flat, slim and atrophied from wearing shoes.

The way that running barefoot felt, and the perceived ease with which I had done it on the day, and the sheer quality of the experience, convinced me that I needed to change what I was doing. I knew that I needed to run, and wanted to adopt any style or technique that would make it a more sustainable solution for me.

It's not all joy in the morning, though. On one of my earliest runs, I discovered that others shared my initial reaction to barefoot running.

I was on the climb out of the bowl of Blackheath village. I had to cross the road, so rather than turn at right angles, a break in the traffic permitted me to keep going on the diagonal. Two respectable-looking women were sat waiting for their bus when one shouted to the other, 'Look at that fucking idiot!' I was on the other side of a wide and quite busy road, and I heard it. Then heads turned, a hundred-weight of embarrassment fell, and I quickened my pace to get out of range, past the Railway Inn and out of town.[10] It is an all-too-common response.

In 1709, when the privateering vessel the *Duke* dropped anchor at the Juan Fernández Islands off the coast of Chile, its crew found a man who had been stranded there for over four years. Alexander Selkirk had been living unassisted, farming wild goats, domesticating wild cats to keep the rodents at bay, and putting his feet up in his shelter at the end of a long day's hunt. He had quarrelled with his own ship's captain and had asked to be left to fend for himself on the island, unaware that it would take so long before he was discovered. His story, one that would become a cornerstone of English literature in Daniel Defoe's fictionalised version of *Robinson Crusoe*, was reported with vigour. And the reports almost always mentioned Selkirk's feet, which had become hard and calloused from his barefoot hunting.[11] His shoes had only lasted a matter of months, as had most of his clothes, and in the eighteenth century he stood as a supposedly real example of what was to become a major philosophical ideal of the Enlightenment: the noble savage. The idea that without stultifying civilisation, 'man' can achieve happiness and contentment.

Daniel Defoe uses this idea to great effect. When Robinson Crusoe finds a single footprint on the beach, he is not overwhelmed with happiness, but is terrified of it.

> It happened one day, about noon, going towards my boat, I was exceedingly surprised with the print of a man's naked foot on the shore, which was very plain to be seen in the sand. I stood like one thunder-struck, or as if I had seen an apparition.

I listened, I looked round me, I could hear nothing, nor see anything. I went up to a rising ground, to look farther. I went up the shore, and down the shore, but it was all one; I could see no other impression but that one . . . I came home to my fortification, not feeling, as we say, the ground I went on, but terrified to the last degree.[12]

It is not a boot print (carrying with it all the promise of rescue and the comforts of society, law and order); instead, it is a barefoot print and as such must belong to the 'savage' that Crusoe later calls Friday.

Ever since the 'return to nature' argument emerged in the eighteenth century, particularly in the work of thinkers like the French writer and philosopher Jean-Jacques Rousseau, it has refused to go quietly back to its room. Rousseau wrote against ideas inherited from the English philosophical tradition of figures like Thomas Hobbes and John Locke who believed that 'uncivilised' meant immoral. Rousseau believed that a return to nature meant freedom from the constraints of morality, but that freedom did not entail violence and anarchy.

Down the centuries, the return to nature debate has rightly stayed with us. We see it now in debates over GM crops, fracking, recycling, agrochemical farming, pollution and global warming. The barefoot-running movement itself is another example of this Rousseauesque desire for sparsity and simplicity to govern our lives, as opposed to consumption, greed and over-abundance. The barefoot-running movement promises injury-free running and a more natural, efficient style.

Tracing the barefoot through the periodical presses of the eighteenth and nineteenth century would require another book, but soon after the publication of *Crusoe*, bare feet frequently appear in crime reports of capers and chases. In these stories, being barefoot is considered a key feature of a pursuit. In rare cases it hinders the quarry, but the reports usually indicate that it gave the villain a flighty advantage over the constables.[13] Bare feet, in these and other reports, also indicate pauperism or even insanity. This is the cultural baggage that bare feet have to carry.

Despite its promises, I have had a complicated and tetchy relationship with barefoot running. It is not the promised cure-all that the streams of books, blogs and magazine articles seem to suggest. I now do it about a third of the time; winter can prove impossible, and in summer roads, tracks or pavements are sometimes just too hot to be pleasant – and if nothing else, running should always and forever be pleasant.

For years I felt that I had to defend this agnostic position, because I was not 'on message' as a barefoot runner, until I realised that barefoot running is not a religion, a philosophy, or even an ideology. It is just a nice thing to do when the environment permits. Some people tend to take baths, while other crazy people whom we walk among every day prefer showers (who knew?), but only the most extreme among us would commit absolutely, for life, to one or the other. We happily alternate between the two as our whim and the circumstances dictate.

That uncle of mine (Jim Hogan, though he also ran under the surname Cregan) never had to put up with any of this. He was brought up in rural Ireland in the 1930s. He was the second oldest of nine children. With 11 mouths to feed there was simply no money for running shoes, but run he did, despite his parents thinking it a complete waste of time and energy (theirs as well as his). He did it with practically no support.

This was back in the day when distance running was for tough bastards. He held Irish records for three, four, five and six miles, as well as the 10,000 metres and ten miles. He still holds the record for the less-popular distance of 30,000 metres. He was ranked fourth in the world over 10k. He ran the marathon at the Olympics for Ireland in Tokyo in 1964 where for 22 miles he harried at the shoulder of the seemingly unbeatable Ethiopian legend Abebe Bikila, who set a new world record in the race.[14] There is footage of the run on YouTube and it looks absolutely brutal – few drink stations, no running gels, just thick grey smog, heat, concrete and a handful of spectators. Just before he pulls out of the race, you can see him begging the crowd, gesturing for a drink of water, before collapsing onto the kerb.

He went on to win a marathon gold at the European Championships in Budapest in 1966. No other Irish competitor before or since has won a European gold on the track. And later he ran for Great Britain in the Mexico 1968 Olympics.

He achieved all this without the kind of world-class competition that runners need early in their careers to challenge them (it was one of the reasons he left Ireland to run under another name). There was no running club where he grew up. My mother and her sisters would mark out a track in one of the fields near the house, and they timed him as he ran around and around and around – they must have thought him mad. He had no training coaches, rigorous schedules that he could follow to improve his fitness or build his strength, nutrition advice or sports physiotherapy, and there certainly weren't any running shoes for him to buy.

It is commonly thought that running shoes were invented around the jogging revolution of the 1960s and 1970s, but this isn't true. They have a much, much longer history than that and they tell us a great deal about our practice now.

Back in the day, runners were called pedestrians. As early as 1831, *Bell's Life in London and Sporting Chronicle* regularly reported on local 'foot-races' – where competitors ran for bets. This is my favourite one, from a reported Hyde Park dash:

> A foot-race took place on Friday for 15l. a-side, between Mr Wilks, alias 'The Little Cock-chafer,' and Davis, 'The Running Groom'. The distance one hundred yards; Davis giving the 'Little Cock-chafer' four yards as starting, and keeping on to get over two hundred yards in thirty seconds, both of which he won cleverly, running without shoes or stockings.[15]

Over the coming decades, stories appeared ever more regularly that suggest running was being employed as a short-con, a scam to trick gentlemen out of their money. One report was suspicious of a Glaswegian competitor running for a – then, huge – stake of £50 against an Oxford chap. Suspicion was aroused because 'it appeared very singular that he should have by him silk drawers and such pretty spiked running shoes'. The paper accused the Scot of being a 'public pedestrian', a pro.[16]

Pedestrianism was so popular by the 1860s it even had its own page in sporting chronicles, with its own heroes and legends.

One report from 1865 celebrates the retirement of a 'pedestrian', who was hanging up his running shoes 'in which he performed the unequalled feat of a mile in 4 min 20½ sec'; his future was not that of a hero: the piece reports that he was starting up as landlord of an ale house.[17]

Throughout the nineteenth century, running shoes remained exotic, and were awarded, sometimes with a bonus ale-tankard, as a prize at athletics events.[18] The way that meets are reported suggests that shoes were difficult to come by – pedestrians seemed as likely to borrow as to own them.[19] They were made by specialists,[20] and could be sought out at connoisseur sporting exhibitions.[21]

Around the same time (18 September 1885), another periodical, *Knowledge* (committed to the popularisation of science), ran an article on 'The Philosophy of Clothing', which while concerned with all manner of goods, showed a significant interest in running-shoe design. In it, the author explained that running athletes were unanimous in wanting 'no raised heels', that running shoes must be 'very light, soft, porous and pliable' and 'as thin as possible in affording the required protection and grip. The foot is nearly free, as if bared.'[22] Minimalist running had its first advocate.

Then, in 1890, among a raft of new sporting patents, appeared an absolutely astonishing one: number 15,344: 'William Archer McCrum and John Griffiths, Raheny, Dublin. "Application of compressed air to leg guards as used in cricket and football, cricket gloves, boxing gloves, football boots, running shoes, and harness and saddlery."'[23] Nike Air, anyone? The twentieth-century running shoe was conceived, if not quite born.

The cost of running shoes, as is still the case at the higher end, was prohibitively expensive. From sports advertisements,

RUNNING SHOES.
Spiked, 3/11, 6/6 ·
Postage 6d.

From an 1890s catalogue for sports equipment

we can see that they were available on the high street, or by mail order. A pair of spikes would, in 1893, set you back around 6 shillings.[24] Monetary conversions of these sorts are impossibly complex – while the cost of items can easily be upscaled, their value is a little more difficult because we have more disposable income than the average Victorian could ever dream of. The figure seems, though, roughly equivalent to the cost of a pair of high-end running shoes today, about £100.[25] Exactly what their construction was is difficult to tell, but a newspaper piece from 1848 has them weighing only 110 grams (about the same weight as a banana skin).[26]

To spend that amount on the hobby of one of nine children was surely unthinkable for my grandparents. My uncle learned to run barefoot because that was the only way that he was ever going to be able to do it. For most of his early training and competing, Jim Cregan was not part of a shoe-wearing running culture, until he emigrated from Ireland to England in 1960. His coaches at White City in London put him into spikes more regularly, and although he did well in them (the 1966 gold came at the peak of his form and was a shod run, as was his Olympic run in 1964), he just never felt at home with his feet tied up. So he ran barefoot marathons.

And through all this, he was never saddled with the identity of 'barefoot runner'. It was mentioned because it was exotic, but no one shouted at him in the street for it.

As I write this, he died just a couple of weeks ago. His health deteriorated in his last years, but he was still running barefoot in the woods, several times a week, well into his seventies. I like to think of him running that forest circuit, belonging to it, his feet flecked with tea-leaves of mud, his breath hard, and leaving everyone and everything behind in a ghost's wake.

In his obituaries, he was singled out as the champion he was, and they nearly all mentioned his bare feet, how he ran in a bygone era. Bare feet are, and remain, an issue for us.

Over the years I have had numerous other little run-ins with people while running, but unlike the Blackheath lout they are invariably men. They seem as if they can't help themselves. They tell me to watch out for the broken glass – nice shoes – mind the dogshit – but mostly they just want me to know that they disapprove. They want to be Crusoe and make me Friday. Putting earphones in without connecting them to anything is an effective measure that discourages the sharing of opinions, but I often forget.

When I stayed on Lundy Island recently, out in the Bristol Channel, I ran by a nuclear family when I heard the teenage daughter say to her mum, 'That's like the weirdest, like, weird thing, ever.' In that place, with its tottering granite boulder towers, outsized mountain goats with their six-foot horn span, and chatty Soay sheep, I cannot believe that a man not wearing shoes on warm bouncy grass on a sunny day was the weirdest thing 'ever' to be seen that day. The truth is, although I frequently wear them, and with all that I've learned, I think shoes are a bit weird.

It was as early as 1991 that research began to appear which suggested that shoes may not be helping us to stay injury-free. Sports scientist Steven Robbins's research suggested that the kind of sensory numbing that shoes encouraged made us less able to judge those forces that we were loading into the ground when we ran. He also discovered a much higher injury rate among runners in expensive trainers than those in cheap ones.[27]

We already ask so much of our feet. We want both mobility and stability from them. We want them to be soft, supple and attractive; while also being strong, tough and able. And then we add unnecessarily elaborate mechanisms to these already unbelievably complex and knowledgeable organs.

In the foot, there are already sophisticated technologies for dealing with the outside world. The sole of the heel is made of multiple layers of skin, and even with a thick layer of fat underlying it, it is still sensitive to pressure. That layer of fat below the heel is clever, too. It has to bear most of our weight when we stand, and when we walk, between 1.2 and 2 times our body-weight. The fat that does this isn't just flubber. It is around a centimetre thick and consists of layers of tightly packed cells a bit like bubble-wrap, and it distributes force both vertically and laterally, providing us with necessary shock absorption while walking.

For all its tech, though, this part of the foot is very unstable. It is basically fat on top of a bone. While running, if you land on your heel, you are putting a lot of faith in the world to look after you, because the number of major gait-stabilising muscles in the lower leg that are activated in this movement is zero – just fat and bone crashing into earth.

Touching down with the fore- or mid-foot engages instantaneous vertical and lateral muscular support and stability structures, and enables sensitivity to balance and terrain, as well as spring-loading the movement with energy all the way through to toe-off. This kind of landing allows the body to read and respond to the movement in a way that heel-impact cannot. One of the reasons for this is that while both parts of the foot are sensitive to pressure, only the forefoot is also sensitive to touch. (If you get someone to tap you on the heel, you will not be able to tell how many fingers they are using to do so until they move much higher up the foot.)

A quick experiment will demonstrate the depths of difference between form and function in the rear and forefoot. Wait for everyone to go out. Put on your favourite song, as loud as the neighbours will stand. Now dance. Throw all your best shapes. Grind out a mythic performance. The only rule is that you have to keep your heels off the floor and stay on your forefeet (the term for this is 'plantarflexed'). You can probably do all the things that you'd like to do. Now repeat the experiment, but the rule this time is that only your heels can touch the floor, your forefeet must be raised ('dorsiflexed'). The full horror of the limited movement of which you are capable should be evident. Whatever our heels are for, it's not this. This kind of primary movement (dancing is so inherent that even babies try it before they can walk) needs coordination and constant sensitive feedback that is not available through our heels.[28]

Think of the high-impact arts and sports that really demand precision from those performing them: ballet, gymnastics, wrestling and the martial arts – why do none of these require big cushioned shoes to protect them from shock? It's because they need their feet to respond exactly and predictably to their world, and they can't do this in thick shoes.

The forefoot landing is also shared by a great many more species than we may realise at first glance. The majority of mammals, birds and dinosaurs that have lived on the planet are thought to have descended from a single pentadactylic (five-toed) vertebrate. Most species today either have these features, or show evolutionary remnants of having once possessed them.

Today, in the structures of their feet, hooves or paws we can see that most animals that run, from zebras to wallabies to squirrels, anatomically speaking run on their toes or fingers – their heels do not touch the ground while running. Horses' hooves are an anatomically absurd extension of the middle finger. Even elephants, whose soles look completely flat, land on their heels while walking (like we do). They have knees (like we do), but they have a fatty layer beneath their heel that is a little different to ours. Our 'fat pad' leaves our feet relatively flat, but an elephant's is so large that it means they actually walk on tiptoe, as if in high heels, because their skeleton is raised by a massive six-or-so inches of solid fat which absorbs the impact of their five-tonne body-weight.

The technology in our feet doesn't end there. When you run barefoot, the callouses you develop are made of the protein keratin – the same as a rhino horn – and we may infer that barefoot running is so natural that the athletes with their hardening callouses are basically growing hooves.

For all these similarities, there remain substantial differences between human feet and those of our nearest relatives. Primates' feet have different uses from our own, with a big toe that works more like a thumb for gripping and negotiating, while our big toe is for balancing and locomotion. But recent research is beginning to show that there are more links between the two than a first impression suggests.

The mid-tarsal (or transverse tarsal) joint in orangutans is a super-flexible set of articulations up towards the ankle. For years, it has been assumed that one of the most distinctive aspects of our species' feet was their rigidity, but new research has begun to question this.[29] The human foot is nothing like as stiff as was previously believed. In most of us, our mid-foot still has a flexible joint. It is the soft tissues that provide the rigidity, and it is this that has made a big difference to our life on the ground. The fact that the mid-tarsal is flexible goes some way to explaining how it is that we were able to make the move out of the forests and onto the plains and veldts, and prove successful in both environments.

The design of our feet is the best that nature has come up with over millions and millions of years. So, if we think back to the advanced supercomputer that is incapable of running, do we really believe that our running shoes know how to? They don't even have Wi-Fi; how can they possibly know our bodies better than we do?

With all that said, I still run in shoes. The ones I have are light and protect the soles of my feet from flints and gravel. They must be flexible to allow my arch to stretch if it wants to, and my forefoot and toes to splay when they land if they need to. I need to be able to slip them on and off easily so I can go barefoot as the terrain permits. I run holding them, like some runners carry a water bottle.

The foot is at the very frontier where places try to acquaint themselves with us. And there is nothing further from our brain than the soles our feet. Perhaps this is why they have their own 'consciousness'. Between the sole and the brain there is a busy superhighway of nervous information that rips back and forth. Alongside our normal five senses there is information of all kinds crossing us from one extremity to the other: proprioceptive (our position in space), nociceptive (pain), magnetoceptive (whether we are facing north, a controversial one at best), equilibrioceptive (balance), and thermoceptive (heat); tension sensors in the body are always active, as are stretch and pressure receptors. The foot is a sensitive member; it needs to be to achieve so much without our having to actively think it.

Anyone who has stepped on a toy soldier or an upturned plug will know how much our feet can hurt. But you rarely encounter anything so hostile while running. When I do step barefoot on a pebble or the corner of a paving stone, something happens that can only happen without shoes. There is a protective reflex mechanism that kicks in before you get the opportunity to feel the pain. During movement, the pistons of the muscles are firing and relaxing. But the moment that something hard begins to stick into your foot, an electrical impulse softens the muscles around the point of impact to minimise the damage. It's an utterly miraculous thing when it happens, and I've never known it happen when wearing shoes of any kind. Our feet are amazing, but they spend much of their time tied up and separate from the world, unlike our hands.

In *The Descent of Man*, in 1871, Charles Darwin noticed that it was the separation of labour between hands and feet that was one of the first differentiating characteristics of the human over the ape, and over the natural world.

> Man could not have attained his present dominant position in the world without the use of his hands which are so admirably adapted to act in obedience to his will. As Sir C. Bell insisted, 'the hand supplies all instruments, and by its correspondence with the intellect gives him universal dominion.'[30]

The hand developed terrific manipulative skill, the feet demoted to locomotion and support. The hands reach out, they caress, they feel, they grip, hold, wave, signal, count, knead, pinch, stroke, play, tap, flick, gesture, comb, slap, clap, cut, type, carve, swear, punch, tickle, peel, cup, promise, embrace, scratch, write, paint, labour, point, heal, mould, speak, and best of all, they touch.

The hand, despite all this wilful business, spends much of its time open, poised to read the outside world for us, forever feeling its way through empty space.

But what of our feet? What are they to make of the world if they are denied access to it?

We use them to balance, walk, run, climb, kick and jump – hardly the endless string of doing-words of which the hand is capable. So they spend most of their time tied up, shod, sandled, or sensually muffled in what is the equivalent of boxing gloves, ear muffs, or a blindfold. All this, when the *barefoot* runner is capable of developing an internal 'materials library' that is specific to the feet, and makes them capable of feeling the similarities between places, even when they look or smell completely different.

One of the many masterly skills of Thomas Hardy was his ability to recall the intelligences of the body, especially those skills long forgotten by city folk. In one of the novels from the middle of his career he wrote knowledgeably and beautifully about the haptic intelligence in the feet of his countryfolk. This from *The Return of the Native*:

> Those who knew it well called it a path; and, while a mere visitor would have passed it unnoticed even by day, the regular haunters of the heath were at no loss for it at midnight. The whole secret of following these incipient paths, when there was not light enough in the atmosphere to show a turnpike road, lay in the development of the sense of touch in the feet, which comes with years of night-rambling in little-trodden spots. To a walker practised in such places a difference between impact on maiden herbage, and on the crippled stalks of a slight footway, is perceptible through the thickest boot or shoe.[31]

Just like experienced runners, who can osmotically absorb information from the ground, Hardy's Heath dwellers demonstrate a peculiar sensitivity to their surroundings. The theme functions as a reminder of the ways that a body experiences the landscape, over and above the merely visual and auditory. Just as it is for runners, the path is not seen, but felt and understood through deeply practised movement.

Our bare feet can help us feel what it is like to be in the world, allowing it to reveal itself to us through all our senses. Our feet can help us understand how our experiences are brief and tenuous, as ephemeral as the single footprint that Crusoe discovers. And this, too, is why Friday's footprint is so perfect. It is a mark left behind of a collision shared. It is also the history of a movement that makes me think of my uncle, and the footprints of his ghost-runner treading the path in that forest. It is both a mark of ownership and of ephemerality – this land is mine until the next tide washes it away. Like the poet Shelley's description of the statue to the once-great 'Ozymandias', 'Nothing beside remains. Round the decay/ . . . boundless and bare/The lone and level sands stretch far away.'

AND SO, AND SO, TO BOSTON WE GO

With all that I had learned about the body, I still wanted to know more. If running is so natural, does that mean there's a natural kind of running? How would I find out? And, if there is, should I adopt it or just keep going? Am I really a better runner than I used to be? I moved towards answering these questions at a snail's pace for a decade (as I said, I'm a late starter), but I didn't foresee that they would eventually drive me across the Atlantic to research laboratories in the States and to meet world-renowned experts in palaeoanthropology.

Many other cities lay claim to being running cities, but Boston isn't like London or Berlin. In Boston runners are everywhere, in the city, down by the Charles River. There are few places that I have been that I have loved as much. No matter what time of day or night you head out there are always runners. It seems to be in the veins of Bostonians. (Even the once beer-swilling Boston rapper, Slaine, is now pounding out sub-seven-minute miles.) It is as European as the US gets. I could, perhaps, do with drinking a little less. I went to a Red Sox match the evening before and it lasted a little longer than I had expected, and I lost my ability to pace myself appropriately. Still, I am not going far today – four to five miles, then I'm heading back into Cambridge to prepare for the next fortnight. For the next two weeks I am either meeting experts in their field, or scratching my head as I read their books and articles in preparation, trying to understand what the right questions to ask might be. Or, if I'm honest, the science behind their research.

Tomorrow, I am going to the Spaulding National Running Center. It is in Cambridge and is the world's most advanced running clinic and lab, using a variety of pressure plates, 3D motion-capture technology to track skeletal movement, tibial accelerometers to track joint-shock, and treadmills to measure lateral, medial, posterior, anterior and vertical force. It is all filmed in extremely slow motion, which along with all the numbers reveals every eccentricity of a foot-strike. In the next few days I will see, for the first time in a decade, what my wobbly gait looks like.

The operation is run by the charismatic Professor Irene Davis. I first read about Professor Davis a number of years ago in Chris McDougall's game-changing *Born to Run*. With degrees in exercise science and physical therapy, she went on to take a Masters and a doctorate in biomechanics. This expertise has enabled her to carve out a career for herself as probably the world's leading specialist in the biomechanics of running, and she has a committed interest in the capabilities of the bare foot. She is as interested in working with elite runners as she is with those who want to run for the sheer joy of it, without ever entering a race.

The research laboratory has a team of postdocs and technicians who all work on various projects to do with running gait. And it is the perfect place for it. Harvard is just round the corner and is a regular collaborative partner, and there are surely more runners here per capita than anywhere.

After a long flight, a good night's sleep, I arrive at the Spaulding National Running Center down the road from Harvard University at a bleary-eyed 7am, which seems exceptionally early to me but turns out to be the start of their normal day.

I instantly warm to Irene when I meet her. We exchange hellos and how-are-yous, but omit names and she immediately introduces me to her colleagues at reception as 'Veebar', but I've had worse. Then, as we march at pace along some corridors, she explains what we will be doing with the morning. She takes me on a brief tour of their two hi-tech labs (both clean, uncluttered and very spacious), then it is time to meet Professor Davis's first referral of the day.

Samuel is an impressive-looking athletic type, tall, strong, with a body that looks like an Olympic rower. He has been referred because of ITB problems (the illiotibial band is a common cause of complaint among runners – it is a long tendon that runs from the glutes all the way down to attach at the knee). Samuel was able to complete an Ironman triathlon, but is now unable to run without some level of pain and does not want to go into another training cycle without having the cause of his injury diagnosed and repaired.

I had expected a 40-minute appointment: a quick go on the treadmill, a look at the video, and an assessment by the experts. But no. It lasts three hours and every aspect of Samuel's long athletic history is combed through and discussed. His body is closely examined, as is its movement and various ranges of motion.

The assessment is carried out with Professor Davis's colleague, Dr Robert Morrison, a physical therapist. Like her, he has a special interest in running biomechanics and has spent his career seeing runners of all abilities in the US. During a quiet moment, I tell him about all the people that I've met over the years who are convinced that they 'can't' run – they would like to but they think they have poor biomechanics, bad knees, hips, ankles, etc. They think that you need a specially adapted body to do it. While I am always ready, with my humanities training, to deliver the 'we possess a body of knowledge' speech, it is nice to hear a scientist's view. So I ask him about the success of the clinic's retraining – are there people who just cannot run?

He tells me that having a limb-length differential, a misaligned hip or flat feet is very rarely a bar to running: 'It is only really neurological conditions that tend to be the deal-breakers.' He explains that something like flat feet is 'more likely to be made than hereditary'. Inherited conditions like this are very rare. 'In any population there is a bell curve for things like height, but just like asthma, too many of us have flat feet for it to be purely genetic.' (About 100 million Americans suffer with flat feet.) There must be another cause. He believes that cause is poor gait; we carry ourselves badly. And much of his work now centres on gait retraining: 'It's normal for us to think of changing a golf swing or tennis serve, but we can change the way we walk and run as well; it's more difficult, but not impossible.' Frequently, with running injuries, 'It's not the body part that's failing, but what we are doing with it; it's usually a driver error. This is a good thing because you can change the driver.'

Whoever has been driving Samuel must have the abilities of Lewis Hamilton. When he climbs on to the treadmill he looks strong as moonshine to me. He has a good posture and sounds light on his feet, but the problems with these kinds of assessments is that the runner is as fresh as a lettuce – not 20 miles into a race, or several months into a heavy training schedule. I also wonder to what extent treadmill running and terra running involve subtly different movements and how much can really be known of one by forensically investigating the other.

During the assessment, Professor Davis deals out astute observations with the alacrity of a practised croupier. 'If people ran the way they were naturally supposed to, I'd be out of business'; 'Training for an event is a high-risk factor for injury'; Competing in a race is 'not a very natural way to run'.

At the end of the assessment, they tell Samuel that he is not using his glutes sufficiently while running, and other muscle groups are consequently having to overwork to compensate for this, resulting in a diminution in his overall ability and stability. Professor Davis explains that although his gait misalignment is mild, the Ironmans have been magnifying this weakness and exposing it over time. They tell him that he needs greater core strength and that over the coming weeks they can retrain his gait for greater pelvic stability.[32]

Later that afternoon, when I meet with Professor Davis, it is immediately clear that she is someone who really loves her job: coming to work, sorting people out, doing some research, barefoot running a little, and going home satisfied from a good day done.

Their goal at the centre, she explains, is to get anyone who wants to do so to run, injury free. She talks engagingly about how weird it is that so many of us get injured. She knows from her own and others' research that getting a running injury ought to be like a fish getting a fin injury, or a bird getting a wing injury. These things happen, but are very rare compared to their frequency in knock-kneed and hunchbacked Anthropocene hominin. The range of reported results for running injury are astonishing: most studies show that the majority of regular runners are injured at least once during the course of a year.

When she begins to tell me that her most recent research paper is about the core, I am about to roll my eyes because I am so bored of hearing about it, but she pre-empts me. She says that we hear so much about having a strong core, but 'I think we need a strong core in our feet.' It is there, after all, that our upright structure begins and if that is not strong, then we are compensating, literally, from our toes to the top of our head. She has a poster on her wall showing the sole of a foot, but instead of an arch it has a tight six-pack.

While strong feet will help, surely they can only be the starting point for biomechanical alignment; it is the whole body that runs, so what other techniques are there for gaining a better gait?

She tells me that everyone loves a quick fix, so retraining your cadence (the speed that your feet hit the ground) to about 180 steps per minute, or working on a 7-degree forward-lean from the ankle, are easy things to do. But the kind of treatment she enthuses about 'takes work'. Many runners do too much too soon and get injured (which is why Vibram – the 'foot glove' manufacturer – got into trouble in the States with a class-action lawsuit and had to change their advertising).[33] Davis continues, 'It takes years to make your calf muscles weak. But you have bigger calves than anterior-tibs [the muscle that runs along the front of the leg and attaches to the shin] for a reason . . . When you run in the way that you do in a cushioned heel, you don't engage those muscles. It would be like going to the gym and not doing what you need to do to lead up to lifting a 100lbs. You would get injured. The muscle groups that need particularly to be fortified are the posterior–medial muscles: calves, posterior tibialis and arch muscles.'

Elsewhere, Davis has used the metaphor of the 'neck brace' to explain our reliance upon shoes and prophylactic support. She sees orthotics as having a place in medicine and podiatry, but only as a temporary measure, like a physio might prescribe a neck brace. Because if we were to wear a neck brace permanently then our neck and shoulder muscles would atrophy to the point where we might no longer be able to support the weight of our head.

She shows me a 'before and after' video of a runner who had been reliant on orthotics and was loading over 120 body-weights per second into his frame from heel-striking.

My favourite, though, is one that she calls 'the eggbeater'. The runner, filmed at foot-level from behind, looks just like a lumpen egg whisk, with the feet dizzily winding around one another, rather than up and over. As I look at 'the eggbeater' I remember the video of my own gait years before and I think *at least she is symmetrical*.

At the end of our chat, I rummage in my bag, because I have a plan to test her skills. I take out my oldest, most beloved shoes – my worn out Nike Frees, which have been on so many adventures, and I ask her, proffering the muddy soles for her to study like a palm reader, 'So, what kind of runner am I?'

She looks at the soles of the shoes, and all around them.

'And you only ever run in these shoes?'

'More than 99 per cent I'd guess.'

She looks at them both individually, compares various bits of them, checking for wear and asymmetries. Then she drops the bombshell.

'Well, you think you're a forefoot-striker, but when you get tired, you fall back onto your heels. You probably do that because these shoes are allowing you to outrun your natural ability.' She assures me that I won't do this in a truly minimalist shoe. No cushioning means full sensory feedback when you're tired. Any cushioning at all on a running shoe will mask this. She explains that the further back on your foot that you run, the greater the likelihood of what they call 'transients', loading-spikes of high impact.

Many minimalist shoes are not minimal enough, in her opinion. Her definition of a minimalist shoe is one without cushioning, which you can roll up in your hand.

She points out that the wear in the forefoot of my shoes is not quite consistent, which suggests to me that I land more heavily on my left side. But she corrects my ideas again and tells me that it's more probable that my forefoot spins off at the end of the cycle rather than lifting cleanly like my right does. (Which I know is correct from the thicker callouses I get on the ball of my left foot.)

I make a mental note to start shifting over to more minimalist shoes and we go on to discuss the technology of the foot, and the future of running. She worries that shoes may get worse. She feels that too many people have turned to barefoot and minimalist running without the necessary preparation or period of adjustment, and that is why we are now seeing shoes like the Hoka.

The Hoka? I realise how out of touch I am with the sorts of shoes that are sold in today's running shops. And I remember that the trainers I've just shown Professor Davis are at least six years old, meaning they have totted up thousands of miles.

She shows me a picture of the Hoka. It is an ultra-cushioned shoe that looks like something that you could jump off a building in. They could double up as a swimmers' float. They are so tall that time travels more quickly up there when you wear them.[34] They are still quite light in terms of weight, but the sheer voluminous mass of the cushioning would make any kind of proprioceptive feedback difficult. The shoes are becoming increasingly popular in the States. They are expensive and, like other running shoes, need to be replaced when they wear down.[35]

If you really want to get into it, leverage is also an issue. Professor Davis talks me through some graphs and images to explain how shoes that may seem built to protect may exacerbate certain conditions. The lever that we are interested in can be understood if you imagine looking at the foot from behind at floor level, as with 'the eggbeater'. With a bare foot, the length of the lever is measured from the floor to the ankle joint. If you are running barefoot, and pronating a little (10 degrees, say) then the lever turns inwards (medially) when you land, the ankle joint is pulled with it by only a few millimetres. In 'barefoot' shoes with no heel this lever is lengthened, but only by a few more millimetres (from the rubber sole), so although it adds to the medial motion of the ankle, it is only a miniscule addition. But a motion-control shoe or a deeply cushioned one can add centimetres to the floor-to-ankle lever. With a much longer lever, the ankle joint is forced through more motion, the irony being that this is the motion that it is supposed to be controlling. So despite the extra cushioning and the motion control, it is the extra height of the ankle joint that can place extra stress on the entire mechanism.

Time to break out the maths skills that didn't get me through those exams. Basic trig.

With a lever-length of 8cm, and a modest 10 degrees of pronation, then medial ankle movement will be tan $10° \times$ 8cm. This means the ankle rolls medially about 1.4cm with each foot-strike. At about 1,400 steps per mile, on a 10-mile run, therefore, the following figures apply in the case of a barefoot runner:

1400/2 (i.e., total steps divided by number of ankles) = 700
700 × 10 miles = 7,000 steps
× 1.4cm (8cm × tan 10°)
= 98 metres of total medial ankle motion

Now a shoe with a good heel with lots of extra cushioning could add as much as 35mm to the lever:

1400/2 = 700
700 × 10 miles = 7000 steps
× 2.03cm (11.5cm × tan 10°)
= 142 metres of total medial ankle motion

The lengthened lever could add an extra 44 metres of medial roll to your ankle – every millimetre of which has strained and pulled on your tendons and ligaments because they are not used to the additional movement that the lever has added.

That is quite a difference given that the cushioning is supposed to protect the wearer from injury.

Then, with the vehemence of a slam-poet delivering their final hammer-blow, Professor Davis tells me, 'Twenty-six bones, thirty-three articulations each with six degrees of freedom of motion, twenty muscles, four layers of arch muscles, a beautiful structure that is meant to be a mobile adaptor, a rigid lever for push off, a base of support, spring-like: all those characteristics and we contain it in a shoe that doesn't allow it to move as it should? And we run in those shoes, and it changes altogether our landing pattern and the way we run, and we are a surprised that runners are getting injured at the rate up to 79 per cent each year?'

I resist the temptation to hold out my fist for a 'bump'.

At the end of the interview Professor Davis invites me to be their 'special guest' at Harvard Science Week, where I get to play scientist for the night and talk to the public about running gait. I also get to come back for a more detailed tour of the facilities and a series of presentations by the technical staff. She takes the trouble, too, to equip me with a nice route for a barefoot run round the Charles River, downtown. Most exciting of all, she books me in for a gait-analysis the following week. But before that, I have another world leader in their field to visit, at Harvard, a man whose work, more so perhaps than anyone else's, makes the biological case for our bodies knowing best.

About a decade ago, around the time that my physio and I were watching the video of my wobbly legs, palaeontological research was beginning to appear in the States that suggested we may not need specially efficient biomechanics to be able to run. All we might need is to be human. More than 2 million years of evolution have prepared our bodies for this activity. To paraphrase the Daoists and the phenomenologists, your body knows more about running than you ever will.[36]

If our bodies' design is so good, though, why are almost half the adults in the UK on prescription medication (that figure balloons to 70 per cent in the US)?[37] It is not that Palaeo-hominins did not get sick, of course they did. But the modern human knocks it out of the park when it comes to illness. Preparing for my next interview, I started to read up on 'mismatch theory', which seeks to explain what happens when an organism that is evolved and adapted for a certain environment finds itself in another one.

In the UK recently, doctors were urged to promote the 'miracle cure' of exercise, because it can often be more beneficial than medication. The report (*Exercise: the miracle cure*) says that regular exercise can assist in the prevention of strokes, some cancers, depression, heart disease and dementia, reducing the risk by at least 30 per cent (a better performance than drugs for these conditions).[38] The risk of bowel cancer drops by 45 per cent, and osteoarthritis, high blood pressure and type-2 diabetes by a whopping 50 per cent.[39] These figures are staggering.

I was recently called to the doctors for a health check (for early signs of heart disease, etc.). I went along, assuming that people like me were a self-selecting group of goody-goodies who go to be told that they are doing OK. But I was wrong. He told me I had inherited from my father a 5 per cent risk of suffering a stroke or heart attack in the next ten years, but when I told him how often I exercise he was pleased. And I saw him click a drop-down menu and select the last option on the list. Suspecting that it was only the healthy ones who actually came in to see him, I asked how many did no exercise at all.

'Most of them. About 80 per cent of the people I see do nothing. Drive to work, sit at a desk, drive home and sit down to dinner.' Basically, a whole day in a range of sitting postures. The latest figures published by the Sport and Recreation Alliance bear testament to this. They discovered that while 40 per cent of men thought they met the government targets for physical activity, only 6 per cent of them actually did.[40] 'People are much less active than they think they are.'

Fifty or so years ago more than a third of the miles travelled using a machine were done by bike. That figure is now estimated at 1–2 per cent.

We need to move more than we do. And despite the numbers of people that turn towards running at New Year, or after watching a big-city marathon, many find it difficult and stop within the first few weeks because, like I used to, they go at it too hard, and have little technique, making it completely unsustainable as a long-term form of exercise.

As Robert Morrison had told me, any one of us may have a mild genetic predisposition to flat feet (or type-2 diabetes, for example), but the way we live now is exacerbating what is probably only a mild genetic tendency, exposing it in us where it remained hidden for our ancestors. Such diseases of misuse ravage the west. Alzheimer's, acne, apnoea, asthma, athlete's foot, Attention Deficit Hyperactivity Disorder and acid reflux are all commonly believed to be evolutionary-mismatch diseases. If this seems like quite a high number, well, these are just some of the 'A's, from a list the length of an elephant's trunk.

Modern medicine is a miraculous thing. Without it, I would probably be dead by now. I am not *quite* a chronic asthmatic, but have had the conversation with my doctor a couple of times. I have to medicate for it twice a day, without fail. If I do, I can live normally; if I don't, I can't do things like exercise or laugh at a joke, for risk of bringing on an attack. So while the drugs I take are wonderful, there is an odd feedback loop because it is modern life that has created the condition for which so many of us need the medication. There are no asthmatics in Shakespeare, Austen or Walter Scott. It is, like so many other conditions, a recent epidemic.

The idea of dentistry before painkillers seems utterly horrific (it's bad enough with), but there is no evidence of cavities or malocclusions in the pre-agricultural fossil record in our and other related hominin species. Recent research has shown that malocclusion (tooth/jaw misalignment) has emerged in our species because our jaws no longer have a chance to mature and develop and grow in the way they once did. We spend a lot less of our time chewing, and the amount of processed, mashed, juiced, boiled, grilled, smoothied food in our diet is thought to be to blame.[41]

For millions and millions of years our bodies have responded and adapted to their environment, but in the last few hundred years that environment and the ways we live in it have changed dramatically. The ways that we move through it have changed dramatically, too.[42]

I make my way along Kirkland Street on a cool spring morning. I had been genuinely excited about meeting Irene Davis, but I feel a bit nervous about meeting my next expert. He is Daniel Lieberman, professor of human evolutionary biology at Harvard, and I have come to find out more about his research and the impact that his work has had on the running community.

I arrive at the Peabody Museum of Archaeology and Ethnology a little too early, so take a stroll around the quad. There I see a sculpture entitled *Gilgamesh*. This is a sign. My last book was about *The Epic of Gilgamesh*. I go in, and am directed up numerous flights of stairs, so arrive, despite my fitness, a puffing wreck. After a cross-purposes, slightly breathless, introduction where I try and talk about the statue outside but fail to realise that he is talking about a different one entirely, I start by asking him how his research had become so important in running-science circles.

In 2004, he and Dennis Bramble published a remarkable paper suggesting that our species' running ability has shaped our evolution over the last few million years.[43] Evolution by natural selection is the process where, over long periods of time, certain traits brought about by random mutation prove to be favourable to survival and reproduction. Previously, running had not really been considered to have a key role in our evolution, but Lieberman and Bramble's comparative examination of the fossil record of extinct hominins suggested otherwise. The genus 'Homo' was found to possess some meaningful characteristics.

When I ask Dan to go through some of these adaptations he says, 'Well, there are so many that it's difficult to know where to start. We have features all the way from our heads to our toes.'

First up is short toes.[44] Our toes are minute for our body mass when compared to other apes, but this feature is believed to create greater locomotive efficiency: longer toes require bigger and stronger muscles and therefore more mechanical work with a greater metabolic cost.

The Achilles tendon and the arches of our feet are, likewise, not necessary for walking (most mammals have neither). Both are efficient technologies that use the weight of our body to create propulsive energy while running.[45] Lieberman tells me that there are numerous adaptations in the foot for both running and walking. He has conducted a study into the relative stiffness of the arches in subjects who regularly run barefoot versus those who run in shoes. He discovered that those that don't wear shoes have stiffer arches – a good spring has to be strong as well as reasonably stiff: the strength and stiffness 'help the spring to function better'.

As we move up the body, he tells me that many of our joints (from the ankle through to the knees, hips and lower back) have a larger diameter (relative to the body mass of other primates), suggesting a greater need for shock-absorption in the running human body.[46]

The primary function of the gluteus maximus (so called because it is the largest muscle in the body) is to hold us upright through our stride and when we stand.[47] Other animals have similar muscle formations, but the size differential is nowhere near as great as it is in humans.

We also have, as Lieberman vernacularly states, a 'very twisty waist', along with 'adaptations in the shoulders and the neck' that allow us to counter-rotate.[48] This is essential for balance, as are the canals in our inner ears, which are significantly larger than in other species.[49] They also allow us to stabilise our gaze as we run.

Even our faces make us good runners: small teeth, flat features, shallow snout, each pushes our centre of gravity back so that it is easier for us to stay upright while running.

Moving on up, the nuchal ligament 'acts as a spring to stabilise the head'. The ligament is not found in chimpanzees (for example) and runs from the upper spine to the bump on the back of your head. This ligament prevents the head from pitching forward on impact and is unnecessary for walking.[50]

Physiologist and palaeoanthropologist Peter Wheeler in 1991 first introduced the idea of the thermoregulatory advantages of hominin bipedalism: that we have a sophisticated cooling system that historically gave us a distinct advantage over other predators.[51] Because we are upright, we are hit by less sun when it's hottest.

But we also carry an efficient cooling technology. Our foreheads may seem to sweat more than is necessary. It is not that our brow gets particularly hot: it is the evaporation of sweat that helps the circulating blood to cool around the brain (thereby maintaining an effective working temperature).[52] Lieberman says that it's a system that 'allows us to dump an enormous amount of heat' while running. For example, if a litre of sweat evaporates entirely from your skin, you can lose as much as half a million calories of heat.

I ask him about his own experiences of barefoot running: what is the strangest thing that someone has said to him? He has two stories. He recalled running on a path with lots of space – 'No one was in anyone's way' – when a cyclist passed him, turned and shouted 'Jackass!' as he pedalled away. The second was a woman walking her dog, who exclaimed in disgust, 'How can you run in bare feet?' He replied, 'How can you let your dog walk in bare feet?'

I'm not sure what the cyclist meant, but the dog walker seemed to be saying that it is not safe to be barefoot; if that were the case, we would never have made it off the plains of Africa. Running barefoot is not something to be afraid of, and it amuses Lieberman that so many people are warned away from it because they might hurt themselves, but people in shoes hurt themselves, too, and are doing so at a colossal rate.

We talk a little about people's hostilities; I think it is to do with the taboos of poverty, primitiveness, sensuality and masochism, and a desire to punish attention-seeking. Biologist that he is, Lieberman feels that people's disgust is rooted in hygiene. We don't wash our shoes when we come in from the outside, but barefoot runners always feel the need to wash their feet.

He and his colleagues have now run numerous trials that suggest we already have all the technology we need in order to be healthy runners. But just like Professor Davis (they are both barefoot runners), he urges caution: 'There are no simple answers to anything. Barefoot running is not a panacea, it isn't going to solve all your problems, but wearing shoes won't either.'

He, along with others in his field, is frustrated by the fact that there are researchers out there that simply refuse to believe that huge impact-loading (particularly of the kind found in heel-striking) is injurious to our bodies. It has become a kind of dogma. The idea that someone cannot see that impacts are harmful astounds me: 'Have they not heard of car crashes?'

We finish up talking about the neurological and psychological reward systems that our brains share with other mammals (but that is a discussion for the neuroscience chapter), then we say our goodbyes, and I head back to prepare for my stint at Harvard Science week.

Human adaptation for running is not just one aspect of the body; it is not a distant tune played on a single instrument, but a Mahler-ready orchestra of body parts still very much in daily, hourly or minute-by-minute use. And while most of these running traits evolved in all hominin species, they are most particular to *Homo sapiens*. Humans, more than any others within the hominin family, evolved to run.

In modernity, running is all too often seen as a behaviour that we might choose (like sharing rather than hoarding, saving rather than spending). Whereas the truth is that, as a *Homo sapiens*, you have evolved to be one of the best running animals that the planet has ever witnessed. Running is not what we might do; it is who we are as a species.

For example, if you were to imagine the age of our species as represented by Tolstoy's *War and Peace*, the amount of time that we have *not* been regular runners may be represented by a short experiment. Imagine holding that kilogram of book in your hand. Now find the last page and tear it out. That page roughly corresponds with the period in which we have been sedentarily living in cities, working while sitting down, with food relatively easy to come by, wearing comfortable shoes.

On the torn paper, this is what you will find:

> In the first case it was necessary to renounce the consciousness of an unreal immobility in space and to recognise a motion we did not feel; in the present case it is similarly necessary to renounce a freedom that does not exist, and to recognise a dependence of which we are not conscious.[53]

Tolstoy was arguing that our lives are contiguous, relative, dependent upon and connected to our moment and our surroundings. I want to argue this, too. We are becoming static and our bodies are neither built nor prepared for it.

Evolution is slow; tectonically slow. Slower than it is possible for us to imagine. It is fair to estimate that it will take our bodies a few million years to adapt to these quite substantial changes in our ways of being – by which time we will be long gone. What Tolstoy is really concerned with is the force of history, but we really could be doing more to renounce our immobility, and to recognise our 'dependence' upon what is around us; a dependence which we are either not conscious of or willingly indifferent to.[54]

A few days later, and I am back at the Spaulding National Running Center, about to be measured (and found wanting, I worry). My limb lengths are checked by the lab technicians and I'm ready to go. An accelerometer is attached to the base of my tibia (to collect 'shock' data) and I am given a few motion-capture beads to track the movement of parts of my feet through the cycle. Slow-motion video is to be set up to film my gait in profile, and more dreadfully, from behind. The video footage (forgive the pun) will then be synced between shod and barefoot, providing a side-by-side comparison of how different my running is in shoes versus without. The videos will also be synced to a live graph that will show my impact gradients (how smoothly I land and load my body-weight through the step cycle).

Heel-strikers' gradients are not smooth. An ideal foot-strike has the runner's body-weight loaded consistently (where the force of landing is slow and performed with less shock to the joints and skeleton). On the graph, this produces a smooth curving gradient, a neat parabola, like a child's drawing of a mountain. With heel-strikers there is a very sudden spike where the initial loading happens too quickly as the calcaneus (heel bone) crashes into the ground.

When it's my turn to run on the treadmills, Hannah Rice (one of the researchers at the centre) explains what I am seeing on all the screens in front of me. They are live feedback graphs from the pressure-sensitive treadmill I'm running on. Because I am already a forefoot runner (well, predominantly), the graph arcs are quite smooth. When I change deliberately to a heel-strike the graphs become vicious and jagged. It only takes a few minutes for the technical team to collect all the data they need. It seems a very short time for a running sample. The hypersensitive pressure plate is only about the size of a paving slab and you need to stay within it as you run. And, because the technology is so proprioceptively weird, it is difficult to know if you are doing what you would normally do when running on an actual paving slab.

The reports have to be prepared and processed; the videos and graphs synced. All the measurements checked. So I go back to see Professor Davis again as we wait for the numbers to come through. I feel a little nervous, classic impostor-syndrome stuff, like I'm about to be found out.

I stand outside her office and I feel like I am waiting for the headmistress (but a really nice one). I start to regret having done this. All the advice I've given to people over the years flashes before my eyes – what if I'm a terrible runner? This is going to go in the book, and if it's really bad I can't leave it out, as all these people here will know.

Professor Davis arrives, clearly having rushed from a previous appointment to meet me.

'OK, I got it. We need to get the video, too.' That arrives by email, and we're ready to go.

I have photographic proof that when she told me my scores my jaw dropped in disbelief.

As we look at the video she tells me, 'You look perfect-perfect-perfect. In shoes, you are landing mid-foot, but barefoot you have a tendency to land on the ball of your foot. This is what I think of as "natural running".'

She continues, 'Your rates of loading [body-weights per second] are kind of low in the thirties and forties. Your medial-lateral forces are good, too. Good cadence [178 – the ideal steps-per-minute figure is believed to be 180].' My graphs are super-smooth ski slopes. When I was wearing shoes, there was a tiny ridge on the rising slope, but you'd only see it if you knew to look for it. I now know from the computer readouts that my left and right stride-lengths are identical, to the millimetre; my 'flight' times (the bit of running when both limbs are off the ground) identical to the millisecond. It all looks unbelievably symmetrical. Professor Davis explains that there is usually a small impact-transient with a mid-foot landing, and that's what my shoes were encouraging me to do. She recommends that I try to transition into something with a little less cushioning. She also tells me about my medial-lateral forces, which look good. I look at the squiggly graphs that have 'right' and 'left' data, and I ask her to explain again. But no, I simply don't have a scientific mind and I cannot make any sense of it beyond understanding that it has something to do with force shifting from side to side along all three axes. On the third explanation (Professor Davis is very patient) I admit defeat, and she finishes with a reassuring, 'You're *good*.'

But she also suspects that I was *being* good, that I was behaving for the cameras. She doesn't say so, but I think she can see from my lower-leg musculature that I am not a barefoot marathoner. I don't have bulging peroneals. And she's right, I still don't run double-digit miles barefoot – more for reasons of practicality than anything.

When we watch the video, I am struck by how similar it all feels to the horror show that was my video assessment ten years before. And when we switch to the rear-view video, I can see that my gait may have improved hugely but my leg-bend is still there, even if it is not as bad as it once was. It isn't stomach-turning any more. But I am surprised that such visible motion did not show up in the numbers anywhere.

The x axis in the following graphs is the number of body-weights, from the moment the foot lands on the plate; the y axis is time.

All runners' strike patterns and levels of impact vary. Run badly and you could load greater amounts of force beyond the figures on these graphs. Figure a is my own foot-strike.

Professor Davis tells me that I don't have a bowed leg, 'It's a varus thrust. Does your knee give you trouble?' I tell her it doesn't. 'Well if it does, you come back and see me because we can correct that, too.' Although my hopes had been unduly raised by the symmetry of the numbers, it could have been worse. The numbers don't make me strong or fast, or give me more stamina, but they do explain how I went from struggling with just a few miles, all the way up to some of the very long distances I cover in this book. And it's not that I feel proud or strong, more that I feel all set to keep on running while I can. Running, and learning how to run well, are for me a sort of

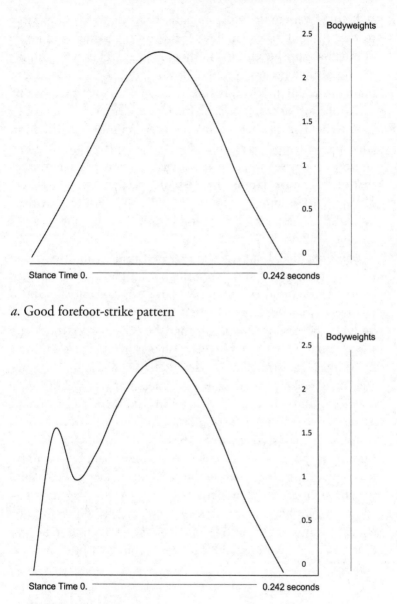

a. Good forefoot-strike pattern

b. Typical heel-strike pattern

insurance. I want still to be running the forests in my seventies like my uncle, but as the doctor told me, I probably share more genes with my father.

Before I went to Boston, I thought that there wasn't a right way to run. After all, there are few people on the planet who know as much about the running body as Daniel Lieberman, and his feeling is that because biology is variable ('We have different brain sizes, different tooth sizes') then why shouldn't there be variations in the ways we run? It's a nice, democratic approach to movement, but when I think of other running animals, dogs, cheetahs, antelope, deer, and the rabbits outside my window at work, I can see none of the huge variation in their species that exists in ours. Do fish of the same species swim completely differently? Do birds fly differently? I'm more birdwatcher than biologist, so perhaps I am wrong in this, but my observations seem to say not.

The term that I can't get out of my head is one that Irene Davis kept using: 'natural running'. Landing on the forefoot is, for her, 'natural running'. We have big calf muscles and a relatively small anterior tibialis (the muscle next to the shin bone) for a reason. One thing that the calf muscles (both the soleus and the gastrocnemius) excel at is negating those collision forces that heel-strikers seem unable to avoid. Collision forces are damaging, and the persistence of those impacts spells trouble down the line. (That said, sitting and reading a book is much harder on your joints than good running is.)

While it may seem that the message of barefoot or natural running is that our bodies know best – and I believe that to be true – that knowledge can be buried deep below newer habits that have emerged in modern life. The way we live now has educated our bodies out of form with a daily diligence and tenacity that, were we in training, would be Olympic standard. Our bodies know more about how to be in the world than we ever will.

2.
SENSES AS LENSES: HOW TO TRAIN YOUR SENSES

THE LAKE DISTRICT AND SEATTLE

When you come back you will not be you.
> – E.M. Forster, 'The Other Boat', 1957

Leave behind you your high-seasoned dishes, your wines and your delicacies: carry nothing but what is necessary for your own comfort . . . Custom will soon teach you to tread lightly and barefoot on the little inequalities of the ground, and show you how to pass on unwounded amid the mantling briers.
> – Charles Waterton, *Wanderings in South America*, 1825

WRITING MOVEMENT WITH THE BODY

We don't just see with our eyes, but with our whole bodies. Neither are our senses easily separable. They are processed and transmitted, sometimes in separate parts of the brain and body, sometimes the same. A few weeks ago, when I was chatting to a friend, he said: 'Hang on. I need to put my glasses on so I can hear you properly.' Our perceptual technologies are much more sophisticated than an 8k HD digicam with surround sound. All the more so because our senses are upgradable. This chapter is about our senses, the ways that they become refined through use, how they can help us know the world that we move through. It is about how learning to run long distances changes your body. But more than that, as your body trains itself into its new activities, there will also be fundamental changes in the ways that it engages with the world around it. If we see with our bodies, and we change our bodies when we learn how to run, that means that we see things, or understand them, or feel them, or experience them and come to know them, in ways that were hidden from us before. These are not new discoveries, and they do not belong only to runners. The Romantics, that loosely defined group of poets, artists, thinkers and writers that emerged to counter the overwhelming rationalism of the eighteenth-century Enlightenment, were among the first to understand the frictive relationships that exist between the landscape, the body and the mind in motion.

COLERIDGE'S FINGERS

I am running with my eyes closed. This is not a recognised training strategy, merely a practical solution to the needle-sting blur in my vision. I wipe and wipe but it only gets worse as I wring the sun-creamed sweat deeper into my eyes. So I close them, gripping them tight shut for two steps. This seems to work, so I try four. I open them to another sting, so I try ten, then twenty. Finally, I close them and stop counting. Now blind, it is like a sluice of sensory intelligence has been freed and the world beneath my feet and on my skin breathes to life.

Running like this, with my eyes closed and my other senses open, reminds me that there is a history to how places feel. With refined senses we can read these histories. Lifetimes may come and go, and the architecture of cities may rise and fall, but there are aspects to places that we visit or inhabit that outlive us and are passed forward to coming generations, or even for thousands of years. These aspects are not written in any traditional way, but they can be read nonetheless. We are primed, ready for them.

The French word for a track, *sentier*, carries with it the wonderful idea that pathways are like scent trails for us to follow. *Sentiers* are the trails that we have taken because, for one reason or another, we have found ourselves 'on the scent'. Whether it is the 'scent' of a view, food or comfort, our bodies snuffle out experiences, employing our available senses to read or succumb to our environment or to what the American writer Henry David Thoreau called the 'subtle magnetism' of the path. Over hundreds of years humans are drawn to the same places and sights. We take the same routes, past the same natural fingerposts, and without realising, we become part of that larger story of human activity in which we as individuals only play bit parts. A path cannot be made by one explorer; instead, it will emerge if it succeeds in luring those who are nose-to-the-ground, readied to follow the scent.

I am not talking about ley lines, telluric currents, mysterious archaeoastronomy, geomancy or divining, but the idea that if we exercise our senses (like we do our bodies) then they change the way that we see the world. 'See' is not the right verb to finish off that sentence, because what we do when we go out to confront these places and environments is so much greater than just 'seeing'. At the most conservative count we have five senses (more on this later), but when I sit at home browsing news and social-media sites, I am using only my sight, as my brain's pistons fizz and whistle behind the scenes like the Wizard of Oz. And sometimes I do this for hours at a stretch. I know that when I go running it wakes me up from a kind of hibernation. But the experience of sitting at a computer is an inversion of the language used to describe it: instead of feeling *refreshed* by sitting still, I feel exhausted by it, like I have been holding a weight with my arms outstretched. The stiffness in my limbs as I start to shuffle back to life is part of that same complaint: my body is trying to tell me that movement is what it needs. There is an irony to writing a book about movement, especially running, as writing prose must be one of the most stationary employments possible (except perhaps for those silver-painted fellows who have elevated standing still into a tidy earner in the Times Squares and Covent Gardens of the world). At least poetry can be mulled over to the rhythm of one's footsteps and quickly noted down while on the move. Or you may be like Wordsworth, who could write hundreds of lines of blank verse to be recalled when needed – or 'recollected in tranquility'.[1]

When running, thinking plays sixth fiddle to sensing – for hearing, seeing and feeling how places present themselves to our consciousness takes precedence over careful consideration.

William Wordsworth and Samuel Taylor Coleridge frequently share the same breath. They were contemporaries, friends, collaborators, and poets of 'the common man'. But the intensity and inevitable dissolution of their friendship is indicative of how very different they were under the skin. Wordsworth was roundly praised as the philosophical poet of the imagination, producing many thousands of pages of ambulatory poetry throughout his writing life. Samuel Taylor Coleridge, by harsh comparison, and despite a promising and productive beginning, was barely able to complete anything.[2] He contributed only a handful of poems to their revolutionary shared literary endeavour, *Lyrical Ballads* (Wordsworth was determined to be the lead singer of these power ballads and so relegated Coleridge to the maracas). Wordsworth became comfortable with the idea of his own poetry (some would say, with the sound of his own voice), went on to become Poet Laureate and productively ploughed his way through all manner of short- and long-form verses. Coleridge's restless imagination, though, was always pushing at the boundaries of what was plausible or possible in prose and poetry – if he was not striding across the Lake District, struggling with opium addiction, plagiarising, sexually fantasising, planning communes, dabbling in mysticism, or disappearing for jaunts in France and Germany for months on end, leaving wife and newborn behind, then he was party to the invention of new ways of describing the world.[3] In his essay on the two of them, William Hazlitt explained that:

> Coleridge's manner is more full, animated and varied; Wordsworth's more equable, sustained and internal. The one might be termed dramatic, the other, more lyrical. Coleridge himself has told me that he liked to compose in walking over uneven ground . . . whereas Wordsworth always wrote . . . walking up and down a straight gravel path.[4]

A quick browse along the shelves of Coleridge criticism and the words that leap from the spines are 'visionary', 'imagination', 'mind', 'intelligence', 'sensibility', 'psychology', but it is not his mind that I am interested in, but his body. Although he was a lazy and easily distracted fellow (the ADHD Romantic), he could get up and walk 40 or 50 miles in a day or scale mountains without preparation or equipment. His work also showed him to be something of a literary *flâneur*, a saunterer and observer, nibbling here and there morsels of philosophy, poetry, political economy or chemistry. These aspects of his personality were admired and despaired of in equal measure by his circle. Late in filing articles for the *Morning Post*, late with the manuscript of *Lyrical Ballads*, late with his biography of that exceptional dramatist Gotthold Lessing, Coleridge set off to tramp the hills and mountains between Keswick and Grasmere. In his notebooks from the period (July–August 1802), amid maps, diagrams, squiggles and sketches, and in some letters (particularly to his beloved Sara Hutchinson), Coleridge recounts the rich and embodied experience of climbing and walking and records the effect this movement had upon his psychology.[5]

> I had a glorious Walk – the rain sailing along those black Crags & green Steeps, white as the wooly Down on the under side of a Willow Leaf, & soft as Floss Silk/& silver Fillets of Water down every mountain from top to bottom that were as fine as Bridegrooms. I soon arrived at the Halse – & climbed up by the waterfall as near as I could, to the very top of the Fell – but it was so craggy – the Crags covered with spongy soaky Moss, and when bare so jagged as to wound one's hands fearfully – and the Gusts came so very sudden & strong, that the going up was slow, & difficult & earnest – & the coming down, not only all that, but likewise extremely dangerous. However, I have always found this *stretched & anxious* state of mind favorable to depth of pleasurable Impression, in the resting Places & *lownding* Coves.[6]

While many find the formality of Coleridge's public writings wearing, with their distressed arguments extruded with great effort and the hairpin bends in some of his opinions, these writings are different – all those faults disappear in the immediacy of these private, spontaneous jottings.[7] Elsewhere in the same period in the notebooks, recounting a climb up Helvellyn, Coleridge wrote that, as he bounded down, he noticed the moving stones under the soft moss pinching at his feet. The tone may seem prosaic, but the power and originality of these descriptions effectively heralds a new form of nature writing, one that broke down that fourth wall of the Enlightenment picturesque, which sought always to enframe the landscape and put it on show, like Wordsworth does in his poem 'Tintern Abbey'.[8]

We runners know that once you settle down deeply into pace, you settle just as deeply into the landscape; you huddle into it. The reason that the experience of the landscape can be so intense is that you become part of it. What you are feeling is an analogue for what the place is feeling as it feels itself, and you. It's not that landscapes are conscious, but there is something sentient to them. They have a life so complex as to be invisible in our language (it's the dark matter of the environment); we find ourselves wordless in accounting for the sheer diversity of it. And as the writer George Eliot said, we are not attuned to hearing the squirrel's heartbeat or the grass grow; that roar of life that lies on the other side of silence cannot be made sense of in a human alphabet.

In Coleridge, movement itself is elevated into a philosophy. The Romantics were the first among Westerners to remember the pleasures, gains and joys of movement.

A little before them, Dr Johnson's *A Journey to the Western Isles of Scotland* recounts the reveries of 83 days on the move, but so little of it is actually about motion itself. In other words, for Johnson walking was utterly pedestrian. For him, and the monied classes, a walk was work; to travel was literally a travail. It was for tinkers, not thinkers.

Even worse, Johnson complained on one visit that his body got in the way of appreciating fine views. At Ullinish on the Isle of Skye he recounts that he and his companion Boswell 'walked through a natural arch in the rock, which might have pleased us by its novelty, had the stones, which incumbered our feet, given us leisure to consider it.'[9]

By the time of Walter Scott's *The Heart of Midlothian* (1818) things had changed a bit. In the novel, our heroine Jeanie Deans walks most of the way from Edinburgh to London to see Queen Caroline. The purpose of Jeanie's journey is to plead clemency for her sister, who has been found guilty of infanticide. But even here, the drama tends to be a stationary affair, something that happens in between the walks. 'With a strong heart, and a frame patient of fatigue, Jeanie Deans, travelling at the rate of twenty miles a day, and sometimes further, traversed the southern part of Scotland, and advanced as far as Durham.'[10] Are we to believe that not a thing happened, nor a significant thought crossed her mind betwixt the two? This was surely unlike the real journey on which it is based, which was stamped out by Helen Walker of Irongray, Dumfriesshire, in the 1730s. Today, in stories like Rachel Joyce's *The Unlikely Pilgrimage of Harold Fry* or Cheryl Strayed's *Wild*, the journey is the story.

Unsurprisingly, when a culture has yet to fall in love with walking, that lack of affection also applies to the places walked through – places which we now, in modern times, visit in order to walk.

The Lakes were not always loved. Daniel Defoe, in *A Tour Through the Whole Island of Great Britain* (1724–6), complains of the lake country as 'the wildest, most barren and frightful of any that I have passed over in England, or even Wales itself'.[11]

Whether the new pedestrianism began from fad, fashion or fondness, once consumer culture got hold of it, there was an explosion of stuff that could be bought to enhance the experience of walking.

There was a popular gadget which assisted in the creation and stylisation of the picturesque in the landscape. Just like the walking practice of Dr Johnson, the gadget encouraged movement between places to find views of interest, but it did not help the user to think about or focus on the movement itself in any way.

The gadget was called the Claude glass. Named after the painter Claude Lorrain, it was a small handheld device like a powder compact, and it flipped open to reveal a convex mirror. One would stand, turning one's back on the view, to regard its distorted reflection in the glass, moving this way and that to achieve just the right artistic effect. The poet Thomas Gray was an enthusiast. Writing of a sunset, he claimed '[I] saw in my glass a picture that if I could transmit it to you, & fix it in all the softness of its living colours, would fairly sell for a thousand pounds.'[12]

The Claude glass was also known as the 'black mirror' and was responsible for a number of minor mishaps. This is where history catches up with us. Our version of the black mirror, carried in the pocket, used by millions to 'see' rock concerts, fireworks displays and sunsets, is the smartphone. We look through it to make sure we are catching grainy footage of the wondrous thing we are missing. And we are not very good at it. Each year, the number of people going to casualty departments with injuries caused this way is increasing by an astonishing 50 per cent.[13] The similarities between the Claude glass and the smartphone don't end there. Runners like smartphones – I've run with mine, and have seen others with theirs in hand or clamped to their arm. For runners, the smartphone entertains or distracts them, just like the Claude glass, but it does it in different ways. It allows runners to keep in touch with work or family. Some people also feel safer with one. It will also GPS-track the run so, just like the Claude glass, the landscape may be reframed in another way upon return.

Thomas Gray took a nasty tumble while using a Claude glass. After lunching at an inn, he 'straggled out alone to the Parsonage, fell down on my back across a dirty lane with my glass open in one hand, but broke only my knuckles.'[14]

The painter Charles Gough was not so fortunate. He fell to his death on Helvellyn in 1805, where his body lay undiscovered for months. When he was found there were only a few clothes, his gnawed skeleton, a pencil and *two* Claude glasses. The search for picturesque distance could be a dangerous business. These accidents tended to happen because one had literally to turn one's back on nature to enframe it in the glass. For these eighteenth-century adventurers, the landscape was a strictly visual feast, but not for Coleridge.

He did not like the containing effect of the Claude glass. In his notebooks he expresses a kind of reverie of perspective only offered *en plein air*:

> One effect of the magnitude of surrounding objects – it gives to shapes a narrowness of width, exceedingly favourable to boldness, and approximating to a sharp point, which being comparative loses its effect upon paper – because you can scarcely give the real shape, preserving its true relative dimensions, besides in a picture you only take a part of the view; but in nature the whole, perhaps 20 fold more than you draw, appears to you, each part modified by all the rest.[15]

For Coleridge, the landscape is immediate, physical, and fleshly. He talks of the forms and shapes he eyes on his travels as seizing his body.[16] It is only this movement through the lakes and mountains that creates for him a state of mind so 'stretched' as to shape another kind of impression beyond the merely visual.

Navigating our way through a landscape changes the means by which we may experience it. If our heart-rate is raised, if endorphins are flooding our system, if our veins and capillaries have dilated to increase the flow of oxygen to the muscles and the brain, if we can feel the microtexture of the earth changing beneath our feet, the world becomes a different place. The world stops being a picture for us to gawp and yawn at, and the relationship between our insides and its outsides becomes a dynamic one in which the rules can change, data may be gained or lost, connections can be made, shapes and symmetries noticed. Running reminds us that our bodies and the world are made of the same stuff. A runner's sense of place, of reachable space, their vision of themselves in the landscape – all of these things are altered by a kind of movement that brings about real changes in the physiology of the runner.

Is this just another way of saying that running makes the body 'fitter' or 'stronger'? While that is true, it is more than this. A runner's way of knowing and experiencing the world alters (I might even say 'is enhanced or upgraded') precisely because he or she is a runner. Their way of seeing and feeling has changed because the matter that is doing those things is, or has been, running. Sidestepping the debates concerning Euclidian optics (where light may travel to or from the eye), we can safely say that light does not land on the retina like an arrow quiver-thudding into a target. If the target is the eye, it is attached to our nervous system and our bodies. A target doesn't experience drops in blood sugar, it doesn't fall in love, it doesn't laugh so hard that it cries, it doesn't itch on summer days, it doesn't have to wear spectacles, it doesn't wince when sweat runs down from the forehead and stings it into a squint, it does not read, and it doesn't look back at you. Consciousness is not just affected by the body; philosophers as far back as the Greeks have argued that it *is* the body.[17] Running provides us with an opportunity to indulge in a kind of kinetic empathy with the world around us. Just like Coleridge, who was able to better present a more rounded and informed bodily assessment of place, running offers up the possibility of connecting with the world in unpredictable and creatively productive ways.

The body's senses are like lenses to our consciousness. The experiences that we have are filtered by our senses.

Lenses can often cost hundreds, even thousands, of pounds more than the camera to which they are attached. This is because a camera's ability to record visual data is made or broken by the quality of the lens; equally, the picture that results is stylised and framed by it. But imagine a dynamic lens that could learn from the way that you used the camera, that could focus tighter, let in more light, or sink down into itself when it wasn't being used. How much might such a camera lens be worth? Our senses are forceful, bold, active and wilful, just like our bodies can be. They undergo changes when they are exercised. As one of E.M. Forster's characters warns in his short story 'The Other Boat', 'When you come back you will not be you.'[18] Running changes who you are, and how you see, feel and sense the outside world – how can you still be you if you run?

PHILOSOPHY IN THE MIST

It was a half term in 2014. Outsiders usually see it as a break, but for lecturers it is a brief opportunity to catch up on all the things that you have fallen behind with in the previous six weeks, while the students beaver away at their essays. But I was exhausted, and I had lost the last few days, not to drink and reverie, but to correspondence, requests, reports, references, quality assurance, governance, approval, the list went on and on. Like a slow liquid that comes to occupy all the available space in a vessel, I barely had room in my head for anything.

I was also aware that I had only a short amount of time in which to try to get some energy back for the gathering wave of marking due the following week. Not making headway, I was failing to hold back the tide.

I didn't know why, but I had been thinking about Coleridge all day. My mind kept coming back to adventures, climbs, rains, mists and infinite space – but these daydreams, all indistinct, generic and placeless, were all I was capable of. My brain felt like the soggy brown mass of a forgotten lettuce found in the back of the fridge.

I made some tea, and when I went back to my computer, instead of clicking back into emails, I huffed as my fingers began a bid for freedom. I typed 'Moss Force', 'Greta Hall' and 'Keswick'. A few more clicks and it was all arranged. I was free.

The next morning, a warm November day, I set out to run the pathways, hills and mountains that Coleridge had trodden 200 years before near Keswick in Cumbria. The hazardous escape had worked for him; surely it could for me, too.

He had packed a shirt, some socks, a nightcap, paper and pen, some tea, and a book to read. For a walking stick, he stripped the bristles from his broom, leaving them strewn on his kitchen floor. He packed it all in an oilskin knapsack and off he strode.

My own packing, though a little more laden with charger cables and toiletries, was just as hasty.

After a few hours' driving, and with a back so stiff it made my legs hurt, I stopped off at a service station in Stafford, where a mural boasted the region's cultural alumni of Samuel Johnson, Josiah Wedgwood and (sharing such esteemed company) Robbie Williams.

By early evening I had made it to Lake Windermere, and when I arrived, spine-locked and creaking from my car, I noticed the smell of elemental smoke and I saw hatted and mittened families ambling along the pavements. I had forgotten it was Guy Fawkes Night. One of the many British festivities that cast a dark shadow.

The previous week I had been reading some John Ruskin. In late career, the art critic and social thinker had written a short piece, 'The Extension of Railways in the Lake District – a Protest' (1876).[19] In it, he railed (forgive me) against the rampant materialist expansion that he saw everywhere in Britain in the period. The introduction of railways into his beloved Lake District (he lived on the east side of Coniston Water) irritated him, not as a Nimby, but because he held a passionate 'wish to improve the minds of the populace'.[20] These may seem easy words to say, but Ruskin did expend most of his career (without any need to earn an income) writing tens of thousands of pages on trying to improve the lot of the worker. He rallied for social improvements like universal free education, national insurance, national health care, even our beloved National Trust. He despised the profiteering of the rail companies who wanted to rip through the crags and lakes to deliver tourists to the region's hotspots. While the capitalists pretended a democratic intent of making the area accessible to the masses, Ruskin argued that it was accessible already. Anyone who wanted to go, could. He was concerned, too, that the arrival of the railways would change the way that people experienced the landscape. Being bundled out of a train for a couple of hours would predetermine the kinds of experience available to the visitor (I know what I am tempted to do when I arrive at a railway station with an inviting pub just next door). Small-'c' conservative that he was, Ruskin thought the railways would change these places.

The campaign against the extension of the railways failed – the lines were laid, viaducts erected, and stations constructed. Then, 70 years later, the profits made, the area saw many line closures as part of Dr Beeching's famous post-war cuts. The train lines were no longer economically viable.[21] The cry for democratic access had passed. All that was left were disused viaducts, ghost stations and old railway lines.

I make my way down into the town and find what Ruskin would most have feared. Fine jewellers' shops abutting 'Bargain Booze', and the steamed-up windows of ice-cream parlours across the road from Tesco Express. There's another shop with a long list of access restrictions (no ice cream, no kebabs, no reading, no laughing). As I turn the corner to the lakefront I see a man; beside him is a swan. The usually perfect curled 'S' of its neck is stretching straight up like the trunk of a silver birch sapling. I have never seen a swan do that before. As I get a little closer I can see that it is hooking its bill into something the man is holding. It is a creamy-orange polystyrene box of ketchup-squirted chips, and the man laughs as the swan dives in, snapping at the potatoey mush. Hungry ducks gather round. Behind this modern vignette is Lake Windermere and it looks like miles of mercurial silk.

That night I buy a pint and plonk a pile of books onto my table in the pub. As fireworks fizz and pop outside to 'oohs' and 'ahhs', I spread out my OS maps and start tracing the route from Greta Hall that Coleridge would have taken in 1802 all the way to the inaccessible waterfall of Moss Force.

The next morning, I gather up what running gear I've remembered to bring and aim for Keswick. It's raining. It's always raining. If the sun's ever out in the Lake District, it's because it's about to start raining. Anyway, there is no sun, so it is raining.

I drive past Rydal Mount (a home of the Wordsworths) while it's raining, and later past Dove Cottage (also a home of the Wordsworths), and it is still raining. Bantock's 'Celtic Symphony' is on in the car and it's perfect music for this landscape. The movements are filled with a kind of airy buoyancy mixed with the gritty, cold, wet texture of moss when it's squeezed between your fingers. It's lush and ferny. Perfect music for when it's raining.

When I arrive in Keswick, it's raining. I climb the lane up out of the town to Greta Hall, which feels far away from the bustle of the high street. It was originally designed to double up as an observatory. Coleridge stayed here from 1800 to 1803. After that, his friend and soon-to-be Poet Laureate, Robert Southey, took it on for the next 40 years, which means the literary who's who of the first half of the nineteenth century visited here, including Walter Scott, the Wordsworths, De Quincey, Hazlitt and Walter Savage Landor. The chickens in the yard are new, but there are a couple of yew trees surely old enough to have been here back in the day, and the view, though a little busier, is unchanged because overlooking the house is the 3,000-foot summit of Skiddaw. Its great hulking shoulders seem to surround the town in an arc – Coleridge called them 'a whole camp of giant tents'.[22] What it must have been to have such a mountain looking into you every morning and night.

Robert Southey never left Greta Hall (probably because it was always raining). He loved the place and stayed until he died here in 1840. I've never been able to understand why he was so respected as a poet. He even had the gall to discourage a young Charlotte Brontë from a career in writing because it was not a business for women to get involved with. She took it well and was evidently undeterred, and perhaps we should forgive anything of the man who gave us the story of Goldilocks and the three bears.

I stand at the gate of the hall and look at the yellows and golds in the trees. The rain falls. I think, *I can't do fifteen miles in this. I'm a road- not a fell-runner. Once I hit the hills, my normal mileage would be halved anyway.* I look at the flimsy 'London' running kit I've brought with me and procrastinate a little more by deciding to walk down into the village to find some breathable waterproofs (in every town throughout the Lakes there are numerous shops crammed with red and blue Gore-Tex for the ill-prepared, such as me). Coleridge did his walk in clement August, not this biting wet.

I do that curious thing where I have to negotiate the shop assistant 'up' because I want the best waterproofs I can get: 'I'm going to be running in them – and this isn't just a shower,' but she can probably hear that the steel in my voice is already a bit rusty from all the rain.

Hard negotiations over, I proffer a card for payment. 'Is that a Norwegian name?' Cue that conversation about my name that I have every day of my life.

I change in the shop. Then, with the wind and mizzly rain in my face, I climb back up the path to the hall.

I get back in the car, and the rain has changed its status to audible.

I sit for ten minutes, as I sometimes do in a gym car park – unable to face either the misery of attending or the defeat of leaving. I look out towards Keswick Bridge, which Coleridge strode over when he set out. *I can't do this*, I think. *It's going to be awful. It's dangerous. I shouldn't take a mobile because it'll get wet. Even if it didn't, it wouldn't work. No one knows where I am. No one knows what I'm planning to do.*

I remember the Claude glass casualties. Then I turn the key in the ignition. Admitting defeat, I start driving out of town. The warm light of the cafés of Grasmere and Rydal Mount suddenly seem inviting. 'Having a tea at the Wordsworths', that's research. I could finger a copy of Dorothy's journal with one hand and butter a hot crumpet with another. I would be rediscovering the phenomenology of warming one's feet by the fire while scoffing a muffin.

But something stops me; perhaps it's the rousing Bantock still on in the car. Unsure of why I'm doing it, instead of turning south towards Windermere, I pull in at a pub car park in a village called Braithwaite, only a mile or so from Keswick. In my distracted state, I get out of the car and then, as a gust of wind blows, the car begins to roll and I realise I've forgotten to put on the parking brake. I manage to jump back in and crank the handle and then re-park.

I go into the pub, dressed for a run. I order a tea, and ask if it's OK to leave my car there for a few hours. Unknowingly, I have disposed of my main reason for not going: now someone knows I am here. Warmed by the tea, I am ready to go.

I go back to the car, dump my belongings, and spread the OS map over the passenger seat to get my bearings, and I make the odd decision of leaving it here because I don't want the map ruined in the rain. If I head south-west out of Braithwaite, there is no way I can miss Moss Force, surely.

Whoever heard of anyone getting lost in the mountains, in bad weather, and without a map?

The rain has calmed into something between precipitation and a heavy mist. The sky is heavy, intense and low. I head out of the car park and turn south. The film of water between my feet and the concrete on the road slurps and slaps like glue. My weatherproofing rustles. I am only just out of the village when I look at the cues of my surroundings and realise I'm already lost. I've gone the wrong way. In front of me is a valley with Coledale Beck running through it, when what I want is the steep climb to Stile End. I turn and return. After only a hundred-or-so feet I am attacked by Porsche winds that accelerate from 0–60 in a couple of seconds. I am only ten minutes into the run and it is confirmed to me that I have not overdressed or spent unwisely on extra clothing. I am not going to have to look hard to find some of the 'unhospitable terror' that Daniel Defoe found here.[23]

The rain stiffens from mist to needles. It comes down hard as I reach the crown of Stile End, my legs aching from the ascent of only a few hundred feet. I lean in to the teeth of the wind. I have got miles to go, but I feel like I can only manage a few more yards. I want to turn back, back to the pub, and the fire, and a pint.

I follow the path towards High Moss and Crag Hill. My breathing has settled. The rain softens again. All around me are the Cumbrian Mountains, and I am overwhelmed by their preposterous size and impassivity, and the sheer heedlessness of them. When you look at a mountain, what you take from it fills you up. The ticks and sparks of daily life are crushed under the weight of the rock, and I begin to feel the experience of the place as Coleridge may have done.

I lived in Sussex for 20 years, and the chalky summits there are always walkable, even in bad weather, because they drain so quickly. But even hundreds of feet up, here, the tops of the mountains are black and wet peat bogs.

At the cairn on Sail, I know I am supposed to cut south, but another hundred feet or so will take me to the summit of Crag Hill. When I get there, I can barely stand up because the gusts attack from every direction in which I try to move. I crouch down in supplication to the gods of wind and rain, afraid I might tumble over Scout Crag. 'Please, don't kill me.' But I gasp in the exultant pleasure of the fear of something real.

I idle along, crouched as if under gunfire. The rain billows in the wind as thick as smoke.

Back at the cairn, through the rain I can see four pathways (one of which quickly splits again), but the visual clues of the skyline have disappeared. All I can see are green leviathan mountains with mottles of copper-brown fern and claws of stone.

The rain dashes against my face and I have to squint to try and work out which path I came up. They all look the same, wet, dark, and disapproving. A panic begins to rise. The light has dimmed, not because the sun's going down, but because the clouds are heavy like they are carrying volcanic ash. I have a compass. It is warmly tucked away in the glove compartment of my car. I shout in exasperation tinged with fear: 'You twat!'

I pull up my hood and I can hear the anger of the rain, firm, decisive. I stop panicking and start thinking. The clouds are too thick to be able to tell where the sun might be in the sky. I look round for trees or walls that might be able to give me an indication of north from the growth patterns of moss, but there is probably too much air movement, anyway, for this to be a reliable indicator. A single, correctly placed puddle in a field, can sometimes be enough to help indicate north, but there are hundreds around me. There are no trees leaning, battered by the prevailing wind, towards the north-east. All I've got are nearby visual clues. I realise that if I stay in the long grass by the paths, I can try to see my own footprints in the mud.

In the mix of mud and grass they are almost impossible to detect, but after a couple of minutes I find my own little waffle imprint. This is the path I came up, so there is the path I need to take.

I take a more careful note of the visual clues and skip south. I descend, then climb to Ard Crags. I know I'm in the right place, because I can just make out between the mists a winding road, hundreds of feet below. If I stay up on the crags, they will take me towards Moss Force. The small advantage of the weather is that, because of the rain, the cataract will be roaring. My fingers feel snapped at and bitten by the cold.

I stop at a small outcrop patterned with mosses, lichens, grasses and alpines. There are the tiny paddles of crottle (*Parmelia saxatilis*) huddled in against some pistachio-green map lichen (*Rhizocarpon geographicum*), which likes clean air and altitude, so this place is perfect for it.[24] Focussing on its little landscape, the lichen's tiny perimeter coastlines, makes me feel big, and it seem small. It gives me comfort. Then when I look up at the mountains again, they seem so big, and I so very, very small.

Back on the path, wraiths of cloud crawl over the peaks ahead of me. The path is waterlogged, and the puddles lead in a line to a precipice. They reflect the grey sky above so they look like apertures that I could step through to be in another world entirely. Over the edge of Knott Rigg and through the mist I can just make out a thin white lightning bolt among the mushy green – Moss Force, and it is raging on the other side of the valley.

When I begin the descent, there are footholds, burrowed out by use, all the way down the slope towards the waterfall about a mile away. I think of Coleridge and the fact that no such footholds would have existed 200 years ago. Walking for pleasure did not really exist before then. These footholds have come about because of the region's hundreds of thousands of visitors over the years. So what has changed so much between now and then? An explanation, as is so often the case, may be found around the period of the Industrial Revolution. Why is this area being used like this? The terms of the question provide a clue to the answer.

Martin Heidegger is one of those philosophers who is as famous for his impenetrability as for what he actually said. He is inclined to the sort of neologisms that enrage readers. But he's a genius at seeing round 'things as they are' to the concealed machineries of modern life.

As part of a series of lectures given in the 1940s, he sought to unpick our relationship with technology – understandable, given the recent invention of the atom bomb.

Outside the context of the Industrial Revolution, invention is a relatively harmless thing. For example, we do not think of the invention of the cup, during the Neolithic period, as bringing about the destruction of the planet. But the idea makes me think about Stanley Kubrick's career-defining jump-cut in *2001: A Space Odyssey* (1968), where the early primate throws the recently used 'tool' into the air, and we jump forward 2 million years and it becomes a passenger space ship.[25] Creativity and invention are fine things, but when we mix them with industrialisation problems may begin to arise. The essence of technology is the journey towards what Heidegger calls enframing, a process where everything is reduced to its use.

He uses the example of a chalice, a cup rich in design, association, ceremony, value, custom, memory, meaning, which is also handy for drinking from. The process of enframing involves the chalice being stripped of these relations and functions. The chalice, with its complex social, fiscal and religious web of relations, becomes, in our modern, technology-dominated world, the cardboard coffee cup. A thing stripped of all association. It has no maker, no family, no owner, no design or monetary value; it is used once and discarded. This process is the essence of technology and it has become a way of life for us. And for Heidegger it also applies to the world as we see it. The world becomes a kind of standing reserve of energy or usefulness-in-waiting.

One of the most straightforward illustrations of how the world as a 'standing reserve' might be figured comes from a poem by Alexander Pope, 'Windsor Forest', in which the trees that line the River Thames are seen by the poet as 'future navies'.[26]

Is this a wild landscape, the one that my trainers occasionally disappear into – the one that wants to blow me off my feet? Or is it a kind of standing reserve? Is this space being used or experienced? I would want to say the latter. But these Cumbrian Mountains are part of the 'Lake District National Park'. The *Oxford English Dictionary* tells me that a park is 'any large enclosed piece of ground . . . used for recreation, and often for keeping deer, cattle or sheep'. That verb is the killer, 'used'. The use that has been ascribed to this environment is exactly what I am using it for – to have a kind of recreational experience that feels real. This is no freer than going into Bargain Booze and buying some bargain booze, and while drinking the said booze celebrating what a very good bargain it was. Further consultation of the *OED* only worsens things: 'an extensive area of land set apart as public property, to be kept in its natural state for the benefit of the public and the preservation of wildlife'.

These definitions make me feel like a little cog in a machine. These footholds, as I descend towards Moss Force, symbolise the path I have been on throughout this journey. It might have been dangerous and a bit blowy, I might have momentarily feared for my wellbeing, but I was on designated footpaths, having designated experiences, in an area designated for recreation from work. I haven't escaped at all. It's all so grim.

As I descend, the air temperature suddenly rises. The Cumbrian Mountains surround me in a crescent and I realise that it feels like I am welcoming an embrace from the sweet, warm rain.

The descent complete, I cross the road (yes, amazingly, there is a road) and begin the short climb towards Moss Force which gets ever larger as I approach. My head is spinning. My lungs pumping hard like a bellows – my blood must be redder than claret. Out of the wet turf, slate juts like flesh-stripped bone. I wind around a couple of paths. The torrent has been worth the wait. The water is brilliant white against the grey sky, the black slate and the wet, mossy baize. It's like the mountain's heart has been lanced and it's gushing snow.

I start to climb the slippery-wet rock because I want to see the source. My curiosity driving me like I want to climb inside its heart. My hands are white, wrinkled and cold, as if the bones are protruding from them just like the sharp slate from the earth. My smooth, waffle-soled Nikes have no purchase on the wet rock and although I feel like I might be able to go further, I am not at all sure that I could make it back again. The fall would be ankle twisting rather than body breaking, but after a couple of slips and grazes I accept that this is the end of my outward journey from my study. So I stand and watch the water bounce and dance and turn its way down the mountain. And I look at the beck that runs for miles down the valley, with these peaks flanking it like protective siblings. I look into the distance and realise that I am all temperatures: fingers and nose freezing; thighs cool; cheeks and body warm; lungs scorching; and my heart is blazing.

I follow the stream down the valley, along the road. My legs are dead. My blood sugar dropping, and everything in my vision has a penumbra. *It's the mist, surely.* It's a long way back, but I grant myself the luxury of not doing another climb, so I run the road that is as wet as a rill. The light is disappearing and the last place I want to be is on a mountaintop when the sun goes down.

I try and keep a good pace to stay ahead of the darkness chasing me out of the valley. As I tramp along I think through the dead soreness of my feet, the splintery cold of my fingers, and what I don't feel is trapped or deadened by my seemingly predetermined use of this space, by my escape from modern life. As I look back, I must be a mile from Moss Force, and I can still hear its voice calling through the rain. The light has changed, and the crags cycle through yet more colours, from grey and orange to deep blue and black. And still, it rains, but never have I loved rain so much. Now it feels gentle – sweet, even, welcoming. We are old friends because it cannot wet me any more than it has. Perhaps an hour passes, and as I turn a bend in the road, I realise that I have made it back, and I'm left with an enduring respect for the young Coleridge.

I am stiff-kneed. Night has fallen, but it was easy to find my way. There were no cars on the road, only sheep. I am tired and delirious with an electrochemical joy for which there is no word.

Several days later, and I can still feel the crags in my fingers. Their biting cold and their sharpness have left splinters in me that I couldn't gouge out if I wanted to.

A couple of weeks pass and I'm driving someplace, and when it begins to rain, the articulate click-clack on the windscreen transports me back to mountaintops like I had been hypnotised and that sound was my prompt. I remember getting back to the pub, drunk on exhaustion with my hair matted to my head like a victorious pearl-diver come up for air. And, I realised that my body had taught me something: that there are ways out of modern life. Heidegger thought that poetry and art were the only escape, but as I remembered the billowing rain, the feel and smell of the waterfall, the sight of it shooting from the mountain like a white sabre, and watching the torrent gulping at itself in great hungry mouthfuls, I realised all this was missing in Heidegger – where was the flesh, bone and sinew of the body? Where was the mad, drunken euphoria of it all? It is not found in any writing; it is inside us.

PHENOMENAL SEATTLE

There is no possibility of taking a run today. I am in a coffee shop in Alki, Seattle. It is 5am and I can't sleep. I have brought some books by the French philosopher Maurice Merleau-Ponty (which I am finding offensively difficult – continental philosophy and jet lag seem to have the same effect on the brain), and although a run is about to teach me that the book's lack of clarity is sort of the point, I find myself drawn instead to watching a table full of very old-age pensioners discussing last night's game.

Later, walking back to the B & B, I notice for the first time that a way off there is a wonderful sea/island view trying to make my acquaintance from between the rooftops. I acknowledge the winks and nods that the view is sending and try to set them off against my desire to go back to bed. It's nearly seven and I know I shouldn't give in so easily to jet lag, so when I get back to the B & B I find that I am just in time for a second breakfast. I decide that I will go and explore central Seattle. Revived, I set out again and as I climb the hill to the high street, I glance back over my shoulder to eye the landscape once again.

The way that we experience the simple pleasure of a view or a landscape, what it offers and what it promises, is not in the least straightforward. Every schoolchild will have learned in their basic science lessons that the Greeks used to believe that the eye was like a lamp that projected out on to the world. This is called an emission theory and it was popularised by the Greek philosopher

Empedocles and later taken up by Plato.[27] From Euclid (whose work on optics, *Optica*, dates from about 300 BCE) onwards it was widely believed that something travels from the object to the eye (an intromission theory). The particles or waveforms of the 'view' come to us through air, eyes, and optic nerves, and are finally blended in the brain. Like punching data into a computer, sight and sound in this model is reducible to the 1s and 0s of a JPEG. But were the Empedocleans entirely wrong?

An experienced runner will tell you that the process of looking at a view is more complex than data travelling into the eye. This is because our bodies play a significant role in what we see, sense or think.

The area of tightly packed photoreceptors on our retina is called the fovea, it is what gives our sight such high-resolution detail. Like pixels, we pack about 200,000 of these into that square millimetre at the centre of our vision. This makes us one of the most acutely visual animals on the planet (though bettered by many a bird of prey, which can have twice as many photoreceptors). About a third of our brain activity is given over to the processing of visual stimuli. But clarity and quality are not the same; it is not just about pixels and resolution. We see with our bodies, too.

Part of the way in which we learn to exercise bodily skills, such as running, is in our ability to recognise opportunities (and environments) which will allow us to use or perform those skills. We are unlikely to go for a run on a pebble beach, say, or in a bog. We become attuned to recognising environments in which it is possible to have qualitatively valuable running experiences. But is this just a case of personal judgement, or is it the environment itself that offers the opportunity?

The places in which it is possible for us to have a rewarding running experience are not the same. Instead, they share attributes and arrangements that we become attuned to recognising and wanting. Just as a pianist has knowledge of the fingers, we all have knowledges in our body that are inherited, but also ones that are learned, hard-acquired through practice.

Years ago, when I was starting up as a runner, I had many failures, but eventually the movement found its way into my bones and I was able to stick with it. Once I was up to a regular three or four miles, I was more capable and sure of myself, confident that I could cover the distance. But this exercise doesn't endow a runner with any particularly special skill. If you are not a runner, you could try this experiment. Without checking a map, try thinking of something three miles from where you are. Now imagine covering that distance to get there. It's not such a stretch, is it? If you had to walk the three miles you could almost certainly both picture it and manage it. As long as they don't wear those shoes that really pinch, and it's not raining, most people could happily manage this distance.

But if you keep on being a runner, get better, develop a taste for distance, you will have changed more than your muscles and the soles of your feet. What if you were to repeat the experiment, but were to think of something, say, 11 miles away? Would you be able to do that? You need the right body to have those thoughts, being one that can cover that kind of distance so that it is possible for you to be able to recall the climbs and falls, the variety of camber, and the changes of surface you'd need to cover. Can you honestly do that?

If you are a distance runner, I suspect you will find this task relatively easy. Without checking, I can tell you that it is that distance to Notting Hill from my house. A quiet route through south London would get me there in about two hours. I wouldn't need any special shoes. The weather wouldn't matter that much, either. I was pretty sure that if I headed in the opposite direction, 11 miles would take me to Darwin's house in Kent. When I went to check this I discovered I was wrong, but I was blisteringly close; it was 10.9 miles. It's not just this spatial relationship that has changed for me since I became a runner. I can't look at pictures of a landscape, of almost any kind, without thinking about running through them, over them, to the side of them, beyond them.

Our bodies are much smarter than we give them credit for being. When we exercise a kind of bodily movement or a motor skill this is evidence of a kind of understanding of the environment in which we are moving – the landscape is 'runnable', or 't'ai-chiable'; some septuagenarian climbers that I chatted to on Lundy Island also confirmed that they see it as 'climbable'. In this way the landscape offers up a particular kind of sense-experience that is exclusive to those who are readied to partake in it. But even then, these landscapes and environments are not just painted, theatrical backdrops to runs or activities. Merleau-Ponty, whose book I had been reading over my coffee and doughnuts that morning in Seattle, had leapt off the page at me when he explained that for 'the normal person every movement and its background are "moments of a unique totality". The background to the movement is not a representation associated or linked externally with the movement itself, but is immanent in the movement inspiring it and sustaining it at every moment.'[28]

So the landscape is not just a backdrop to my run, but as long I have the skills necessary to negotiate the landscape, it actually beckons to us. It creates the desire, and makes the movement within it possible, too. This means that as we move, we are not the passive recipients of sense-data; Merleau-Ponty believes that we 'summon' those beckonings to behave or act from the world around us.[29] So we are less the film in the movie theatre and more like the projector, casting an opportunity out onto the world around us. A landscape is not a view that we receive; our consciousness has to compose it, and it does this through our senses and our minds, but most importantly through the abilities and awarenesses of our bodies. The landscapes that we see are already embodied because we do not see them just with our eyes, but our bodies, our abilities and our potential.

In short, we don't receive the world as atomistic sense-data, like the sensor panel in a camera, but directly in relation to our ability to interact with it in various ways. Senses are lenses: change them and they change the world they perceive.[30]

By late morning I still feel a bit ghosted and out of step with the weather, which is clear and fine. Too tired to run, I take a bus into the city. I'm not much of a sightseer. I just like to stroll around feeling what a place is like. Today that will mean daisy-chaining between book- and coffee-shops in the college district. I lose a fine few hours doing this until I pass a running shop advertising its own 'fitlosophy', which I cannot resist. (I desperately want it to be called Sneakers in Seattle, but it isn't.) I'm not going to buy anything. I am at the beginning of a three-week trip down the Pacific coast where I will finish by teaching for a couple of weeks in California. I don't need any extra luggage. But, I start to riffle through the clothing. A young assistant bounds up, asking if he can help with anything. 'Have you got these in a medium?' I hold up some overpriced grey shorts that seem to weigh about as much as a dollar bill.

'Oh, these are great aren't they? They're very popular. They're, like, "naked shorts".'

'Naked shorts?'

'Yeah, like barefoot shoes – these are naked shorts.'

That's it. He's sold me. I want them.

I take the bus back to the B & B, quickly change, and goddamn! They are like wearing nothing, but in a good way. I am going to find that view.

Because Seattle is new terrain, I have my trusty Nike Frees that I have ripped the stuffing out of and trimmed the fat from, and whose laces I have replaced with elastic so I can slip them on and off easily as I encounter changing surfaces. They are feather-light because there is so little left of them. I don't bother with socks.

As with any other motor skill, the better one becomes at running, the easier it is to perceive the possibility of covering certain distances on certain terrains.

I look at the map. There is indeed a coast road. But maps' greatest design flaw is that they are too concerned with destinations, not journeys. They are full of roads without any information about what it is like to be on them. They attend to interconnection while ignoring experience. They tell us what is there, but not if we can see, smell, taste, hear or feel it. A landscape is all of these things, and it is more. It is about the time of day, the changing humidity, the rising tides, the direction of the wind, the scent of what is in season, or about how the light hits the water. Maps do not look like they were designed by humans, more like by computers performing a kind of spreadsheet geography.

The door clatters behind me. I jump the gate, and begin the long arc down towards the sea. As so often happens, my body sits up and takes notice as soon as I shift into the comfortable and familiar 4/4 running rhythm at the elastic pace of 180bpm.

Suburbia is recognisable anywhere, but each country, town even, has its own interpretation of it. This place reminds me of the creepy openness of John Carpenter's film *Halloween*, where everything seems open to view, but nobody is there to see it. I follow the soft curves that lead into other streets, which look inviting but identical. There is still no sign of the coast, and now that I've lost height the view of it has gone. Another turn and another street, and another. Has the coast been built over entirely, so that only private houses back onto it? After a mile and a half, I am getting warmer. I have passed hundreds of houses and not seen anyone that I can ask, but it seems like the road cannot descend any further. Disappointingly, this must be the coast road. I am a mouse in a maze who's caught a whiff of the cheese. I can hear and smell the sea but cannot see over the walls and fences. Just out of reach, only a few footsteps away, is the edge of the 170 million cubic miles of the Pacific. So great is its size, we know more about the surface of Mars than we do of the Pacific's deeper ocean beds.

The first slivers of sweat sting my eyes. The road begins to curve back inland. I feel like I want to give up. Am I about to be driven back up the hill to the cycleries, senior centers, animal hospitals, teriyaki joints, and all of that real-estate-hogging, real-estate-selling real estate?

Then suddenly, in a flash of blue, the wood-panelled houses disappear and there is the Puget Sound. This is a complex estuarine inlet of the Pacific Ocean, consisting of basins, channels and marine waterways. It protects the area (across its hundred-mile length) from the Pacific's pummelling storms, and helps to regulate the climate in and around Washington. Running this coast, it looks oceanic. Commas of islands speckle the seascape. Rising above a light mist from far out to sea are the snowcaps of the Olympic Mountains. The suddenness of this open space leaves me breathless.

Evolving to avoid other land predators, our eyes are particularly attuned to working laterally, paying special attention to how things appear in juxtaposition with one another. When we are presented with a stretched view such as this, our ability to make sense of the information overload is challenged beyond its capacity.

The road ahead is clear, so I slip off my Frees, and as always, some connection between the foot and the brain flips a switch so that I become more attentive to what is on the ground in my path.

In the concrete are bronzed diagrams of constellations. The shards of sweat keep stinging at my eyes, blurring them up. I gather a slub of my shirt and gouge at them with my fist, but the sting returns within seconds.

As I settle back into my rhythm, I realise that one thing that surely brought early settlers here thousands of years ago is the colour of the place. There is sea or greenery almost everywhere else in the world but here it is different. It looks like the sky and landscape have been underpainted with a hue chosen by one of the great masters.[31]

The smell is sweet and warm, mixed with the citrus salt of the sea. A low-level Pacific wind whips up suddenly and I am riding a thermal. Maybe it's the sleeplessness but my legs feel light and tensile. My eyes sting again. Checking the lie of the land ahead, I close my eyes for a couple of steps. The ground is warm, the concrete is not sharpened by gravel and, rare to say, I can feel my blood in my veins. A jasmine scent glides by me. I close my eyes briefly – experimenting with how far I can go, and whether I can 'know' proprioceptively how far I've gone without opening them. I take a quick look to check I haven't wandered into road or sea, and I close them again, and again, and again.

I can feel more constellations beneath my feet. A ship's klaxon sounds, penumbrated by its distance. And just like you can hear the muffling effect of fog or snow in the atmosphere, with my eyes closed I believe I can hear the depth of the view. Can it really be that to see a place truly, we must close our eyes? Then I remember, from my reading this morning, Merleau-Ponty's warning that if we really want 'to see the world and grasp it as paradoxical, we must break with our familiar acceptance of it'.[32]

So I keep my eyes closed and find that I am more equipped to feel. I think about Wordsworth's 'spots of time', relished moments to be recalled later for rejuvenating effect. I think of Keats, too, extolling the delights of planning a jolly:

> I purpose within a Month to put my knapsack at my back and make a pedestrian tour through the North of England, and part of Scotland – to make a sort of Prologue to the Life I intend to pursue – that is to write, to study and to see all Europe at the lowest expence. I will clamber through the Clouds and exist. I will get such an accumulation of stupendous recollections that as I walk through the suburbs of London I may not see them – I will stand upon Mount Blanc and remember this coming Summer when I intend to straddle Ben Lomond – with my Soul.[33]

These are moments of sensual pleasure written in the ink of memory, to be read and reread – of a life savoured rather than frittered like pocket money.

As I reach the peninsula of Alki Point, it is odd to think that I am standing on the spot where the modern settlement of Seattle began in 1851. These 'first' settlers only stayed a year (through an uncharacteristically hard winter) before they realised the weather was too inclement, and port access too shallow, prompting them to go east across the bay to where the city would later bed down.

The shoreline reveals a beach, so I throw both my shoes and myself over the railings. My toes sink into warm sand and I am arrested by the idea that this is what has been felt on days like this for thousands of years. 'Alki' means 'someday' in Chinook jargon (a pidgin trade language); the place was named in 1851 by these first settlers from New York. And as I draw my toes down into the sand, feeling the same sand that they will have felt, seeing the same colour sea and sky, I feel moored to those countless other days, and those countless others that have seen and heard and felt these things here. This is a kind of knowledge that penetrates us in a way that no reading ever can. It is a physical empathy that is impossible to know intellectually.

I look back up along the coastline and in the distance just above a thicket of trees that rise steeply from the shore I can see what can only be a hovering UFO.

Later, when I am making some notes I realise that I can't write about the anthropogenic mush of buldings and telegraph poles around which the UFO appears – I know it was there, but I don't remember it. Our retinas are spherical and our lenses cannot focus on all of an image for us, only a tiny part, so we do the rest of the work ourselves – our brains fill in the blind spots both of what we don't see, and what we simply can't be bothered to see.

Sensing is not a transparent and straightforward process of reproducing what is happening in the outside world. We work, pulling the strings like Geppetto, behind the scenes in conjunction with the information our senses receive, to create a sense-experience. In the world of sensing and perception 2+2 never equals 4, but always something more. In one of J.G. Ballard's short stories, 'The Zone of Terror', a psychologist is trying to explain a kind of temporal hallucination experienced by his patient by using the metaphor of film. In this metaphor, many thousands of hours of footage are stored in the brain, as if the eyes are a film camera.[34]

But our experience is more like the photographs in Ridley Scott's film *Blade Runner* (1982). Harrison Ford's character, Deckard, is following up a lead and finds some photographs in a possible perp's apartment. At least they look like photographs to us. He feeds them into a scanner and is then able to enhance the original image and navigate through the room away from the picture's original perspective, through to other rooms, recovering details that no glance at the photograph could possibly deliver. Our perception is a bit like this in that we are presented with some scant information, and from it we perceive a much fuller and detailed picture. Running has taught me that our perception occurs as in a stream or a path – we do not take in a single scene all at once, we move through it. Our bodies affect the visions and sounds of external reality, placing them in time and sense-making sequence. Even in the act of perception, we are trying to arrest something that will always outrun us. To capture whatever reality might be, other faculties than ours seem necessary to the task; whatever those faculties are, we as a species do not possess them, and they certainly cannot be written down. The very difficultly of explaining such an idea is part of the argument for its existence.

I set off along the beach, and as I round the bend, the recognisable Seattle skyline begins, drawn like a polygraph. The flying saucer reveals itself as the upper deck of the Space Needle, then there's Columbia Center, and finally the altar-boy's snuffer atop Smith Tower. The scene changes quickly, as if I have stepped over a border. The population increases a hundredfold; this now seems like a miniature resort. I have gone far enough, so I turn back, south, and practically the first road I find is the other end of the one with the coffee shop from this morning's 5am jaunt, now many miles away.

Long runs with long views and long beaches cannot fail to minimise any troubles or worries, even if I still have over 200 pages of Merleau-Ponty to wrestle my way through. But I am OK with not 'understanding it'; like running itself, Merleau-Ponty and his philosophy of embodied thought cut like a razor through our belief that the world and our relationship to it is logical and can be made sense of from an objective distance.

I know that running is all too often seen as an introspective activity, but running breaks down the barriers between what we think is inside us and what we see as being outside. Running unites us with places and creates emotional connections with them in ways that are not easily accounted for.

It seems obvious to say, but becoming a runner (rather than just a walker of the land) has an impact on the kinds of choices that you make. Your body's changes will permit access to experiences that would otherwise prove impossible. Just as we learn to read words, our senses learn to read places, and the more we do it, the more attuned they and we become to collecting and collating how places look and feel, and how they live with you, within you and without. With its sensitive potential, your body can be your means to freedom, if you will only allow it to become itself and escape the received wisdom that separates it from the mind.

Runners know in their hearts that when thoughts move, we think them differently.

PART II
REASONING

3.

WHAT'S RUNNING THROUGH YOUR MIND?: RUNNING, NEUROSCIENCE AND ENVIRONMENTAL PSYCHOLOGY

THE COTSWOLDS, BRIGHTON AND ANN ARBOR, MICHIGAN

I have such a stressful job that the only way I can get it out of my mind is by running hard.

– Alan Turing, 1947

These two branches of education seem to have been given by some god to men to train these two parts of us. They are not intended the one to train the body, the other the mind, but to ensure a balance between energy and initiative on the one hand and reason on the other by tuning each to the right pitch.

– Socrates speaking in Plato's *Republic,* 380 BCE

If you could manufacture a pill that was guaranteed to make you smarter, it would make you a billionaire. We would rush out in our millions to buy it for our ageing parents, our children and ourselves. The drug companies are hard at it, but in the meantime this is exactly what exercise is capable of. With a few tweaks to the way we do it, we can optimise the experience of running to harness the benefits it brings, long after we stop moving. Put simply, running makes you smarter.[1] It is not quite as easy as that, but that ought to be enough to turn the head of anyone considering running, but there's more – much, much more. If performed in a softly fascinating (more on this later) and natural environment, running can make you better at your job,[2] more independent,[3] a more attentive friend or partner,[4] care more for the environment,[5] enhance your concentration levels, improve exam results,[6] and feel more attractive to – well, whoever it is that you want to attract.[7]

Neuroscience's analytic technologies are not yet at the point where advanced brain-scanning equipment can be placed on a runner's head like a baseball cap, to read exactly what is going on during a real outdoor run. Nonetheless, there is a huge amount of research data already out there that can help in understanding what running means for our psychological wellbeing. With the help of some recent advances in neuroscience, palaeontology, and behavioural and environmental psychology, I focus in this chapter on understanding what is happening when we are out on a run. In what ways exactly might running provide essential respite from our digital, on-screen lives? The runs I undertake in this chapter demonstrate some of the essential ingredients to help us understand why we are less likely to achieve a euphoric and restorative state on a treadmill than when we are running outdoors. These runs will get to the bottom of the runner's high.

For years it was assumed that the runner's high was just a flush of endorphins in the brain, but if this were the case we would be able to achieve a euphoric state by stomping about our living rooms to workout DVDs. The idea of endorphin (body-made morphine) release was first queried in the 1980s, when subjects who had been given naloxone (an opioid inhibitor) in experiments reported the same 'high' as those subjects who exercised without. The expectation of the 'high' was also thought to precipitate it.[8] Thirty years later, a link between exercise, endorphins and mood is believed to exist, but is described in a recent meta-analysis as merely 'plausible'.[9] In John Ratey and Eric Hagerman's book *Spark!* it is referred to as a 'fuzzy notion'.[10] Gina Kolata, science-writer for the *New York Times*, writes it off as a myth,[11] and the psychobiologist Huda Akil thinks it a 'total fantasy', borrowed from pop culture.[12] Can this be correct – can thousands of runners have been making it up for all these years?

The short answer is a definitive 'no', and serves as evidence of the all-too-easy way in which the sciences can be mobilised to dismiss waves of anecdotal evidence that are contrary to a supposedly proven opinion. Our Boston biomechanics expert, Irene Davis, said in an interview recently that we have to beware of the truth that 'research' reveals, because the truth changes. The truth 50 years ago is not the same truth as today.[13]

MISMATCH ENVIRONMENTS AND YOUR BRAIN DURING EXERCISE

In 2014, my partner and I, with a writer friend of mine called Elle and her dog, The Captain, travelled back in time for a fortnight's holiday in the Cotswolds. We stayed in a beautiful old seventeenth-century house surrounded by grounds in which cricket and badminton could be played between the giant walnut trees, apples from the orchard could be plucked and cooked, and the only thing we had to watch out for was The Captain's pathological hatred of horses.

We arrived on the wrong day and had to sleep the night at a local pub, where we binged on food, drink and Wi-Fi. The next day we and the mounds of books we'd brought with us (in which the local 'Dymock poets' featured quite heavily) took possession of our analogue house (no landline, no mobile signal, no TV, no Internet).

The recent weather had been patchy at best. The night was unseasonably cold, so the next morning we got some logs in, organised lunch and I headed out onto the paths.

I am in the wrong shoes. They have thin soles made for London running, not these stony pathways. In only my first mile, the ground gives way to such a steep declension that I have to walk the single-track road. I start to run again and the tarmac joins with a footpath leading to the tiny hamlet of Nag's Head. It has a plaque on a wall listing the 18 men from here who died in the First World War – about a quarter of its inhabitants – one of whom was only 17 years old.

Down the side of a cottage, three men are working and they smile at me as I dance down a path littered with chalky cobbles protruding from the earth like femural heads. Then I realise why they were smiling: the way (after only a few metres) comes to an end in a steep hillock like a 20-metre tsunami of grass. The psychology of the runner will not let me retrace my steps so early in the game, so I start fighting back to find my way.

The wisps of grass are so tall they brush against my face, and beneath their horizon are nettles that I feel before I see. My legs up to my hips start tingling with stings (which go on to last for days). I angle my way up the hill in a Z, only to discover there is a clean and clear path that I somehow missed.

I catch up with myself and spend the next couple of miles under the dappled luminosity of beeches. Summer is in its last phases and when the breeze blows, the leaves sound a little more sibilant than usual, readying as they are for autumn. It makes me think of that arresting bit in Thomas Hardy, when he talks about the range of character in different trees' voices: 'To dwellers in a wood almost every species of tree has its voice as well as its feature.'[14]

And I'm *still* climbing. To my left is a shorn meadow, golden, with great drums of gathered hay. There is something colour-wheel perfect about the three shades of the landscape, gold, green and blue, that feels like a mental or optical sluice, rinsing out my eyes, and mood, rinsing the words right out of me. As I soon discover, environmental psychologists and neuroscientists have begun to explain that it's a bit more complicated than this.

As I run through these landscapes that inspired the Dymock poets, it's easy to feel how places and what we do in them alter our mental states.

The Dymock poets were a group of youngish writers from the early twentieth century (among them, Edward Thomas, Robert Frost, Rupert Brooke and John Drinkwater), who, for one reason or another, found their way out of London to their quiet hideaway to enjoy the comparative freedom of the Gloucestershire and Herefordshire borders. Although Thomas was closely connected with them, he wasn't yet writing poetry when he visited Robert Frost, Lascelles Abercrombie and Wilfrid Gibson. The Dymocks set themselves against the modernist turn that was emerging in London. They were part of a loosely defined collective of 'Georgian Poets' whose work would appear in several anthologies of that name, published between 1912 and 1922.

The Georgian Dymock poets were rustic and simple, employing the language of the everyday, imitating the natural cadences of speech. It's hard not to get behind an aesthetic whose founding principle was so democratic. But, like pages of history tossed into a fire, most of the Dymock poets were consumed in the First World War. Edward Thomas, with a career spent in prose, did not live to see his first collection of poems in print. He had the sensibility of a shark. It seemed that as long as he could stay in constant motion, walking, walking, walking, he could survive the terrible depressions that he, and consequently those around him, suffered from.

The rustling beech cover breaks and I'm in a gulley that has been recently sheared back. Stubs of weeds snap and poke at me underfoot; and the nettles, sensing their chance for dominance, are creeping back into the empty space left by the cutter. After another mile I am back on single-track tarmac. It looks like an Eric Ravilious painting: the road, lined with hedges, runs straight to the horizon, then gold and green fields appear either side.

A tractor ambles over the hill and I have to flatten myself into the side of the road as it thunders past. And it is only then that I see a caterpillar, in the middle of the road, perfectly perpendicular, in full sprint to the other side. It oxbows and stretches in a line, as if it has done this journey tens of times. I laugh at the dynamic heedlessness of one thing for the other, the tractor and the caterpillar.

Signs of modern life are ahead. I reach a junction which signposts one way for Bath, the other for Cirencester. After a few yards, I decide on neither. There is no pavement and the booming traffic is so fast and heavy that the distraction of a dinging text in a lorry-driver's cab would be enough to kill me. I am running for nothing, so I turn back onto the footpath and retrace my steps for a while, hoping to be diverted once again.

After Edward Thomas's death, Harold Monro's collections of *Georgian Poetry* continued until 1922, that hot year of modernism that saw the publication of James Joyce's *Ulysses*, Virginia Woolf's *Jacob's Room* and T.S. Eliot's *The Waste Land*. Even though editions of *Georgian Poetry* sold more than 70,000 copies, its moment had passed and it was already seen as conservative and backward-looking. What chance did a verse form, so sense-making, so clear in its expression, have of surviving the chaotic lunacy of a war that slaughtered so many?

The modern world and modern warfare changed everything. They did away with the idea that the world made sense, that it could be understood easily, that we could look inside ourselves and know what was there. Modernism was the open expression that we were not who we thought we were; that we had fundamentally changed and that pastoral poetry could do little to make sense of the way we live now. The modernists were right: the *world* had changed. The way we lived in it had changed. But had we?

The world may have changed but our bodies have not, and we are firmly related to the places that we came from. Environmental psychologists call our place of origin the 'environment of evolutionary adaptation' and aspects of modern life that differ from it are seen as 'discordant'.[15] Discords in music are bad notes in a harmonic key, the sound of a misplaced finger in a stunned guitar chord, and in environmental terms they represent what can individually be only a small aspect of our life that is, consciously or not, out of step with our complex evolutionary function. A discord describes those aspects of the environment which are not 'natural' – one of the barriers to recovery in a hospital, for example, is its lack of homeliness, because we are out of place.[16] In discordant environments we are like depressed pandas who refuse to mate in captivity because the conditions are somehow wrong.

The city is, of course, a discordant environment, and the city is a psychological experience as much as it is a physical one. *Homo sapiens* evolved around 2 million years ago, shortly after the Pleistocene epoch began. The Pleistocene, though, ended 11,700 years ago with the last ice age. So although we live in the Holocene epoch, we don't really belong to it – to return to music, perhaps we are an evolutionary *sostenuto*: a note held long after the movement has finished.

There have been numerous studies in recent years concerned with the effect of technology on our cognitive function and our sensibilities, on our aptitude for learning and socialising. For centuries, almost every technology's introduction has been accompanied by concerns for the wellbeing of its consumers. Around 2,500 years ago, Socrates railed against the 'forgetfulness' inculcated by the technology of writing.[17] In the sixteenth century, Conrad Gessner worried about the information overload that lay in wait after the printing press took off.[18] More recently, in the 1920s, the worry was the passivity of the picturegoer's gaze.[19] In the 1940s, parents expressed concern about children's addiction to the radio.[20] In my childhood, TV was the great enemy.[21] (My mother, harried as a result of running her own business while bringing up the four of us, used to check if the TV had been on while she was out by testing the back of it for warmth. Unaware of the danger, we soon learned that a cleverly placed ice pack after *Top of the Pops* did the trick.) And it is not only parents who now worry about what the Internet – and especially the behemoths: email, SMS, Wikipedia, Facebook, Twitter, YouTube – is doing to how we learn, socialise and think. It is little wonder that we expend energy in the search for activities and experiences, like running and walking, that will allow us to escape off-line.

Running is analogue. It is hunter-gatherer. It is Palaeo. It is linear. It is long-form thought. It is an uninterrupted conversation with yourself. It is a journey back through modernity to your body. It is a way out of technology. It is a way to be free.

We now live in an environment that is very difficult to switch off, and our brains have evolved in such a way that they need to switch off from time to time. We flock towards the interruptive technologies of smartphones, smart watches, and things like email, when all the time what these technologies are doing is allowing us to deplete our finite resources of concentration and attention. It takes willpower to turn off your phone, not check your emails or sign out of social media. So even if I manage to resist these things, it still takes mental work. The supposed relief from alleviating the potential distraction can be offset by the mental effort that it requires.

Our brains have an inbuilt desire to extend our maps, to better understand the world. In a natural environment we have some control over our levels of attention. In modern life, where we exist in a veritable ecosystem of interruption, this is more difficult.

A strong analogy can be drawn between attention and diet. We are all different, but our appetites evolved in an environment where sugar and fat were not easily come by. If a hunter-gatherer hominin were to stumble across a pile of doughnuts while roaming the savannah, they could happily tuck in to raise their blood sugar and muscle glycogen, and whatever wasn't used could be laid down as body fat for a day when no cairns of Krispy Kremes were to be found. The obesity epidemic in the developed world is basically due to the fact that we have changed the environment so substantially that we can buy a bag of doughnuts, for a couple of quid, every day of the year – and all the milkshakes, coffees and chocolate bars that we choose. Food scarcity may have become abundance, but our bodies don't know that, and our Palaeolithic appetites (that evolved for our survival) persist in an environment that is no longer resonant with them. And we well know that liking something doesn't necessarily mean that it's good for us.

We are so addicted to distraction that computer applications are now available that force us to stay disconnected for a specified period. These programmes are basically the informational equivalent of a gastric band.

Since the day I got my FitBit, I have been meaning to disable the little tap on the wrist it gives me when a phone call comes in. But I haven't done it. I also find it really hard to leave my phone on silent, not check my emails, and to resist Facebook and Twitter. I am hardwired for this, it seems. I have had a number of cross-purpose conversations with people about email – 'But why don't you just not check them?' they sensibly ask. What they are talking about sounds so easy, but I don't know how to do it. My personality is good at doing things, and really terrible at 'not' doing them. So I am happy to try and exercise more to shift some weight, but eating less? No chance.

One of the great myths of the modern world is the belief that we are good multitaskers. That's not true, but what the brain is really good at is self-delusion. Switching between tasks, checking email, deleting one or two along the way, replying to a text – in the completion of all these micro-tasks the novelty-centre in the brain is stimulated with a little hit of dopamine, which is both pleasant and mildly addictive.

And it is all so very tiring because it's all so coercive. This is even true when reading, usually a relaxing experience: I find that when I read on an electronic device, something as seemingly innocent as a hyperlink tries to bump me off the page to explore somewhere else.

It is this mode of living that can make activities like running seem more alien and peculiar, boring even. So we try to turn it into something else by paying to run on treadmills, or listening to music, or competing against ourselves or others. The idea of being alone for an extended period of time – without interruption of any kind, without aural entertainment, without the diverting promise of an arriving text, asks us to *be* in a way that is the unmetrical fifth beat in the rhythm of modern life. Without long breaths of silence, we lose sustained access to ourselves; we risk forgetting what it is like to be alive in this shard of time flanked by eternity.

The brain will survive – it is highly adaptable. But for now, as the enemy is within the gates, what can we do? Put the kettle on and invite them to tea? Or resist and run?

Meanwhile, back in the Cotswolds . . . As I run up a lane pheasants cross my path and defecate with fear as they flutter into the air. It's taken me 30 minutes or so to get back to the house but I'm not quite ready to stop so I veer outwards once again on another bearing. The sun had been warm, but a sudden bite came into the air and now there's a flash shower. As I look across a shorn crop of hay, I can see that the rain's deep – twinkling in the sun for miles.

In the distance a church spire rises from a copse like the mast of a ship in a tempest. I am relying on the sun for my direction, so inevitably I lose my way when I come to an unclear junction, and take the most defined route. Down a long pathway there is a handful of poppies and elder. The fields are bleach clean. Ever since intensive agriculture began, the diversity of wildflowers and colour seen in the fields has been diminishing. On a square mile of land all I can see are eight wispy poppies huddled together. We are suffering from a kind of generational amnesia where every 30 years, the baseline for what is called 'nature' retreats further and further, becoming blander and blander.

After another mile, I arrive at a farm, convinced I have gone wrong. Two dachshunds eye me from across the paddock. Their tails curl up, their hackles rise and they start, well, I suppose it is sprinting but it looks more like a kind of angry see-sawing towards me. Their owner can't see or hear any of this as she is engrossed with what looks like a giant vacuum cleaner sucking up horseshit. The sausage dogs' confidence wanes and they slow as they approach me. The woman finally sees me and runs over to tell me that I have indeed gone wrong, and she sets me back on the path.

The rain stops. I go up and down vale – through gulleys, over hillocks. When I finally see a village I recognise, a funny thing happens: without prompt or warning – bang! Hormones flush through my bloodstream and I'm having another of my supposedly non-existent runner's highs.

The rush always seems strongest in its first moments, but the euphoria and its painkilling effects continue. My lungs fill deeply, as if a third one has opened up somewhere in my thorax.

Freud had a term for how we self-monitor our behaviour through the internalisation of cultural rules: superego. And just like when drunk, the runner's high can encourage uncharacteristic conduct where the superego retreats into the horizon. This time I'm lucky and the only effect is that I find myself raising my arms in joy, as if I'm crossing a finish line.

In the final mile, I pass an old red telephone box that has been stripped and relined with bookshelves. As if we need any more books, I see a hardback of Rohinton Mistry's *Family Matters* – a book I bought in paperback just two days ago. I smile to myself when I realise that this is the most natural form of running: I am foraging, hunter-gathering.

The finish is a steep climb which I gamely attack. A man sees me carrying the tome and yells 'Bravo!' from his garden. I smile, but as soon as I'm out of sight I splutter to a stop – it's too steep (the superego returns).

On one side of me is a golf course – another kind of bleached landscape; on the other there are nettles, celandines, clematis, all kinds of grasses; the wild berries are out, too – so I stop and grab at some; they are round and sweet. Then I notice that the diversity missing from the fields is here in microcosm. I wonder if the 'edgelands' (those half-urban, half-rural placeless areas that have been of such intense interest to more recent writers) are now so small that they cannot even appear on a map.[22] Have they shrunk to this slim fillet of weeds by the roadside? What will the next generation's edgeland be?

I arrive back at the house still woozy, grab my laptop and start pounding out all the thoughts that have ambled through my head for the last hour or so.

Almost any writer will tell you that writing while drunk doesn't work. I'm a morning person, so I haven't really had the opportunity to test this theory; I just can't face it. But the hangover from the runner's high is something different altogether. Why is it that in this state, creative and organised work like writing comes so very easily? You feel drunk, but you don't think drunk.

They are funny things, these highs. The earliest ones I can remember were from when I was running the South Downs in Sussex. They are as strong as bootleg whisky. They make you want to stop everyone that you pass and tell them how beautiful they are, what a wonderful world this is, isn't it great to be alive?! I tend not to do this, but I do manage something just as creepy: unmediated smiling in public places while I gasp in exhortations of ecstasy. I throw my arms wide to open myself up to the universe, because I feel suddenly like the conduit for all its energy.

The fact that I am willing to seem completely idiotic is testament to the raw power of the high. Only someone under the influence of some quite heavy-duty chemicals would give in to the temptation of such clichés.

When I first discovered these highs, on the South Downs, it wasn't only them that I was chasing, but they were an important part of the relief running offered from my own sense of feeling stuck in life.

The highs do have a darker side, too. My friend Scarlett Thomas, the novelist, went through a phase when she exercised a lot, and I mean a lot. It got to the point where she might play tennis for several hours a day, then maybe skip a meeting and go and workout, too. She rarely took days off. Why would she? She loved her practice, doing all sorts of things: weights, running, Pilates. Just before she became ill, she had a battle rope coiled like a serpent ready to bite at the asphalt on the seafront of the town where she lives (I have it now, and it causes much eye-rolling among mums and dog-owners in the local park). She was about to go off to learn how to slam tractor tyres with sledgehammers, but her heart rate slowed. She began to feel tired all the time. She had burned out. It looked a lot like overtraining syndrome (which is hard to diagnose) and it laid her out for months.[23] But something else also seemed to happen to her. The pleasure and reward centres of her brain even now still fire with the electrical conductance of gold. Her synapses flick and spark almost as soon as she starts any exercise, so that she no longer has to work patiently for the 'high'. Nothing feels so good, nor comes so easily for her. Her condition prevented her from partaking in competitive sport for nearly a year, and even now her behaviour around exercise seems overwhelmingly cautious, not unlike a recovering addict.

While many studies have attempted to give credence to the runner's high, one of the principal problems with the endorphin theory is that our brains are protected by a fatty wall known as the blood–brain barrier. This barrier is necessary in maintaining a constant working environment for the brain, and in preventing blood pathogens (like viruses) from entering it. Among the many things that cannot pass through to the brain's neural receptors are endorphins, and so they cannot be responsible for the runner's high.

Though some questions remain, the mystery was recently solved; the runners had not been lying. A high is experienced when the endocannabinoid system is activated,[24] releasing the neurotransmitter anandamide.[25] Anandamide bypasses the blood–brain barrier easily, providing pain relief and feelings of relaxation. The reason that I felt like I was accessing a third lung is because the neurotransmitter helps to dilate veins and arteries, allowing an increased flow of oxygen in the blood.

The Palaeolithic persistence hunters out on the veldts of prehistory could be out for hours at a time, chasing down their prey, until the animal (unable to lose heat as efficiently as the human) collapsed with exhaustion. Humans are thought to have evolved these mechanisms to make hunting more successful and rewarding, and less painful. But there are still anomalies in the data. In many of the tests completed so far the euphoric response of outdoor runners scores more highly than for people taking an aerobics or spinning class, for swimmers, or even cyclists. What is it that is specific to running that encourages this accentuated 'high'?

A recent trial looked at the extent to which, as well as being born to run, we might be wired to do so. Research also shows that our endocannabinoid reward-system is an old one; so old that it is shared by other species. One study looked at whether the system was found to be active in dogs (a running animal) and ferrets (a non-runner). The endogenous neurotransmitters believed to be behind the runner's high were of course active in the pooches but not the ferrets. The provision of a neurobiological reward linked to high-intensity exercise is thought to go some way to explaining why it was that, as hominins, we indulged in the risky, potentially injurious, and energy-hungry behaviour of running.

The three big guns of mood control are serotonin, dopamine and norepinephrine. Serotonin is the elder sibling, keeping the party under control, trying to make sure nobody gets overstimulated or too excited. Dopamine is the reason so many people become addicted to the challenge of computer games like Tetris and Candy Crush; it is a learning-reward neurotransmitter and focussing mood-controller, which plays various roles in different parts of the brain. Norepinephrine is able to indirectly elevate perception, attention and arousal. Through drugs like methylphenidate (Ritalin) and fluoxetine (Prozac), these neurotransmitters can be controlled, but it is more complex than this. Imagine a car in which a chemical has been added to the petrol to prevent the exhaust from rusting; if not added carefully it is likely to have all manner of unpredictable effects on the behaviour of the engine as the chemical makes its way through to the exhaust pipe. This is why these drugs are so difficult to prescribe, because the human engine is so complex. But exercise is also able to do this job, to balance these neurotransmitters in a way that is currently not really possible with the blunt scalpel of medication alone.

We all know that stress is not good for us. It is poisonous, but even at the level of the brain cell, stress acts like a kind of rust. Depression is even known to shrink parts of the brain. Exercise, though, can have a hugely positive impact on how our brains work, and while it is not a cure for depression, it can return to us an element of control over misbehaving brain chemistry. The sad irony is that saying 'Hey! Why don't you try some exercise?' to a depressed person is like telling a hungry mouse that there is free cheese on Jupiter.

It all seems like fuel to the argument that modern 'discords' are out of step with our old relationships – that the ways our lives are organised in modernity are not compatible with the complex biochemical needs of our bodies.

Exercise has been shown to produce neurogenesis (the process where new brain cells are created) in the hippocampus (involved in memory formation and spatial navigation).[26] This may sound like exercise will make you more intelligent. Well, it will and it won't.

While intense exercise will create brain cells, they are basically stem cells, hanging around waiting to be put to use. If you exercise and go straight to bed, chances are, for all the other benefits you will have derived from your training, you will have missed out on this one.

This is because what exercise actually does is to make you *ready* to become smarter. It prepares the hardware and the pathways needed for learning, but you have to actively do some learning yourself, too. Integrating exercise into your working or studying day would seem like a sensible option if this particular benefit is of interest to you.

Another way that exercise helps to make you smarter is that it encourages the production of a protein called brain-derived neurotrophic factor (BDNF). It encourages the growth of new neurons while supporting existing ones. John Ratey (a Harvard professor of psychiatry) has called it 'Miracle-Gro for the brain'.[27] Once BDNF is released on the brain's axons (the conductors of electrical impulses) and dendrites (that process the impulses generated by other neurons), what is present there can thrive.[28] If a brain cell is like a tree, BDNF allows its roots to grow deeper, its leaves to catch more sunlight and grow larger, and makes sure that the tracheids that send water to the leaves are not clogged or withered, but ready to exchange information with root or branch. Unsurprisingly, quantities of BDNF decrease with age, and lower levels are found in Alzheimer's sufferers, schizophrenics and chronic depressives.

Your brain can never blaze on full capacity. Imagine trying to get every muscle in your body firing at the same time. The brain is just like this. While a part of you might be lifting a heavy weight, many of your muscles will be at rest. In the brain, processes are fired as quickly and easily as they are deactivated once a process is complete. So by getting our brain to do something else other than focus on the warning signals of worry and anxiety that are being pumped out by the limbic system, we can actively relieve stress symptoms by firing up another part of the brain, which is precisely what we do when we exercise.[29]

You will also be doing something really valuable and important for your wellbeing, which while not directly connected with the intensity of exercise, is still a powerful by-product of it. It is to do with what psychologists have begun to call 'soft fascination': a mental process that allows us to reflect, think freely, and be at home to ourselves. It won't make you smarter, but as with the stimulation of BDNF, you'll be more ready to learn as a result. You'll also be be significantly less stressed. Here's an example.

BRIGHTON, MICHIGAN AND EXERCISE SQUARED

Having been away for years, I've come to Brighton to visit friends, and I'm fitting a run in between seeing them. I've forgotten to bring any shoes, but it's that time of year when I've spent so much time out of them that it doesn't matter, I can manage it barefoot. Our memories of places, even those that we love, seem only ever to be partial. Their overwhelming presence and the intense simultaneity of our sense-experience of them are never quite possible to recall. But it's not just their presence; all the things that you've done and seen in those places seem written there.

As soon as I step on to the seafront, the air seems heavy with the glitter of damp scents. The rain has brought the blood of these billion stones and pebbles to life. And with it, they stir up random excess memory. The sky is grey with patches of peach; soft rain floats in the air like chaff. For 20 years I ambled, ran and cycled this track of seafront between western Hove and Brighton and it bursts with recollections of reading while walking, football, skateboarding, and fumblings between the beach huts. When I lived here, the storms could be so violent as to drive pebbles up the beach, across the promenade and the lawns, around the shacks, over the dual carriageway and hundreds of yards up the neighbouring streets.

Now, even though the concrete seems impermeable, the tarmac, the grey and pink flagstones, the pebbles even, have all been brought to life by something in the air. Their mineral tang is swirling and diving like a cloud of starlings. But it's not the rain; it's something else. The word for this smell is petrichor, from the Greek *petra*, 'stone'; and *ichor*, the golden fluid that runs in the veins of the gods and the immortals.

Up ahead, by the bombed-out pier, I can just make out waves of starlings as they tidally swoop and swirl. The movement is uncaptureable, the soaring, stunning four-dimensionality of this dance of clouds. As Ruskin said of water, 'It is like trying to paint a soul'.[30] It is overwhelming: centrifugal spinning and turning like a tornado churning in a washing machine.

As I'm running and watching, what I am doing without realising is exercising a 'soft fascination' with the environment. It is one of a few kinds of attentional capacity that we exercise.

The most obvious kind is called 'involuntary attention', which can be characterised by our reaction to a loud noise, seeing a snake, or hearing our name in a crowded room (narcissists that we are). Involuntary attention requires no mental effort; it is more like a reflex that comes from a very old part of our brain.

There is also something called 'directed attention'. This is the kind of attention that requires work: things like exam revision, but it also includes things as seemingly innocent as watching a film or gaming, or even looking at advertisements. (Conservative estimates suggest that we are exposed to between 600 to 625 adverts per day,[31] while another estimate puts the figure at about 3,500.[32]) Our ability to concentrate wears out in ways that I'll come back to, and those abilities need to be recharged.

The best way to do this is through soft fascination, which is a sort of meandering, free-form mode of thought inculcated most successfully by natural environments. Instead of the mental work associated with reading, writing emails or even watching TV, 'soft fascination' is exemplified by something like leaves rustling in the wind. Time spent offline is essential for effective mental functioning. Letting your thoughts run as freely as you are is good for a healthy, working brain.

I am brought back to the surface of the present when I see plumes of sun-darkened seaweed thrashing in the air. It takes me a moment to recognise a crow so bedraggled it looks like it's been shot by a blunderbuss. It tries to climb, but the wind is too strong and it gives up.

The smell hits me again. The oil, sodium, pollen, magnesium, bacteria, lichen, potassium, soot, skin, calcium, loam, dust, diesel, lead, wood, ash, mould and sand; elements of them all sink and burrow into the magmatic caverns, atomic in size, made billions of years ago in every pebble and stone. All kinds of memories of the place flood back to me (like the petrichor's arid scents, tucked tightly away, waiting for a stimulus to release them). And all of it is still here: playing football with a great friend that I lost touch with, David, on our way into town to celebrate our degree results; walking in to watch a £1 mid-afternoon film when I was on the dole in 1990; chasing after my young nephew who, in the winter cold and rain, had stripped and bolted because 'It's the seaside!'; sitting in the moonlight listening to the music of This Mortal Coil and watching the stars after my father died; wading through *Middlemarch* on the beach; walking my dog who used to try and bite at the waves as they broke; watching the 1999 lunar eclipse. It's all here in this smell of rain.

And then I remember possibly the funniest run I have ever done; but the way I remembered it mattered, too.

Shortly after the time of my South Downs runs, I was living in a flat near a friend, Aylla, who was undergoing chemo. I used to walk her abominably behaved dogs, so we held each other's keys. In post-millennial, austere text-speak, I called the dogs the '0E Girls' (as in 'naught-ee' girls).[33]

One morning, instead of lying in bed for hours, nursing a well-grounded sense of self-disregard at the ongoing chaos I had created after flitting from that long relationship, I threw back the covers and danced to the front door singing, 'Oh yeah, it's my birthday.' There would be cards downstairs; I was sure of it. I stepped into the shared hallway. I latched the door and it clicked behind me as I bounded to the mail-box. I opened it to find one letter: my car insurance was due. And when I went back upstairs the door was not latched; it was locked.

Phone, keys, money, shirt, shoes and trousers were all on the wrong side of the locked door. For five minutes I refused to believe it. I had latched it; I heard it click. It wasn't fair. I couldn't possibly be locked out. For a further five minutes, I tried to rouse anyone I could from the other flats. Nothing. I rummaged through the uncollected junk mail in the hope that I might find a plastic card so that I could lever the lock. Empty. Then I gave the door a couple of pathetic kicks. Hopeless. Happy birthday!

Just as I had been made to do when I had forgotten my school PE kit, I would have to make a run for it in my pants. I could probably make it to Aylla's, but even if I did, she might be at the hospital. Then, I would be a man alone in his underpants, in the street.

But hey, it's Brighton! So I ran.

I know that it happened, but I have no memory of this run. I remember it was – lucky for me – a sunny day. I don't remember the route I took, the looks that my appearance no doubt coaxed; passing the newsagent (who knew me), climbing the steep hill, knocking at the door? Nothing. I remember that the 0E Girls were very excited to see me standing on the raised porch high above the street expecting me to take them out for a walk.

Aylla answered the door bleary-eyed, post-chemo, and requiring very little in the way of explanation, handed over the keys, and I ran back.

Later that day, when she had resurfaced a little from the chemo stupor, I got a text from her: 'I wish I had been awake enough to enjoy that this morning.'

Of all the runs to remember, I would have thought that running there and back should be prime candidates – but all I know is that I did them. Why is this?

I think it is to do with instrumentality: the purpose of the run was not itself, but to get through the streets as quickly and quietly as possible. My attention was not at rest and primed for experience, it was as overly directed as amateur theatre, focussed entirely on the hope that Aylla would answer the door.

The run's purposefulness has erased it from my memory, whereas I will remember that crow trying to take off in the breeze for decades to come. It is like the brain can only do one thing at a time, either focus on the experience *or* the intention. And, when directed attention begins to rest, other more reflective and observant processes are fired up. And there is a great deal more to this than just being able to lay down new memories. It is to do with our emotional functioning and our wellbeing.

Throughout our childhood we are encouraged to 'eat our greens'; it seems that we ought to be '*among* our greens', too. Waves of psychological, environmental and behavioural research have gathered in recent years to prove that spending time in 'natural' environments is good for us, even if the processes involved are yet to be fully explained. This missing algorithm, the mysterious cause, the potent x, may also go some way to providing an answer as to why runners are reported in trials to experience a better 'high' when outside in fields or parks or on hills than when using cross-trainers or treadmills. The missing link might be found in ART.

Attention-restoration theory has emerged as a means of explaining why it is that so many of us are unconsciously desperate to get away from our screens and out into the air.

In the last few decades there have been repeated environmental and psychological studies on the effects of nature in reducing stress,[34] improving attention,[35] benefitting health in various other ways,[36] and even increasing longevity.[37] With such evidence, we should be open to the idea that the influence of the natural world on our psychology is not a wholly conscious one. Just as we have an instinctual involuntary fear response to, say, snakes, in a recent meta-analysis, environmental scientists Bjørn Grinde and Grete G. Patil suggested that a region free of plant life might also be experienced by us, unconsciously, as an unsafe environment (having no vegetation or food as means of sustenance).[38] And Richard Louv's recent book, *Last Child in the Woods*, warns against denying the next generation their right to a freerange childhood, linking attention disorders, obesity and depression to the observable decrease in the extent to which children are permitted access to nature – to go out and play.[39]

The field of environmental psychology has blossomed into a new discipline. It explores and repeatedly demonstrates the unexplained positive impact on mental wellbeing of being outdoors, in particular environments, instead of locked inside with your web-connected buddy.[40] The data is so persuasive that we must accept that even in the grumpiest console-loving adolescent, there is (though rarely expressed) a deeply genetic love of the outdoors.[41]

One of the most persuasive and conclusive bodies of work to emerge in recent decades that supports this idea comes from two scientists at the University of Michigan in Ann Arbor, the Kaplans. Rachel and Stephen Kaplan have spent 40 years testing and measuring the ways in which humans respond to natural environments, and they are key exponents of ART.

Attention-restoration theory is a simple idea: we function better when exposed to natural environments. Our cognitive abilities can be restored by them. In Stephen Kaplan's 2008 study, he and his colleagues explored the cognitive benefits of interacting with nature, in various forms.[42] The earlier trials of the Kaplans riffed on these themes, but the more recent tests are most persuasive.[43] This later paper reports a full-blown trial of ART. In the first experiment it describes, subjects had their mood assessed, and were then given some mental tests to fatigue their cognitive abilities. The participants were then given a break, during which they were asked to walk for 2.8 miles in either Ann Arbor's Nichols Arboretum, or downtown in the city (it is quite a nice college town). When they returned to the lab they were subjected to further tests to assess mood and cognitive function. A week later, the trial was repeated, with the participants this time swapping the arboretum for the city, and vice versa. Unsurprisingly, the subjects that got to take their break in the arboretum performed significantly better in the post-rest activities. This is not so conclusive: the arboretum's natural qualities are by their very nature also more peaceful.

So when I arrived in Ann Arbor, having flown from Boston, the first thing I wanted to do was run in that very same arboretum, to see exactly what it was like.

I was expecting somewhere miles from the centre of the town, but this was not so. Still, it was a varied and sunny space widely used by all ages. It was early on a summery Sunday evening, so I decided on a quick run followed by a reward dinner at the legendary Zingerman's Deli.

The air had a pungent quality to it. It was idyllic. I don't know if this is the case, but I would bet that site-specific performances are staged there of plays like *A Midsummer Night's Dream*.

As I stepped across the threshold between city and country, the only background noises were the hum of the extractors at the children's hospital nearby and the occasional bark of Amtrak trains as they crossed the River Huron. I got no funny looks for being barefoot. And when I made it down to the river I saw people had erected hammocks for the day and had obviously been sat reading in them for hours. Others kayaked or canoed or explored on and off the trails. It was not possible to imagine a less stressful environment than this that didn't involve a marble bath and jugs of asses' milk. That the trial's subjects were restored by a walk in that environment was of no surprise to me.

I also found steep climbs and declensions in the arboretum, where the downtown walk was comparatively flat and regularly interrupted by traffic lights, so had the experiments ended with this comparison then the argument could easily be made that it was the level of exercise that was restorative, not the space itself.

But there was genius afoot in the trial.

In the second wave of experiments, in controlled and equally peaceful surroundings, the subjects completed the same tasks over the same two weeks, but this time they were shown 50 images (displayed for seven seconds) of either urban scenes (Detroit, Chicago or Ann Arbor) or rural ones (Nova Scotia).[44] The scores were again conclusive. The subjects exposed to 'natural' stimuli fared better in the second bout of cognitive tests. Nature had restored them in the first test, but its power was so great that even a simple visual representation of it reproduced similar effects.

When I first read the study, it left me bursting with questions. I thought its implications were huge.

A few weeks before, I had contacted two of the leading environmental psychologists working at the University of Michigan, Dr Avik Basu and Dr Jason Duvall, and arranged to meet them today. It rains and rains as I walk up to the campus. The town is quiet and, as is so often the case for travellers overfed on American cinema, many bits of it already look familiar.

It is an old university that looks like a nice place to come to work. It is in the centre of town, but the quads are so large that there is little traffic noise. They must be on some break because there are almost no students around anywhere. I've done my background reading and yet again here I am at the top of a building, out of breath, ready to meet my experts.

We start by talking about their projects and research interests, which in each case seem to be focussed on making life better for people, whether they are working, resting or recuperating. They ask me what a literature professor is doing writing a book about biomechanics, psychology and the environment, and I joke that I'm not really sure, but I think my answer would be the same as theirs: because I think it matters, it's worth doing, and it gets me out of bed in the morning.

I have so many questions for them that I don't know where to start. But it is not until later in the interview that I understand that the reason I have so many is that there just *are* that many. Environmental psychology has turned up a great deal of evidence, but that doesn't mean that all of it makes sense.

So I ask Avik, 'What is attention?'

It's like concentration, he explains. 'You can use a muscle analogy. You work it, it gets tired, it depletes at different speeds depending on the task. Directed attention is not something that you can use indefinitely without any cost. While it's questionable that directed attention can be strengthened like a muscle, the analogy holds that, like a muscle, if it's tired the best way to restore it is to let it rest.'

What is its role in making us human? Are we all wired to find things interesting, and go looking for things to engage our curiosity? Has it helped us survive?

The answer is both yes and no. Our ability to hold our concentration is, if anything, as much a risk to our survival as boredom and lethargy is. Avik explains: 'If early humans were OK with not needing new information, then they would not have had that evolutionary edge.' If food became too easy to come by, the uninterested hominin would not have had the knowledge and ability to seek out other food sources or predict contingencies. 'The only way to do that is to tap into our basic human desires, where we want to understand things, extend our mental models, avoid confusion, and avoid boredom.'

It all sounds like the H.G. Wells fable *The Time Machine* (1895), with the Eloi and the Morlocks. They are two deep-future species of hominin that, at some point in their evolutionary past, split. When Wells's Time Traveller meets the Eloi he notices that they live a leisured life. They eat a good diet, yet don't seem to need to work or have much curiosity about the world. As the novel progresses, the Time Traveller realises that this is because the sweet-natured, vegetarian Eloi (who he thought were the future humans) are being farmed by the Morlocks, who periodically come up from their underground kingdom to take one of the Eloi away to be eaten. Their food comes easily because they are being farm-fed.

To survive, early humans needed to be inclined to seek new information, Avik tells me. 'Just like you need food, you need to have information that extends your mental models of the world.'

'So this is like the neuroplasticity in the brains of newborn humans, where the brain comes into the world incapable but ready for culture and new information?' I ask.

'Not ready,' Avik tells me, 'but wanting, actively seeking new information. It's a desire, like food or sex.'

He then goes on to tell me that the fact that our attention weakens over time is not a design fault, but an inherent necessity to keeping the whole system working efficiently. He is talking about depletable directed attention.

Our brains evolved in an environment where meandering distraction wasn't a bad thing. Fascination with a task or activity is helpful for getting things done, but if you become fascinated for too long, it may prevent you from knowing or exploring the environment. Our abilities to momentarily tune out save us from all manner of mishaps and dangers: everything from the over-involved reader returning to a good book while their bath overflows in the next room, to the tribesman who is so involved in whittling his spear that he fails to hear the approaching leopard. Even poor Narcissus would not have drowned if he had taken a moment to notice the risk that proximity to water presented.

Moments of ambient distraction are good; they are natural; they are healthy. Those moments, as well as allowing us to pull the plug just in time, also permit us to rest the depletable muscle of our concentration. That rest is not a weakness. It is desirable, necessary and rewarding.

There is also a social benefit to not being able to concentrate. Not being able to focus on a single problem for hours on end practically predetermines a sort of social engagement with one's peers that enhances the likelihood of cooperation. Our inability to focus totally on something basically means that a solution is more likely.

'What other kind of work is involved in directing our attention?' I ask Avik.

Between them, he and Jason explain that we possess an inhibitory ability: if you're concentrating on these words on the page at this moment, then you are using that ability. Assuming you weren't bored by the last sentence, your brain is still working while you're reading this sentence, holding a bit of the last sentence in your memory while you add new information to it as you continue to read this one. It all sounds rather taxing. What you are also doing as you read this, while holding this entire passage in your working memory, is blocking out all kinds of stimuli from the noise of the passing train, the ticking of the clock, the coffee-shop chatter, or the hum of your central heating. This inhibitory ability is additional mental work which we need rest from (sorry, kids, you don't study better with music on). One of the reasons that the modern epidemic of mindfulness is so successful and relaxing is precisely because it works to weed out these inhibitory responses to the environment to allow mental rest.

This is not a completely new field of inquiry. There have been hundreds of studies and trials over the last few decades that bear out these theories.

Studies (particularly of children with ADHD) have shown that indoor activities such as watching TV or playing video games drain directed attention. Parents reported that these activities exacerbated their children's symptoms, whereas playing outside, demanding less voluntary mental work, proved more effective in getting them to cope with their symptoms. While it would be easy to assume that it is physical activity (the kids burning off energy) that is restorative, comparative studies have also been done that compare outdoor play in urban and natural environments, with the latter performing best.[45]

This is all very well, but I know from speaking to runners that many of them get bored. Recent research (by Dr Rachel Hallett, researcher at Keele University) shows that while runners who listen to music might run slower, they will, if they are beginners, have a greater chance of adhering to their exercise routine.

I run with music probably less than 5 per cent of the time. I enjoy it when I do it, but invariably it is a cadence-training aid for me. I listen to music with about 90 beats per minute, so that I can make sure my cadence hasn't fallen into bad habits. The music literally keeps me on my toes.[46]

I ask Jason and Avik why, if the natural environment is so good for us, so many people get bored when they're running in it.

Avik explains that people are different, and may find all manner of things either interesting or not. But once they become 'acclimated to the environment' then 'the mind is wired to seek new information at that point, so you're psychologically hardwired to find something different to do'. The activity that is being disconnected from could be of any kind, whether walking, running or conversing. He explains that running with music is an easy way to introduce constant novelty to an experience without having to work at it.

Jason says, 'The alternative is that you could try more actively to manipulate the levels of interest yourself, but that's not necessarily the easiest way to go.'

'No, that sounds like work,' I say.

But Jason has recently published a study that backs up his suggestion. Entitled 'Enhancing the Benefits of Outdoor Walking with Cognitive Engagement Strategies', it measured the effect that outdoor exercise with 'awareness plans' had on half of his trial's subjects compared with those who did the outdoor exercise without such plans. The awareness plans were a simple set of mindful instructions to the subjects to be aware of their senses, or imagine that they were artists looking for beauty in everyday things, etc. The latter group 'experienced significant improvements in multiple dimensions of psychological well-being, including attentional functioning and feelings of frustration'.[47]

It seems to be the case that runners get bored because they conjure that state within themselves, and are maybe denying themselves some of the psychological benefits of their exercise in doing so.

Jason is also a runner, and he explains to me yet another version of 'just because you like it, doesn't make it good for you'. He is convinced that the negative feelings he experiences in anticipating a midwinter run, and even during it (Michigan winters are notoriously bad), are irrelevant to the restorative benefits that the run will proffer. This seems hard to believe, but when you think about it, an unpleasant midwinter run is an essential part of most marathon runners' training. Whether you like it or not, the run will have made you fitter, stronger and your heart a little more efficient. The benefits are there regardless of how we might feel about them. This applies on a physical level, but equally to the psychological benefits.

Music allows us to be a little more absent from the run, but as Jason says: 'How much can you get out of any experience if you're not really present?'

There is a longstanding research interest in this field, concerned with environmental enrichment. Throughout the twentieth century, numerous studies, starting with some quite informal trials in the 1940s and 1950s, have shown that cage-bound lab rats had lower intelligence and were less adept at problem-solving than those that were permitted environmental, sensory and social stimulation.

In a plain, featureless lab-rat environment (perhaps a treadmill in a gym), the BDNF released by the exercise may to go to waste. Likewise, the new stem cells may expire without finding a purpose. Stimulation is what is needed; real experiences, novelty, life. So if you want to get smarter, run. Better: run outside. Or best of all: run outside in a stimulating and immersive environment.

We conclude by talking through the impact of ART.

Understanding the attentional systems is key to understanding ART, so I ask them what kinds of environment would allow our directed-attention system to rest while engaging the fascination systems. 'Content matters,' Jason says, and Avik continues, 'It turns out that natural environments have the effect of engaging the involuntary system in a way that allows the directed-attention system to rest. We have been seeing leaves, trees, savannahs and rivers for most of our evolutionary history, so it makes sense that we are naturally engaged by those things.'

Jason finishes by telling me that the expectations of what counts as a natural environment can be as simple as a lawn and a few trees.

I'm left with the lingering frustration that, beyond the incredibly persuasive data, there are few answers to what the real psychological mechanisms that restore us might be. Nevertheless, the evolutionary argument seems to be rearing its head everywhere I look.

What stimuli count? Almost all the tests that Avik and Jason talk about are ones that prioritise our visual abilities. Visual processing accounts for about 35 per cent of brain activity, so it is an important sense, but what of the others? What about people who are visually impaired? Has anyone begun to think about the reported potency of the runner's high in natural environments? There were no answers.

I'm not a scientist, but I am convinced that there is more to green than meets the eye. Green is the colour which our eyes have adapted to see more shades of than any other in the rainbow. It is the colour that our brains have to do least processing to be able to see. Green is the room temperature of our visual spectrum. When we see it, we are home.

GREEN EXERCISE

Back in the UK, I had heard that there was work going on in precisely this 'green' field of enquiry, with research taking place that might help to refine the role that the individual senses play in these processes of restoration. Based at the University of Essex, the Green Exercise Research Group comprises experts in physiology, public health, psychology, environmental sustainability and sports science. They all work on understanding the numerous benefits of natural environments, asking what additional benefits we can gain from our exercise if we do it in particular places or surroundings.

When I first heard about them I got rather excited. Here were the people that might be able to put together everything that I'd learned about the potency of the environment, with the sorts of physiological and psychological reward-systems that I had also learned so much about. But I had second thoughts when I read the first study of theirs I came across, concerning the 'green, grey, red' test.[48] In this slightly odd trial, subjects were asked to cycle while being shown three videos: one of an actual rural ride, another of the same ride but in black and white; in the third film the ride was screened through a red filter. The cyclists were tested for levels of tension, depression, anger, vigour, fatigue and confusion. The natural environment provided the most positive means; the red, the least. One major advantage of this trial was the extent to which it was able to test the effect of greenness, because it used the same video in each of the tests. But it was not stated whether the subjects' response was influenced specifically by the 'green' of the video they were played, or whether it was connected more to the fact that the 'green' video was the only one that had not been colour-filtered in some way. The 'red' and the 'grey' landscapes are not ones found out in the world, and their inherent unfamiliarity might conceivably have given rise to altered levels of stress while exercising. Those viewing the 'grey' landscape reported better mood than the red, but equally this could be as much to do with our daily familiarity with grayscale imagery.

There tended, too, to be a focus (as in environmental psychology) on outdoor pursuits (running, cycling, canoeing, etc.), and that also leaves the question as to what extent it is the activities themselves that are being measured, rather than the stage on which they are performed.

I began to have my doubts, but made my way to the oldest town in Britain, Colchester, to meet a pair of the group's researchers.

The campus is almost identical to the one I work in across the water in Kent. I stress about parking, then make my way to an unbelievably noisy coffee shop and wait for Mike Rogerson. When he arrives, he looks like the Jim Morrison of sports science. Not only for that reason is he immediately likeable, and we end up talking for hours about the mechanisms that underpin the seemingly positive effects of immersion in nature that the Kaplans' experiments had already reported.

He has a special interest in exercise-adherence strategy – how to get people that have started to exercise to keep going. Mike tells me that a subject's emotional response to exercise is a fairly good predictor of adherence. This is not rocket science: the more someone likes it, the more likely they are to continue. He tells me that a subject's psychological response to exercise can predict whether they will still be exercising in six or twelve months' time. And if the exercise environment influences the emotional response then perhaps exercising in natural environments is the key to increasing adherence to exercise. 'Perhaps we should be getting doctors to prescribe periods of outdoor exercise if we want to have a real impact on public health,' he says.

Environmental planning and public health are part of the same Gordian knot. Graphs that represent crime rates in urban environments show an inverse relationship with ones that indicate levels of access to green space. The greener the environment, the less crime it is likely to have.[49] It might seem that an obvious explanation of this fact would be that rural areas are more affluent, and are less densely packed, but recent studies of housing projects with access to much more limited green spaces reproduce the same results.

In one breathtaking study Mike tells me about, researchers reported that one development that had substantial amounts of greenery had 52 per cent fewer total crimes than those without.[50] Property crime dropped by 48 per cent, and violent crime by a staggering 56 per cent, compared with areas with low amounts of vegetation.[51] Another study draws parallels between access to green space and the impact of stressful life events, with the results supporting the idea that natural environments seem to act as a buffer against the health impact of stress.[52] (The information just tumbles out of him and I find it hard to keep up.)

But these proximities to nature are not all the same. There are different levels of interaction and immersion. Looking at a picture of a natural environment (as the Kaplan subjects did) and walking in one are not the same thing at all.

One of the earlier green-exercise concepts defined levels of immersion:

1. A view of nature – via a window, television or picture.
2. Direct exposure to nature – where the exposure is incidental to another task or motive, like being sat on a park bench reading a book.
3. Direct engagement with nature – active participation in a natural environment such as farming, gardening, or 'cross-country running or horse-riding' (as the paper's authors put it).[53]

It is suggested that at the third level of immersion there is greater mindfulness of the experience of being in nature. Mike Rogerson explains, 'If we think about this in a psychoevolutionary perspective it goes back to what we have always done as a species: engaging directly with the environment for a task, like fishing or hunting.'

I interrupt, 'Or picking flowers?'

'Yes,' he smiles, 'or picking flowers to make daisy chains.' He continues, 'The greater the immersion, the more robust the beneficial responses are likely to be, and they are more likely to be longer-lasting.'[54]

'Do city or urban runners get the same advantages from their exercise?'

He explains that despite some people's positive associations with cities and urban environments, they still demand cognitive work across a number of levels. For example, the amount of processing required to assess the potential threat of a beech tree is nothing compared to that of making the same judgement of an approaching car, or an unknown building on a dark night. But almost any natural running environment is good for you, psychologically, irrespective of how you feel about it.

I tell him that I am interested in the runner's high, that I am trying to develop, not a formula (like a Yotam Ottolenghi recipe), but a loose set of instructions towards what might work (like a Nigel Slater one). I explain that there are varying levels of appropriate exercise intensity – there are advantages to running slowly.

He tells me that some of his work also focusses on intensity. He is trying to find out the point at which the environment ceases to positively influence the outcomes of green exercise.

I press him on the preliminary findings of this research, but Mike will only specify that 'lower intensity' is more beneficial; he will not give a cut-off point because the science isn't there yet.

'Exactly what do you mean by lower intensity, then? What about walking?'

Finally, he gives in and guesses that the cut-off point might be somewhere between 65–75 per cent of maximum heart rate. 'There is some research in peer review at the moment which is looking at the point at which the exerciser switches from external awareness to internal focus on the physiological intensity of the exercise.' More on this later.

He is also interested in doing more work on mood, self-esteem, perceived stress (because it's not the stress that counts, but the subject's interpretation of it) and how appraisal of these factors links to one's physical health. He wants to see if the pleasures of the physical stress of exercise cascade down to real results in the body that are measurable (like reduced blood-pressure).

We now know that for you and your kids, exercising in natural environments is highly beneficial. While trials show that the increased directed attentional capacity resulting from nature-exposure (as in ART) almost certainly facilitates learning experiences, the exercise element also promotes learning and memory (in part via increasing the release of BDNF, which promotes both the creation and strengthening of neuronal circuits – also known as memory). Green + exercise is doubly beneficial to almost any form of learning.

As in other environmental psychology trials, it is the visual senses that are prioritised, and I ask Mike if anyone is working on other senses.

'Yes, John Wooller. Aren't you meeting him next?'

Indeed, I am. An hour or so later, exercise scientist John Wooller pulls up a chair and I ask him about his research into the role of our other senses.

I'd talked about some of the methodological difficulties of these studies with Mike (he was having a problem controlling the precise exercise-intensity of his runners outdoors; indoors it was as easy as putting someone on a treadmill). And this again seems to be an area of science besieged by statistical noise.

One of John's difficulties (as I'd already discovered on my runs) is that our senses don't really work separately; they borrow from one another. But with the judicious application of mood questionnaires, he is creating for his subjects in the trial an environment that has scent, sound and vision.

He hit quite a snag in the early trials with hearing. He explains, 'It's a sense that you can't switch off, so when we tried – using ear plugs and ear defenders to block external sounds – the test-subjects' mood plummeted.' (They were probably deafened by the internal sounds of their own bodies' physiological systems increasing through the workout.) But John and his colleagues have already discovered that the occlusion of vision or smell has no major impact on mood. This is significant because it suggests that a nice view is not as necessary as previous tests have suggested. Perhaps it is more of a 'green awareness' that is needed.

John is also working on some eye-tracking trials that will reveal what it is that people look at when they exercise at different intensities. It is early days with this research, too – but data suggests that patterns emerge at low- and medium-intensity training. With my recipe in mind, I ask what subjects look at during high-intensity exercise. He tells me, 'They do not look at a lot.' The subjects' awareness huddles up into itself. It is no longer a lighthouse looking out into the landscape, but a firefly lit from within.

The depth of immersion that barefoot running permits is greater than that of shod running. I wonder too if depth of immersion might be the chief difference between runners and cyclists, and may account for the attenuated effect of the runner's high that our two-wheeled friends report in trials. While cycling, it is possible to move through a place without actually touching it. You are little more connected to it than when, for example, sat on a bench reading a book. This is why the definitions of immersion need a little tweaking. When farming and gardening, you will get mud under your fingernails, and you will have to scrub the earth from your hands. If you run barefoot, you will have to do the same with your feet, too. I can't help but think that the feel of the earth may create the kind of 'green awareness' that I mentioned above, its effect the same as those natural sights, sounds and scents replayed in John Wooller's lab.

Even if you don't get the runner's high, there is also a state called 'flow', which is increasingly popular as a means of explaining a deeply focussed kind of motivation. It is what is meant when people talk about being 'in the zone'. It usually comes from intrinsic motivations – an interest in improving or performing well, of enjoying the thing in and for itself. The term was invented by psychologist Mihaly Csikszentmihalyi, and his conditions for achieving it were that: *a*) you have a clear task in hand to give structure and meaning to what you're doing; *b*) that feedback is available so that you can automatically maintain the flow state; and *c*) that you possess an innate confidence to continue/complete the job in hand.

As always, there is a bit in Tolstoy to help explain, where the aristocrat hero, Levin, who elsewhere in Anna Karenina acknowledges his need of exercise, has taken up some manual work:

> In this hottest time the mowing did not seem so hard to him. The sweat that drenched him cooled him off . . . More and more often those moments of unconsciousness came, when it was possible for him not to think of what he was doing. The scythe cut by itself. These were happy moments. More joyful still were the moments when, coming to the river, where the swaths ended, the old man would wipe his scythe with thick, wet grass, rinse its steel in the cool water, dip his whetstone box and offer it to Levin.[55]

The state of flow is something almost all runners experience. Once they have the expertise to keep going long enough to reach it, it is part of that cascade of mental refreshment that all runners know to be necessary to them, including the following very special one.

On 25 August 1947, *The Times* quietly reported a marathon race that had taken place at Loughborough. Buried away in fourth place was a runner who had cut a time of 2 hours 46 minutes. This was a really good time for someone who was not fully dedicated to marathon running, bearing in mind that the Olympic gold the following year was taken by someone who ran only 11 minutes faster. The name was 'Dr A. Turing'.

Turing is widely considered to be the father of computing and artificial intelligence. His work in cryptanalysis is thought to have played a key role in the winning of the Second World War. In 1952 he was arrested and convicted for 'gross indecency' and he was put on probation on the condition that he commit to 12 months of hormonal therapy that had horrible side-effects and made him impotent. He was stripped of his security clearances, refused travel to the US, and only just managed to keep his job. He committed suicide in 1954, eating a cyanide-laced apple. Some say that the Apple logo, with the single bite taken from it, is a memorial to his contribution to modern computing. All throughout his brilliant career, he was obsessed with running.

I can't be alone in wondering what impact all that BDNF and hippocampal neurogenesis had on Alan Turing's abilities to decode the Nazi Enigma code. Did endurance running perhaps play a bigger role in the outcome of the war than might previously have been thought?

Because of the numerous and varied benefits of exercise, from intelligence to longevity, and our hard-wired reward-and-protection systems that are activated by green space, outdoor exercise in natural environments has been called 'exercise squared'.

Our bodies and brains are constructed to experience pleasure and come truly alive during a run in ways that we can measure, record and prove, but still do not always understand.[56] The best reason to go out for a run, it seems, is not because it is good for you, not that it will make you smarter, stronger, fitter, more attractive or better at your job, or that it will improve your body-image or make you feel calmer, but because the world is out there, it is now – and, quite simply, you can.

So I have my recipe. This is why I think that low- to mid-level barefoot running works best for me. The different sciences and my experience of them seem to suggest that the most likely conditions for achieving endocannabinoid activation, or the runner's high, are:

- That the run is as immersive as possible.
- That the run is mindful and not instrumental; sensory reception of the present is essential. When I run barefoot I feel that it enhances the immediate stimulus of the environment: it makes the soft fascination that accompanies meditation more explicit and easier to achieve.
- That the run will be longer than 40 minutes.
- That you don't run too fast. The ideal is about 75 per cent of maximum heart rate. Below that, and your body is not likely to be stressed enough for endocannabinoid activation; any faster than that and you will be too distracted by your exertion to notice anything happening (this is possibly the most likely reason that some runners find the chase of the high an endless one).[57] In my own experience, if I am four steps breathing in/four steps breathing out, I am going at about the right pace. (This 75 per cent exertion is also the approximate upper limit for attentive focus on the environment.)
- Easiest of all, that the run takes place in a green space.

4.

IN PRAISE OF IDLENESS: HOW TO RUN AWAY FROM WORK

DORCHESTER, MAIDEN CASTLE AND LUNDY ISLAND

There is no other period in history in which free men have given their energy so completely for the one purpose: work.

– Erich Fromm, *The Fear of Freedom*, 1960

For now she need not think about anybody. She could be herself, by herself . . . Although she continued to knit, and sat upright, it was thus that she felt herself; and this self having shed its attachments was free for the strangest adventures. When life sank down for a moment, the range of experience seemed limitless.

– Virginia Woolf, *To the Lighthouse*, 1927

Working for a university is a job that defies explanation. It's brilliant because it lets you do so many things, and go to so many places, but teaching each term (much as I like it) is the equivalent of managing several projects simultaneously that all last for about three months, while managing others that run year-round (Masters degrees and administration) and keeping an eye on others that run over several years (like supervising PhDs, undertaking one's own research projects, or writing a book). Like many a job, it can be taxing. And the deeper you get into a term, the harder it gets. You start working the odd weekend to keep up, and before you know it, that has become part of your week, too; letters lie unopened, dust gathers, beards are accidentally grown, friends get forgotten, the laundry basket becomes so tightly packed that you might expect to find a stratum of coal at the bottom of it. Like a cumulative weight unnoticed because it is added one pebble at a time, stress can creep up on you and its signals can be subtle. The last time I really noticed it was at the end of the tunnel of term-time, while I was, of all things, looking at a painting.

Sometimes, when I go to an exhibition or gallery, there is usually one image that I find myself hypnotised by. Patiently, I read along the lines of pictures on display, then it happens: I see something and there's a sudden swoop in my guts. The feeling is something between a tug of anguish and vertigo.

On this particular day, I was mentally addled from constant psycho-multitasking. Too busy to run, I hadn't managed to get out for as much as six or eight weeks, and I saw this picture and it was like I'd been bopped on the nose. Tears (yes, tears!) pinched at the corner of my eyes – what the hell was going on?

The painting, *The Siesta (after Millet)*, has the magical luminosity of Van Gogh's greats, as if he had caught the light of the sun on his brush and trapped it in the curls and dashes of impasto. It depicts a couple resting in the shade of a haystack on a sunny day, sun hats pulled down to shade the eyes for a nap. It's simple, balanced and characterful. Why did it make me feel I was about to blub?

Stress does funny things to us, I suppose. But I had already seen at least a hundred other paintings that day, so what was specific to this one? My usual crutch of running had been kicked away, so things had built up, and, here I was – standing in front of a painting that depicted two people resting from work completed – about to cry.

It seems funny, now, but I was so confused and tired that, if I'm honest, I think it was a kind of grief. I had been doing the kind of work that could be managed by a brain in a vat. I hadn't used my body in any way for weeks. I wanted desperately to rest under a haystack somewhere, with that feeling that I had done something, and it was finished.

I don't think I was being particularly soppy in seeing this expression for the desire of mental repose in the picture: Van Gogh painted it, I discovered, while he was interred in a mental asylum.

My response to these workers at rest was personal and circumstantial, but it was part of a wider turn that we can see in modernity, where our relationship with our bodies is shifting, allowing us to believe that we can work mentally for longer than we can manually. I'm not in the least sure that this is true. So this chapter is going to look at the role that running can play in resuscitating us, and how it can get us away from work. It will also consider some of the pervasive ways in which work can squirm its way into our lives when our backs are turned. And how, by going to places completely out of its reach, we can escape it altogether, to get back in touch with who we are.

WHY RUNNING SHOULD BE NEITHER WORK, NOR EXERCISE

As I commence the long climb into Dorchester in Dorset, the sun begins to set high at the other end of town, behind a spinney of church spires and bell- and clock-towers. I have just left the water meadows having run back from Stinsford on a warm summer's evening. My breathing is poor. My lungs sound like two cats fighting in a bag. I will have to double my asthma medication tomorrow. Is this why I don't really seem to be enjoying this run, or am I imagining it?

My distances have been hovering around the six-mile mark. I can't seem to get beyond that because my back or calves complain with muscle knots that come and go like they are a tag-team.

It is July 2014 and I have come here for work. The Thomas Hardy Society runs a biennial conference that I am speaking at. It gathers together academics interested in him with enthusiasts who come from all over the world to attend. It is great fun and a wonderful excuse to stay for a week and run in one of the UK's finest places, sniffing out histories and stories. And, if I'm honest, a few gravestones.

I've booked into a hotel straight out of Agatha Christie, with lots of mahogany, brass, plush carpets and women drinking tea. I was tempted to join them, but I unpacked, changed, and was away.

But as soon as I stepped out onto the High Street I could already feel that the run wasn't quite going to work. I didn't map it in advance, as I had a good idea of where I was headed. Down the town to the River Frome, past the old Hangman's Cottage where the river is rock-pool clear with silky waterweed. I pass the prison and, by it, the meadow where the townspeople used to gather to watch the hundreds of public hangings. (The sight was meant as a deterrent, but was enjoyed by most as entertainment.) Out of the town, following the river, hopefully to Stinsford Church, where generations of the Hardys are buried, including his two wives. A twentieth-century Poet Laureate is there, too – Cecil Day Lewis. I was surprised to see him, given that I often run past his house in Greenwich, about 150 miles away; I later found out that he wanted to be buried as close as possible to Hardy.

But Thomas Hardy is not here. Like an incident from one of his novels, a row broke out after his death, when friends and family could not agree on where he should be buried. Their solution was gothicly grisly: cut out the heart and bury it in Stinsford, but burn the body and send the ashes to Westminster Abbey (where they are now, next to Dickens in Poet's Corner). A cruel scrap of gossip spread about Dorchester that the cat got the heart, and the thing that was buried belonged to a pig.

With all this history beneath, this should be a fantastic forage through the past, but I just can't catch the rhythm of the run and let go of myself. I am trying to remember things to write down later, or to work out how bits will sit together when I write them up.

I pass by the bridge, which has a warning on it that reads: 'Dorset: Any person wilfully INJURING any part of this COUNTRY BRIDGE will be guilty of FELONY and upon conviction liable to be TRANSPORTED for life'. So I tread lightly, and continue along the river past an ambulance station. The architecture has changed suddenly in character and is a bit 'Legoey'. Then I realise that the development has trapped me. At the end of the estate, the path dies, cordoned off with bed frames of steel wire that in turn fence in mounds of soil, mud tracks like dinosaur footprints, JCB diggers and yellowed, plaster-splashed warning notices. Like water trying to find egress, I slosh about, climbing, leaning, ducking, bending and tiptoeing, but there is no way through. I could manage the fence, but the thicket of nettles would do for me once I got on the other side. So I have to retrace my steps. I hate having to retrace my steps, it feels too much like going back to be going forward.

I run all the way back and try another point of access through a park, but no. I have to retrace my steps once again. I hate, even more, having to retrace my retraced steps. I loop back as far as the bridge, and at last I am on the other side of the river, where it absolutely stinks.

The smell is sickly sweet, like a scraped-from-the-bottom-of-the-bargain-bin body lotion. I hold my breath to get away from it. (Two days later, on a walk here with Dr Jane Thomas, Academic Director of the Thomas Hardy Society, she will trick me into pinching one of the seedpods of the stinker. She will tell me it's called Himalayan balsam. It was introduced in the 1830s as a plant for the wetter corners of gardens, and it is now taking over entire banks of the river. And, from the plant's point of view, the attraction of the trick she goads me into is that it is probably ensuring the survival of the species. The seedpods do not pop or burst, they detonate. Their powder-keg scatters the seeds with a bang, making them irresistible to children – and grown-up children – who will flinch and screech in delight.)

I continue across the water meadows, passing the sluice gates used in the past to control the provision of water to the pastures. This is the pathway that Hardy would have taken as a child, an adolescent and an adult – pretty much the only one between his childhood home and Dorchester. I should be reading the landscape, but I don't. I just jog, tread after tread. Into the woods, and I follow the path to Stinsford, scanning the skyline for a candle flame to catch my interest, but it's the same old beat of my feet and mewing for breath. I climb up through the village to the churchyard. I see the graves, Hardy's among them (and for the life of me I don't know why, but I photograph them). Then in the manner of a huffy pilgrim who has too easily found what he was wandering for, I decide to run back. I have been denied the pleasure of the journey, and instead have made it all too easily to my destination. What am I doing?

A fly lands on my arm; with the considered wringing of his limbs he looks like a villain in a melodrama, pleased with having concocted a wicked plan, but then suddenly he skims away like he's remembered he's left the gas on.

I don't think I can articulate how much this run ought to have meant for me. Hardy can seem like misery-porn to the uninitiated, or to those who start at the wrong end of his novelistic career and work backwards. The experience of reading *Jude the Obscure* (his final original novel) has been described as like being continually slapped in the face. It so upset Victorian readers that it both was publicly burned (by the Bishop of Wakefield) and made Hardy a fortune because it was so scandalous that everyone wanted to experience the 50 shades of Jude.

But magic, as well as ink, flowed from his pen, from proto-feminist poststructuralism: 'It is difficult for a woman to define her feelings in language which is chiefly made by men to express theirs',[1] to comedy: 'some folk want their luck buttered'.[2] But he knocked it out of the park when it came to description, to making us feel, see and hear again what the country can be like. 'The lightning now was the colour of silver, and gleamed in the heavens like a mailed army.'[3]

Practically all his work dramatises what it is to be lost in the creep of London, and the rush towards urbanisation; feeling crept upon by London myself, I'm always interested in what he has to say. In all his books, he was invariably trying to capture the workings, wants and wits of our bodies; and particularly, those non-psychological energies and intelligences in our bodies and how they seem to know the world without the mind.

Such was his impression upon me that several years ago, Hardy made me commit the most benign and middle-class form of trespass. I was driving back from the West Country and decided to stop off at his house, Max Gate, near the town where I am today. When I arrived, the house was shut up. But with the momentum I had gathered in coming so far, and knowing that I was unlikely to be back this way for years, I climbed over the six-foot wall. Once over the wall, I had no idea what to do, so I ferreted about in the rhododendrons trying to get a good view of the house and gardens. The reason that the house cannot be seen from the road, and that it has so many trees and bushes planted around it, is that Hardy tried to deter such wall-climbing blighters.

In a couple of days' time, I will visit this National Trust property again, and I will be shocked to discover that when I had been shuffling about and hiding in the bushes, it was being used as a private house.

Back to today, and by the end of the climb back into Dorchester, I am unsure just exactly what has happened. So many of my runs have been like this lately, and I wonder, am I faking it? If I was running before, I no longer think that it is what I am doing now; something has changed. What I am doing now has a taint of exercise, or utility; something is not quite right. When I was running previously, I was doing nothing – I was being idle, I was lazing about, I was bunking off life.

Idling, or even the idea of being able to do it, is necessary, and sometimes we have to find it wherever we can. For example, like a number of book-buyers, I find it difficult to find the time to read quite a bit of what I pick up in the shops, especially the longer books. I love buying them, though. I like the idea of being that person who has read Fanny Burney's *Camilla*, Rebecca West's *Black Lamb and Grey Falcon* or Boswell's *Life of Johnson*, but it has taken me a decade to work out that in the time I've been acquiring these unread doorstops, what I have really been buying all along is the fantasy that I will one day have the time to read them. For years, I have been investing unwisely in the fantasy of bunking off.

Unable to dive into these worlds, my runs have been the only regular crumbs of bunking-off that I have been capable of. But as soon as I started writing a book about it, running became something else. Bunking off isn't bunking off if you have to write about it – most people would call that homework.

It is here, in Dorchester, that I realise what has happened to me. Running is now part of my work. Recently, I have been conspiring against myself to take away the only escape I have from life; and, worse, I monetised it.

I go to bed feeling unrestored and grouchy. I am giving my paper at the conference tomorrow. It's on Hardy and running. I mope with the adolescent disappointment that is felt when you bring two friends together, and later discover that they are fonder of one another than they are of you.

I have stupidly brought work and life together, and they seem to be getting on swell in their coffee shop, as I stand outside breathless with jealousy, in the rain. They have made plans together, and have become intimate. They don't need me any more. So I hatch a plan to break up this new romance between Othello and Desdemona, and I do so with more motive than Iago ever had. Like the fly on my arm, I stand at the window, rain-soaked but wringing my hands melodramatically with glee at the plan I've concocted. 'The robbed that smiles, steals something from the thief.'[4]

Running is mine, *Work*, and I want it back.

It's two days later and my kippers are giving me gip. I over indulged with a hotel breakfast (kippers seemed suddenly exotic and exquisitely Victorian), so several hours later I can still feel it is too early to go running. The sun is getting higher in the sky and if I wait too long I will miss the temperature window. I know from experience that as long as I take it slow I should feel fine in 20 to 30 minutes.

I gave my paper the previous day. It went well, but I'm not sure if I converted any of the Hardy punters into hardy runners. People were polite, but understandably they kept wanting to tell me about characters that have to run somewhere in Hardy novels.

After considering the various talks and activities on offer the following day, and having been thinking about running as work, I come up with a plan to inject some fun into my running. I am tearing apart running and work and am going to play hooky, truant, skive; I am going to slip a run into my shorts pocket and sneak out after the 9am lecture.

I have calculated that I need to bunk off from the idea of bunking off so that I can bunk off it and so use it again for bunking off from what I am not supposed to be bunking off from. All clear?

I unfold the OS map with the desire to chase the heady cocktail of deep history, exhaustion and play, as well as to plan a route that will take me from Roman Dorchester and back through many thousands of years to the Neolithic Maiden Castle.

> There is a joy in this that I find hard to account for,
> There is a pleasure on the heath where Druids old have been,
> Where Mantles grey have rustled by and swept the nettles green;
> There is a joy in every spot, made known by times of old,
> New to the feet, although the tale be a hundred times told.[5]

My fascination with the pre-Roman I dignify with the poetry of Keats, but it probably has as much to do with a childhood dominated by Goscinny and Uderzo's *Asterix*. There is, though, an enduring lure for me in prehistory; it is impossible to resist the vacuum that is created by pre-writing cultures. Their knowledge, expertise and social systems were as complex and nuanced as our own, but they are lost; only the shadows of those things can be reconstructed from sherds and remains. Nothing can be as strange as how they filled their days. They worked the land, they farmed. Family structures were important, and as the historian Francis Pryor confirms, 'the main lesson of prehistory is that humanity is generally humane, but from time to time is subject to bouts of extreme and unpleasant ruthlessness'.[6] How hard, how much, and for how long did they work? Conditions would have been harsher, no doubt, but was prehistory a 50-hour week?

The palaeoanthropology expert whom I visited in Boston, Daniel Lieberman, thinks not. He estimates the working day at about six hours, but bear in mind that this includes things that we no longer think of as work. A like-for-like comparison is difficult, but things like home maintenance, home finances, food preparation, shopping and gardening would be part of this routine.[7]

By the time I set out, the temperature has already risen. The high street is jammed with cars; like sun-tired predators they snarl forward to snap at my heels at the pedestrian crossing.

Dorchester is a town of many pasts, with a glacé cherry of the present placed on top. It has more commemorative plaques than I have seen anywhere. On the main shopping street is the house of Frederick Treves, who was surgeon to Queen Victoria and famous for his treatment of Joseph (John) Merrick (the Elephant Man); his house is now split between a Costa and a Vodafone. Further down the street is Michael Henchard's house (Hardy's fictional mayor of Casterbridge), which 'was one of the best, faced with dull red-and-grey old brick'.[8] You can see why Hardy selected it, with its impressively showy facade. It is the ideal house and, like the character that dwells there, demonstrates an eggshell-thin veneer of respectability. Henchard is a character inherently flawed, who wishes to hide his activities from public view, who seeks publicity for his charity and is angered by those who try to reveal the harder edge of his working practices. He profits from the work of others and seems to enjoy shaming them in their failures, so he cooperates with some while he can use them, but humiliates them with rejection when they try to work independently from him. He takes money for selling that which is not his to sell. He deliberately misleads his community, and bullies and takes advantage of those of lower class status.

It is now a Barclays Bank, which is sort of perfect, really.

I turn down an alley because I know that parts of a Late Neolithic monument are buried beneath the Waitrose supermarket. I bound down the stairs to the car park, and in the angry rippled concrete that shopping trolleys rattle over, there are dyed red circles of cement, each of which depicts where the remains of huge oak posts were discovered (they were about three feet across and twelve high). Thought to demarcate some ritual space, the posts probably fell into disuse in the Early Bronze Age. When the entire site was excavated, similar arced ditches were discovered, suggesting that the ring of oak was over 1,000 feet in diameter. It is contemporary with the Maumbury Rings, which the Romans converted to an amphitheatre, just on the edge of town. Each of these spectacular monuments would have been, like Stonehenge nearby, of considerable regional importance.

It seems early Britons have been settling here since about 3,000 BCE.

Looping back round via Dorchester prison, only recently closed, I pass again the site where the 16-year-old Hardy witnessed the hanging of Elizabeth Martha Brown. A fortnight previously she was said to have killed her husband. She went at him with an axe after he had taken a whip to her. Hardy was ashamed to have witnessed the spectacle. 'I remember what a fine figure she showed against the sky as she hung in the misty rain, & how the tight black silk gown set off her shape as she wheeled half-round & back.'[9] It was the last public hanging of a woman in Dorset.

I continue past the old hangman's cottage,[10] and up along an avenue of trees that encircles Dorchester and demarcates the old boundaries of Durnovaria, as the city was known in Roman times.

At the top of the hill, my legs are aquiver and my asthma tries to fight its way through all the medication (not today, though); I turn east, leaving the avenued boundary of Durnovaria behind to head out of town through a new development called Poundbury.

I hear footsteps behind me – another runner? They are coming in fast. I try not to care about time and speed but a competitive gene is a difficult thing to ignore. I am about to quicken my cadence slightly when I realise that they do not belong to a runner. The feet are too fast, too loud, and there's too much breath. At that point a flabby teenager in long black trousers and school shoes leaves me standing in the dust as he races past with a pendulous rucksack on his back – this is nearly as publicly demeaning as the name badge I have to wear at my conference, which mis-spells my name three times.

The talk in the town is that the Poundbury development is controversial, but it seems a necessary encumbrance to me. They could have done more to make it look like it belonged in Dorchester (or even Dorset), but people have got to live somewhere. Poundbury and I, though, are about to fall out. The road curves to take me south past a large industrial park towards Maiden Castle, and I know that there should be a footpath somewhere here to take me over the A35.

I see two footpaths rising at the side of the road; they form a long, neat isosceles triangle – and it looks like the footpath I need seesaws the axis of the triangle. The moment I step off the concrete, I can tell that the path is not much used. At the top I have the choice of left or right. In both directions the path is crosshatched with angry hawthorns and sycamore shoots. I turn left, because over a roaring A35 I can see the outline of the pre-Roman settlement, Maiden Castle. Immediately, I begin tearing through cobwebs, my feet disappearing into divots; sparrow wings flutter like muffled machine-gun fire, I disturb a couple of damselflies and some common blues, and I feel both wretched at wreaking so much destruction, and a bit like Indiana Jones escaping the Inca cave in the first scene of *Raiders of the Lost Ark*.

It is too much, so I have to walk. Then the path drops out of sight, towards the road, I hope. But no, I seem to be walking around the back of a building. Some office workers look up from their screens. Their faces make it clear to me that these are windows through which no face has ever looked back since that of the glazier. How did I find somewhere so inaccessible? I sink into what I thought was a gravel path, but I now realise is a drainage ditch to protect the damp course of the building. I try to make my way quickly out of sight, but it is a dead end – with the offices on one side and a steep bank on the other. I am furious at the idiocy of this design. It is a path to nowhere, that no one can possibly need. The developers must have thought that this tidy triangle would look lovely from the road, that the path would look walked, peopled, inhabited. The path's design prioritises those that will never step on it, and instead pass by it in their cars or watch it from a distance as they do the washing up. Does development really have to be so myopic and halfwitted?

I make my way back past the windows to the front of the offices to find that I have squeezed round the back of the industrial park I passed earlier. I *retrace my steps* back to the original fork, and at the apex of the isosceles path I take the other route.

Much later, when I get back and upload the map of the run from my GPS unit, what I see, instead of a nice, neat, circular line inscribed on the map, is an angry scribble like a correction in an untidy child's exercise book.

I know that I am getting closer to the A-road because within yards I tread on a discarded Monster Munch packet, quickly followed by a Big Mac box and a McFlurry container. When I look up from the rubbish, I get my first clear sight of Maiden Castle.

On the horizon is a giant jade platform with ridged edges, about half a mile in length. The wheat fields surrounding it offset the lush colour of the grass on the mound. For several millennia, since farming began in Britain, it is these same crops that will have been growing here. Peoples and empires will come and go, but the bread-wheat stays. It takes me back to a time when wheat gathering was a kind of alchemy, making gold out of dirt.

On the path, the grass is dry and the colour of brown paper. It also sounds like paper when I step in it. By the fences on either side plants are given a bit more freedom: there are noisy crickets in the hedges, there are the crane-bill seed pods of herb Robert, enchanter's nightshade (or *Circaea*), and the purple rosettes of field scabious (which was once used to soothe the sores of the bubonic plague).

It is a long and slow climb because the heat is doing for me, so I make the excuse of stopping to take off my shoes. They are full of grass seed (evolution taking every opportunity to exploit the possibility of reproduction, I suppose). The grass here has a silky quality, like it could be spun into gold thread. In the shade cast by the hedge it is still green and cool, and these slithers are refreshing in the heat.

On the approach to the castle, there are steep ramparts and I feel the tiredness in my legs and the fire in my chest that the Roman foot soldiers would have felt as they climbed here 2,000 years ago.

But this famous attack by the invading Romans is only a flint's flash in this structure's multi-millennia history. The ramparts around the castle date from different periods, but by the time the whole structure was active in the middle Iron Age (550–300 BCE), they would have formed a complex maze-like design, with installed obstacles and gates to flummox newcomers. Archaeologists believe that this was only part of their function; an important aspect of the size and complexity of the entranceways was as an affluent display to impress. From the air, the ramparts of the western gateway are so complex they look like the tightly wound coils of an intestine.[11]

I'm a little disappointed that I keep imagining myself as an invading Roman – surely I should be Asterix, or a hardy Briton (a Durotriges), and not some put-upon underling having rocks catapulted at him as he tries to invade the citadel. Why do I want to be the soldier that Asterix's friend Obelisk would whack with a 'Poff!' that would send me straight up in the air, out of the frame, leaving only my sandals and spear still standing?

I skirt the outer wall where the grass is paper thin, with baby teeth of chalk that bite at my feet. I keep stepping on them by accident because I am now distracted by the 360-degree view of Dorset on this fine summer's day. The surrounding country is all hedged enclosures like a green crossword grid, but the light and the wildlife are the same. The upland is bare now, but would have contained hundreds of smallholders when it was attacked by the Romans. Few places seem as hale and lusty as this green velvet corpse of a settlement.

It is then that I remember that I am booked on a field trip this afternoon and haven't cancelled – if they don't know I'm not coming, everyone will be waiting for me. I have my phone so dig for the number then confirm with the office that I am bunking off, can they get a message through? When my name is repeated back to me as 'Beebarn', I agree that it is correct and get back into gear. So I am officially wagging, and it feels like there are no sweeter ill-gotten gains than moments of stolen idleness.

The hillocks and knolls of the fort wall keep taking my momentum and rushing me into the next ascent, so I lengthen my stride and swing my arms deeper and deeper to make the micro-climb each time. Then I start jumping at the end of each climb to see if I can make it to the next declension without having to touch the zenith of the castle. I feel free as air, as I race and jump higher and higher, and I realise that I haven't played like this since I was a child.

I couldn't have known that it would be so easy to take control of my running. All I had to do was pare it back to the thing that it had been before: a kind of lazing about.

The most unimaginable aspect of the lives of those who lived in and around Maiden Castle is what they thought, felt and did when the corn was in and the roof mended. Idleness has fewer accoutrements and physical manifestations of evidence than does work. Idleness is what is in our heads and bodies and as such is one of the least legible historical events. Idleness is without trace.

In our culture, idleness is something that needs to be defended. A rotten trick was played on the populace around the eighteenth and nineteenth centuries: the work ethic.

As Erich Fromm explained in *The Fear of Freedom*, the Christian work ethic now dominates in our culture – but where does it come from? Not from Christ, certainly, whose Sermon on the Mount explains, 'Consider the lilies of the field, how they grow; they toil not.' Idleness is attacked from so many directions in our culture, and I think, like most people, I have internalised this. The only way I can combat it effectively is to run away. Then emails, voicemails and all manner of seemingly urgent things have to wait.

Tension, craziness, even loneliness, tend to be the compatriots of the email or the computer, not the field or the air.

But is doing nothing – lazing, idling – really unproductive? Is it bad for us, our families or our employers?

In a brilliant essay from 1932, philosopher Bertrand Russell spins a tale:

> Everyone knows the story of the traveler in Naples who saw twelve beggars lying in the sun (it was before the days of Mussolini), and offered a lira to the laziest of them. Eleven of them jumped up to claim it, so he gave it to the twelfth. This traveler was on the right lines.[12]

Russell's essay – one of the least crackpot of an *oeuvre* that also contained one in which he advocated a first-strike nuclear policy against the USSR – continues along the lines that so little work is necessary that we should consider reducing our hours of work to about four per day. That this makes readers today laugh is precisely his point. Work, he argues, should be sufficient to 'entitle a man to the necessities and elementary comforts of life, and that the rest of his time should be his to use as he might see fit'.[13] He suggests that it is 'a condemnation of our civilization' that we find the notion of so much leisure time unthinkable.

Throughout the twentieth century, reams of reports and white papers were produced that showed that productivity in a workforce drops off significantly after the standard 9–5 of a working day. Overtime was put under the microscope, and it was discovered that the worker's capacity to ramp up to a 60-hour week was only efficient as a temporary measure, undertaken for a couple of months at best. Among sedentary/knowledge workers, sleep deprivation has a particularly drastic impact on cognitive function, and increases in error rates in their work. Working in the way that so many of us do has more to do with the ever-watchful eye of the superego than it does with accuracy, quality, integrity, productivity or creativity. But with more leisure time, these things have more space to flourish.[14]

After all, wasn't it leisure that produced great thinkers like Ruskin, Woolf, Darwin, Carlyle, Freud, Marx, Newton and Curie. They are all from a similar social class for a reason. In the world Russell proposes, 'every person possessed of scientific curiosity will be able to indulge it, and every painter will be able to paint without starving'. Parents could be more present; workers more efficient; friends friendlier.

It may seem counterintuitive that a form of exercise as all-encompassing as running can be idling, but once you are over the hump of unfitness that presents itself to any beginner, the physical aspect of it isn't nearly as hard as we can make it look.

Running is a way of having fun. Stepping out of the door, you leave behind much more than just your emails: you leave behind all of that clutter, that binding identity that ties you to work, responsibilities and consumerism; an identity that has you pinned like a butterfly, believing that your bank balance, pay rise or job title are the things that really matter.

The work ethic has also begun to cast its shadow over running. The idea of running as exercise is only a recent phenomenon, and exercise is also becoming one of those things that we 'should' do.

People sing, write or paint for all sorts of reasons; so too with running: some people are paid to run, some pay to do it; some do it because it is an easily accessible form of exercise; some do it to raise money for charity, monetising their fitness; some do it because they want to get fit; some do it to compete; some do it to socialise, some do it because they like to be on their own; some do it because they like to be outside; some do it because they are good at it; some do it to see if they can, some to measure their improvement; some simply run to catch a bus; and some just don't care about any of these: they do it because it gives them a kind of pleasure that is not easily accounted for.

When I was chatting to a friend recently about how much time I spend running, she asked the quite reasonable question: 'But don't you get bored?'

Like many, I sometimes suffer from this relatively new phenomenon of boredom. But I very rarely get bored when I am out running. As in Dorchester, I sometimes fail to connect with the activity, but I don't feel like I wish I were listening to music or watching a film as well as running.

And I am sure that the people who think it will be boring, too often, and quite sensibly, confuse it with exercise.

Exercise – being activity of the muscles and limbs performed for beneficial effect – is still a relatively new idea. Distinct from sport (an activity which requires rules and regulations, competition, and the involvement of others), exercise has become part of the dominant ideology, part of a collection of things that good citizens should be doing. And it is work.

In an article from the mid-1980s, the nature writer Richard Mabey asked why it was that no one seemed to walk for its own sake any more. He was suspicious of the dog walkers, the easel carriers, the number-wearing sponsorees and the picnickers. And the activity of jogging in particular he detested for needing more 'planning control than afforestation'.[15]

While I share his sentiments, I wouldn't express them in quite the same way. He feels that the donning of a tracksuit means that the outdoors will pass by in a blur, whereas I think my running has the opposite effect; it brings focus, attention and reward. But I still agree with him. If you are going running only to exercise, you may as well sit at home on a rowing machine from Argos and watch *EastEnders* while you do it.

It is the usefulness and non-immersiveness of exercise that I distrust. Walking is a fine pursuit, but numerous things can be done at the same time: reading, texting, conversing. It can still be a suspiciously utilitarian pursuit. Conversely, running can let you take life at a slower pace, precisely because nothing happens.

Though running has a complicated history, we know that jogging took off in the 1970s and 1980s. It was the period that witnessed the rise of the kinds of hyper-individualisation that were overseen in the West by Ronald Reagan and Margaret Thatcher. Jogging carries with it the freight of this political maelstrom, which confused science and philosophy and cherry-picked the bits it wanted from both.

The era took the idea of the Nietzschean superman (where 'only the strong survive') and the Darwinian imperative ('the survival of the fittest') and mapped it onto so-called ideals like greed and self-interest.[16] But any high-school kid can tell you that the 'fittest' are not necessarily the fiercest or most ruthless. They are those most-suited to their environment, and that could mean 'the quietest' or 'the most empathetic'.

In other words, 1980s wankers hijacked running and turned it into a status symbol as meaningless and utilitarian as their info-filled Filofaxes. This, it seems to me, is at the very heart of the stigma that surrounds the word 'jogging' (I can't bring myself to use the word in everyday conversation).

Mabey's suspicion holds true, but the thing that he attacks is an historical anomaly, like flares or the mullet haircut. Runners may jog, but that doesn't make them joggers. 'Joggers' wore shell-suits; their fat-trainered, pastel head-banded, sunbed-tanned, serious expressions were all accoutrements that transformed running from a beautiful activity into something that belittled those who lacked the appropriate drive and inclination.

Those were running's dark days, and it has moved on. Running doesn't have to be exercise. It doesn't have to be done to make you 'strong' or 'fit'. It doesn't even need to be done as a sport – it can be done entirely for its own sake.

Literary history is quite helpful on the emergence of exercise. Loosely defined, sport may be found at the very beginning of the idea of literature itself, in the oldest, coherent work of epic poetry that has ever been discovered, *The Epic of Gilgamesh* (from around 3,500 years ago), with its wrestling and hunting.[17] But King Gilgamesh never went jogging, or worked out on the cross-trainer.

From then until the nineteenth century, sport abounds in literature, but exercise is practically undetectable. Chaucer, in a throwaway comment in 'The Nun's Priest's Tale', says of a widow in the forest: 'Attempree dyete was al hir phisyk,/And exercyse, and hertes suffisaunce.'[18] (A temperate diet, exercise and a good frame of mind were all the medicine she needed to stay healthy.) Shakespeare is punctuated with sports of all kinds, but no one to my knowledge exercises. There was, in Shakespeare's day, the Dover Hill Olympics (from 1612), but again, this is a sporting event.

Exercise commonly features in Jane Austen. Fanny in *Mansfield Park* is forever 'knocked up on the sofa' as a result of a good walk, but exercise is mostly a pastime for the daughters of gentry, for whom the competition inherent in sport would not be appropriately gendered behaviour. Moreover, Austen often uses the idea of exercise and movement to pass judgement on her characters: generally, those who over-indulge in it are frankly villains or whores, and those who control their appetites for it are usually our hero and heroine. The finest walker in Austen is *Pride and Prejudice*'s Elizabeth Bennet, who seemingly strikes just the right balance when she arrives at Netherfield with flushed cheeks and muddy skirts to visit her sister.

By the nineteenth century, then, exercise emerges as an activity commonly seen around the leisured classes. It is what the body needs when it no longer has real, manual work to do. Is this why we now tend to do it indoors, in specially demarcated places like gyms?

Austen's suspicion of exercise seems to hold true for us today. Running is OK because you are always moving on, but try taking your iPod up to Blackheath and doing an aerobic workout. Public exercise is a complex subject that is now tied up with the sociological and anthropological minefield of territoriality and public conduct, but even in the nineteenth century, exercise lacked dignity.[19] In the literature of that period, it functions like fake tan, in that it seems tainted by vanity and self-regard, diminished by its utility, instrumentality and self-indulgence.

Even though I'm inclined to think it is too easy a target, exercise is almost always part of a comic turn when it appears in our culture. The trope of the dumb jock is a common component in mainstream cinema (from Emilio Estevez in *The Breakfast Club* to Brad Pitt's wonderful turn as Chad the gym instructor with the room-temperature IQ in the Coen brothers' *Burn After Reading*), but even Tolstoy used the trope of exercise to poke fun at the characters that he wanted us to distrust.

The judge that ineptly oversees Maslova's trial in Tolstoy's final novel, *Resurrection*, is given this introduction in his chambers before the day begins:

> The president . . . though married . . . led a very loose life, and his wife did the same, so they did not stand in each other's way. This morning he had received a note from a [former governess]. She wrote that she would wait for him between five and six pm in the Hotel Italia. This made him wish to begin and get through the sitting as soon as possible, so as to also have time to call . . . on the little red-haired Clara Vasilievna, with whom he had begun a romance . . . last summer. He went into a private room, latched the door, took a pair of dumb-bells out of a cupboard, moved his arms 20 times upwards, downwards, forwards, and sideways, then holding the dumb-bells above his head, lightly bent his knees three times.
>
> 'Nothing keeps one going like a cold bath and exercise,' he said, feeling the biceps of his right arm with his left hand, on the third

finger of which he wore a gold ring . . . when there was a knock at the door. The president quickly put away the dumb-bells.[20]

Like many officials in that novel, the judge is vain, unfaithful, and leeches from society, exercising power that is not his own, and failing to understand the gravity of his role (and more importantly, the terrible error of his judgement against Maslova that sends her to a Siberian prison camp). He has to retreat to a locked room to exercise. The indulgence of the body becomes a symbol for the indulgence of the flesh. The president is not an embodied self. Tolstoy teaches us to distrust the judge because he does not live through his body, but only with it – through what he needs from it to impress his lovers. Tolstoy distrusts the judge because his body has become separate from his mind. (And finally, is it just me or would that scene have functioned in just the same way had the judge been watching pornography or masturbating? The self-indulgence, the locked door, the furtiveness, the sexual fantasising, the shame?)

Real running transports us far from the judge's chamber to something more tactile and real. In perhaps their best collaboration, Michael Powell and Emeric Pressburger's magical film *A Canterbury Tale* (1944) has one of its characters (Thomas Colpeper) explain what movement in a particular place can produce in us.

> Well, there are more ways than one of getting close to your ancestors. Follow the old road, and as you walk, think of them and of the old England. They climbed Chillingbourne Hill, just as you. They sweated and paused for breath just as you did today. And when you see the bluebells in the spring [. . .] you're only seeing what their eyes saw [. . .] you're so close to those other people, that you can hear the thrumming of the hoofs of their horses, and the sound of the wheels on the road [. . .] And when I turn the bend in the road, where they too saw the towers of Canterbury, I feel I've only to turn my head, to see them on the road behind me.[21]

I would say that this is one the main reasons that I never get bored when I am running, (irritated sometimes, disengaged, but never bored, because the past is always so present).

The reflections one experiences when one runs are not useful. Neither do they belong to the idea of 'exercise'. They belong instead to a kind of art that expresses a form of historical re-enactment, a remembering that happens through the body and its movement through a particular place.

And for me, this is what running is – neither sport nor exercise, it shares much more in common with the expressive impulse of the arts. The best runs dissolve one's attachment to the world, and allow you to become the run, not just a runner.

Running, like literature, like art, helps you to remember and re-experience some of the impossible strangeness of what it means to be who and what we are, of what it means to be human.

ALONE ON LUNDY ISLAND

I wake at 4am to drive from Dorchester cross-country, in time for the 8am check-in and 9am sailing. This time of day is always perceptually weird, mixing those people who are beginning their day with those who are ending theirs; places are suddenly emptied of the people and cars that are a constant feature at other times. The surrounding countryside starts to repossess them as birdsong, the sound of the river or the rustling trees dominate instead of traffic noise.

I am bound for a place that is as quiet as places were centuries ago. It is devoid of 'stuff' – my books aren't there, neither is my music. There is no Internet, and there is no phone signal. Late at night, there isn't even any electricity. I drive for hours, tuning in and out of local radio (bemusement is a great remedy for tiredness).

I have not seen my partner Adam for several days, and now I'm going for a further week with no phone signal. I like being on my own; I'm used to it, but this is quite a stretch. I feel a bit low when I anticipate what may become island loneliness.

It's now August, and it's raining. I arrive on time at the car park at a local garage – a couple of miles from the departure point at Bideford, but I don't reckon on the local taxi firm not answering their phone. For ten minutes, I listen to an intrusive musical backing track as they tell me how pleased they are that I have called, that my call is very important to them, that someone will be with me as soon as possible. I wonder aimlessly why no one is answering. Have they not been answering all night? Beginning to panic, I run back into the garage to get another number. I dial it, but it's the same music and the same message. After another five minutes of mawkishly expressed gratitude I run back into the garage – what can we do?

'Well, there's a bus . . .' the girl tells me.

'Great, how . . .?'

She continues, 'but I think they only come once an hour.'

'My boat leaves in 45 minutes.'

'It's only about a 15-minute walk.'

I shake my head. No, not with my luggage it isn't. Even if it were, I don't know Bideford that well, and can't be sure that I won't make a mistake on the route.

'Where does the bus go from?'

She points, 'There.'

'Where?'

'There,' stretching her hand, pointing even harder.

I can't see anything, except: 'The lamppost?'

'Yeah, the sign fell off.'

I drop my bags and run outside to investigate the veracity of this statement. But before I get there I see a bus coming. My bags are inside. I think for a second and after considering perhaps too few options I fix on jumping up and down and waving my arms while hopping from leg to leg. Amazingly, this definitively non-London strategy works and the bus begins to slow. I make a dash for my bags and by the time I return, the doors are opened and the driver is waiting and laughing. I explain what has happened and he says, 'Stay on the bus after the last stop, I'll take you right to the ferry terminal.'

We are definitely not in London, and a few minutes later, he does exactly this.

On the quay after check-in, I stand by helplessly (along with a small group of others in a forest of fleece), watching the crew loading up the luggage into the rope crane-sack. I can see my flimsy bag at the bottom of the net soaking up the puddle water, being pushed a little deeper with every rucksack that is bunged on top of it.

It has already rained nine times since I got off the bus.

The early start, the long drive and the stress have all pushed the pleasurable anticipation of this trip out of my mind, so it is not until the boat chugs out of the harbour with its diesel-seaweed smell that I am able to settle into looking forward to a week running on Lundy Island.

Lundy lies about 12 miles off the north coast of Devon. It is less than two square miles and has almost no inhabitants. The puffin colony there is an inherent part of the island's identity: in Old Norse, '*lundi*' means puffin, and the terminal '*y*' means island. It is also rich in other wildlife and has a dramatic smuggling history.

The rain starts again but I cannot bring myself to go back inside the cabin and be deprived of the exquisite optical yoga that is wave-watching. It's like the pixels on our retina are so accustomed to seeing static environments that they go giddy when everything in the landscape is suddenly moving. When another shower breaks hard, the yoga goes deeper as every wavelet is freckled with rivets of rain.

I pull my hood and wrap it hard round my head and face and totter about as the MS *Oldenburg* mounts a few waves, pinballing me from rail to rail like a drunkard.

Anonymity allows us to be whomever we want to be. How we behave when we are around those to whom we need never speak and do not know is a test of character.

I size up my fellow travellers. The group is fairly homogeneous, rucksacks and Gore-Tex, but there are some very smart, linen-clad youths. They sit out on deck and deny themselves shelter. Except for one other young man, I think I am the only lone traveller. By nature, I must seem a rather sad type: middle-aged, with no rowdy friends to share a house with, no companions, no family, and my little fat face peaking out from my hood like Kenny from *South Park*. Feeling a little lonely is one thing, but being seen to be a little lonely seems somehow worse. But there is no one here to remember me.

At least that is what I believe. An hour into the journey and I think I see a face that I recognise. We were undergraduates together. I always liked her. It's 20 years ago now, so it probably isn't her. And when she walks right by me, I'm still not sure. She is with several generations of what looks like her family. My curiosity piqued, I follow them into the galley and as soon as I hear her speak, I recognise her voice and say hello.

She gets up from the table and says, 'Hi, yes, I saw you earlier.' Awkward? *When* 'earlier'? Tottering-about-like-a-drunk-in-my-tight-little-hood earlier? Why didn't you say hello 'earlier'?

'This is Vidor.'

After a correction, a few pleasantries, and the offer of a 'catch up' later, I leave her, because I don't want to impose on what is obviously a family's getaway.

In the Tavern (the island's only pub and eating place) later in the week the coincidences proceed: her sister is part of their group, as are her children, who it turns out are at the same school as my sister's children, many hundreds of miles away in York. The world is a lot smaller on Lundy.

Life here is a dainty affair; an estate agent would call it 'manageable'. My sofa is my bed. The shower is in the kitchen. The kitchen is in the living room. And the living room is the bedroom. Despite being short of space, there is an old broadcasting radio in my room the size of a fridge. The den is built of Lundy granite and has a small table by the window that looks out to sea.

When my bag arrives, I unpack it and hang out my wet clothes. My running gear is dry, so I change. I want to try and catch sight of the puffins before they leave for the year, and before the sun sets for the evening.

My anonymity dashed on the rocks, I feel self-conscious as the only runner in a land of walkers; I can't bring myself to make eye contact with others in the village. And the village is tiny (a shop and a couple of farm buildings, as well as the pub), so I am out of the fray within a matter of seconds, leaving behind the blinking sparrows and the willow warblers with their thick eyeliner like Elizabeth Taylor's Cleopatra. Through the first gate, I am on a harsh northbound trackway that has a strip of grass running down the middle between sugar lumps of granite. Three abreast, a family approaches me, so I arc around them into the long grass. I have been running for less than a minute on Lundy, having planned it for months, when I step on a tussock and my ankle immediately turns with that familiar shard of pain before I catch my weight. The pain passes; I may have corrected it in time, so I continue. I will have to check my ankle in a minute or two for swelling. I know that this wouldn't have happened barefoot. The haptic cues given by unlevel ground would have been detected much sooner without having to travel through sole-rubber.

I continue north through a farm, over the quarter wall and past the remains of the old hospital where there are reed buntings chirruping at one another. The middle of the island is quite marshy so there are also sedge- and aquatic warblers, and *everywhere* there are juvenile skylarks popping up from the ferns, flicking their wings like little brown sparks. The Victorian poet and novelist, George Meredith, described their song as 'a silver chain of sound of many links'.[22] It is as varied as a poem in Morse code, played at ten times the normal speed. If pointillism (the school of Impressionist painting that employed only dots of paint) could be heard, its bright mix of colours and textures would sound like the song of the skylark.

The air is clear this evening so I can see the western coast of Devon in the distance, and that's how far away the world of work seems. Cloud scuds over the waveform heath to my left, bound for the mainland. There are no trees on the upland of Lundy. From the sea, the island looks as raised and flat as a picnic table, with only the spire of the church to trouble the view. Nothing can withstand the fierce easterly wind from the Atlantic that scythes across the island, so there is little that grows above shoulder height. The Yorkshire fog grasses (*Holcus ianatus)*, tall and slender elsewhere, are only inches tall. Even the bar-brawl-tough furze grows in miniature, knee-high mounds, whereas on the South Downs it can reach a few metres.

My ankle checked, I feel lucky and free. On my run, I pass wild Soay sheep, wild ponies, wild sika deer, a pair of ravens, even a peregrine, and everywhere the granite walls are covered in a wide variety of gold, sage, saffron, white, pistachio, opal and amber lichens. So covered are they that some of the granite stones look like sleeping green-pelted monsters straight out of a Maurice Sendak book.

On the path there is a blast of grey and white feathers and a bit of skeleton. It looks like the humerus and radius of both wings of a herring gull. They are spread as if in flight. But there is nothing left. The peregrine must have taken beak, eyes and everything. The bones have only slithers of red flesh still on them, like a licked yoghurt pot.

Nearby, above the ferns, I watch a kestrel hovering, its tail spread below it like a fan. It dives but must have missed its prey because it bounds back up again to repeat the same sequence.

As I approach the northerly Three-quarter Wall, I see that it is noticeably higher than the others. I am about ten metres away from it when a horned head peeps over the top. Immediately, I stop. The eyes stare at me for a second. If I were to throw my arms wide, I might match the width of the horns on this thing. I stare back – a bull, perhaps? It bobs down, but only for a second. With an unbelievably sprightly dexterity, at once impressive and alarming, it is over the wall with a sassy indifference to the feat it just performed. The Beast of the North Wall is only a stupendously large wild goat. With long white hair that looks plumed as if for Crufts, and the size of a pony, it wanders off the path and into the ferns. *This is what you wanted, the wild*, I think; I just hadn't expected it to be so alive, and to have such very big horns.

I climb over the wall. The northern quarter of the island is noticeably sparser, mainly exposed granite and crew-cut heather. At the end of the island I am now settled into my pace. My heartbeat is up but comfortable and the ions of static from daily life feel like they are disappearing. I peep over the edge and see some seals hundreds of feet down, sunning themselves, the light reflecting off the blubbery silk of their bellies. (Later, I check this on my map and the islet is called 'Seal's Island.)' I was shod when I turned my ankle, but am barefoot now, and the pathway, which would have seemed sharp as glass with shoes (sounding like chewing on sugar), is made mostly of tiny beads of quartz, or peaty earth.

Back over the wall and I am on grass again. The sun has dried it in places, but just beneath the surface it is moist and warm. The rain from earlier has woken the peat below. Soft and spongey, it is like running on a tongue, but in a really good way.

The sun is beginning to dip, but I decide I still have enough time to make my way back via the Atlantic side of the island.

There was a puffin sighting at the Devil's Chimney yesterday and I have been told that there are hundreds around Jenny's Cove, but they are shy.

The west side of the island has startling geology. There are huge granite towers, some of which are over 100 feet in height, with a laughably implausible, gravity-defying geometry.

On one of the cliffs I am suddenly overtaken with nausea as I gaze a couple of hundred feet down to the sea between a monstrous granite tuning fork. My Garmin GPS unit's vibrating alarm groans a complaint that I have stopped, and I resist the impulse to unstrap it and throw it into the sea. It is not that I fear I might fall, but, bizarrely, that I might jump, giving into what feels like a rope around my waist that is gently pulling me into the abyss.

I sit down on a pillow of heather, refusing to let the vertigo deny me the view. It is then that the seabirds at Jenny's Cove come properly into focus. My heart is still beating hard, and my breath is deep but slowing. There is that bliss that comes from running, when you feel like every millimetre of your lungs is finally beaten into life and is working efficiently, so that when you stop running you feel like you only need to breathe as rarely as a freediver.

The sun is turning orange. Down at the coast I can make out some majestic shags, long-necked, otter-sleek and black, standing on the edge of the rocks by the sea. There are guillemots, too, and kittiwakes, great black-backed gulls, and herring gulls squawking above my head, and skylarks singing in the heath behind me. When a razorbill, his wings held static, soaring on the breeze, swings into view, he rises and rises out of the cove. Then he banks left, picking up speed as he swoops, still facing the sunset, and goes into a long and deep roll towards the sea, his orientation remaining unchanged towards the dipping sun. He lifts steeply again, rising higher and higher, and then he banks back. Each manoeuvre covers hundreds and hundreds of yards in seconds, and I watch the portly razorbill do it again, and again, and again. His monochrome plumage makes him look like a gliding killer whale. He is not hunting. He is not marking a territory. He is swift, silent and effortless. Like an engine, his wings are idling but I cannot see them move. He is not doing anything except taking and exploiting this confluence of forces, energies and opportunities and feeding off them greedily. Feeling the wind against his nostrils and forehead, the last warmth of the sun on his mantle, the breeze moving across his long throat to his breast and nape, through his coverts, primaries, secondaries, scapulars and tertials, to his rump. Every bit of him, from claw to crown, is in this moment as the sun sets. I could not feel less alone than I do in moments like this. Minutes pass as I watch him and I'm unsure that I've taken a breath.

The sun starts to dim behind the mesh of cloud deep, deep on the horizon, and then for a moment it reappears, crimson now, in a slim thinning ingot. Its corona almost flashes at the sea's edge, and then it is gone. Heedless it has been, on its determined march into tomorrow. The razorbill disappears into the clatter of guillemots and kittiwakes on their commute back to their clifftop roosts for the night.

Clawing at the heather, I climb back up to the heath to find my way back to the hamlet before the light goes, but something about the razorbill's flight has knocked the wind out of me. I feel heavy in the throat at having shamanically shared the exuberance of flight, even for only a moment. I think again of the predator kestrel hungering for its prey in its effortful flight above the herbage and I understand how those two flights are quite distinct. Flight is like birdsong, which can be territorial, or a warning or a mating call, but is also expressive. The bird sings because it is alive and it can. It expresses its skills, abilities and its aesthetic potential. Sometimes they fly because they need to hunt, or migrate; sometimes it is only to enjoy the sensual excitement of flight. This is where joy is to be found: in using one's body and its expressive impulse for its own sake, for no outcome but itself. During that run I realised that we need the receptivity of other life, for without it we are starved of that oxygen that enriches far beyond the boundaries of a single breath.

A week later, when I left Lundy, I didn't regret not having had my puffin sighting. Optimistically, I believed that there would be other opportunities. It all seemed so very far from the treadmill that can be work or exercise regimes. What is more, I didn't regret it, because I knew there would never be another first evening on the island, with that sunset, and that razorbill, playing and dancing free, mid-air.

PART III
EARTHING

5.

THE WORLD AT OUR FEET: HOW THE PLACES WE RUN CHANGE US, AND HOW WE CHANGE THEM

ALDEBURGH AND SANTA CRUZ, CALIFORNIA

The world is nothing but an evolving network of relationships.
– Lee Smolin, *Three Roads to Quantum Gravity*, 2001

I thought of my inner existence, that consciousness which is called the soul. These, that is, myself – I threw into the balance to weight the prayer the heavier . . . I hid my face in the grass, I was wholly prostrated, I lost myself in the wrestle, I was rapt and carried away.
– Richard Jefferies, *The Story of My Heart*, 1883

From what I have seen of Hertfordshire I am inclined to think that the woods there are of a grander type – at any rate the trees themselves – than those in the part of England in which my story is supposed to take place. But I find that in such matters – indeed in any matter – it is not absolute size but the attitude of the observer which makes things great or small.
– Thomas Hardy, Letter to Lord Lytton, 12 July 1887

There is nothing so relentlessly impressive as our environment. It is everywhere we look. Everything we do is in it. Everything we think is achieved because of it. Our bodies come from and return to it. Art is born of it.[1] It feeds us. It shelters and destroys us. Inevitably, the impact that the environment has on our running is enormous, too; but do we also have an impact on it when we run? Clearly there are benefits to our exercising outdoors, but in the following chapters I go far beyond the long series of psychological and neurological rewards already covered, asking what it means for us to exercise in different environments, and also what it means for the places themselves.

In the world of our literature, folk- and fairy tales, everything seems like it used to be forest, from John o'Groats all the way down to the opal Mediterranean. The woods were the magical habitat for wolves disguised as grandmothers, or of Sir Orfeo or Gawain's Green Knight, or a place of enchantment in Shakespeare and Mozart. They were spaces of fantasy until they were all destroyed by the Industrial Revolution, or so the story goes. But the truth is that deforestation has been going on for many thousands of years. It is part of who we are as a species, to build and farm and burn. And this, I was soon to discover while out on a run, may be one of nature's cruellest ironies.

Environmental issues in novels, paintings and poetry are not new and did not emerge only because forests of chimneys began to spring up from our urban centres with the sudden ferocity of leylandii. For thousands of years, humans have been in the business of altering the landscapes around them. As long ago as three or four millennia, at the very beginning of recorded history, in our favourite ancient poem, *The Epic of Gilgamesh*, there is a scene which basically recounts an early exercise in deforestation. It is the sequence in which King Gilgamesh and his new friend Enkidu go to the forest to collect cedar wood and slay the demon-ogre Humbaba. For this the gods punish the pair by killing Enkidu and exposing Gilgamesh to the anguish of grief for his friend. But I learned on my run that there was a great deal more to be had in the forest than cedar wood, and that there are ways of rabidly plundering places that, far from destroying them, may even help to ensure their longevity.

Although it has been around for about 4,000 years, parts of the poem are still turning up in the sands of Iraq to be translated, casting a new light on its meaning. Only last year, some lines were discovered that made more sense of that deforestation/male-bonding 'lets-cut-down-trees-and-kill-us-some-demons' sequence from Tablet Five of the poem.[2] It was discovered in these new lines that Humbaba (killed by Gilgamesh and Enkidu) was not a demon-ogre at all, but a foreign king and protector of the forest.

The poem itself tells the story of someone discovering that, just like everyone else, he is going to die; Gilgamesh learns to accept his fate and rejects the myth of immortality. For this and so many other reasons, it marks a turning point in our sentience as a species. It is the beginning of written records, and so of literature and history as we know it. But what, after all, does it say of us that our first major poem recounts environmental plunder and the slaying of a forest's protector so that the bond between two men may be forged?

Given that they are synonymous with fairy stories, it is all too easy to think of natural places as sources of wish-fulfilment and fantasy. Sigmund Freud argued that part of our development from child to adult was the acceptance of the reality principle and the necessary renunciation or deferral of pleasure. And for him, our desire to preserve natural environments was as indicative of our refusal to accept reality as a daydream in which we calculate how we might spend the money from a lottery-win.

But renunciation of pleasure has always been very hard for man; he cannot accomplish it without some kind of compensation. Accordingly he has evolved for himself a mental activity in which all these relinquished sources of pleasure and abandoned paths of gratification are permitted to continue their existence . . . In phantasy, therefore, man can continue to enjoy a freedom from the grip of the external world, one which he has long relinquished in actuality . . . The creation of the mental domain of phantasy has a complete counterpart in the establishment of 'reservations' and 'nature-parks' in places where the inroads of agriculture, traffic, or industry threaten to change the original face of the earth rapidly into something unrecognizable. The 'reservation' is to maintain the old condition of things which has been regretfully sacrificed to necessity everywhere else; there everything may grow and spread as it pleases, including what is useless and even what is harmful. The mental realm of phantasy is also such a reservation reclaimed from the encroachments of the reality-principle.[3]

Places are more potent than this, though; they are more vital and more real. Freud was right in that they do have a psychological value for us, but it goes deeper than that. Running through the following chapters is that notion that I keep coming back to: curiosity. And the environments in which we exercise have a big impact upon the kinds of wonder that the world might encourage in us. These are all ideas that I would brush up against on an upcoming run on the bulging beer-belly coastline of East Anglia.

SUSTAINABLE RUNNING IN ALDEBURGH

To get to Aldeburgh I drive A-roads, B-roads, and roads without any status, finding myself in the heart of the seaside village with barely any suburban prologue. For years, I have been reading about its associations with Benjamin Britten, E.M. Forster, Ronald Blythe, the Tennyson family, George Ewart Evans and George Crabbe. There's a pageantry to it, managing to look old and new all at once.

It's the end of the winter, February. It's shudder-cold and breezy. I pull up on the north edge of town. It's just after lunchtime, and having worked all morning it's now too late for me to eat if I'm to do a longish run. Knowing this, I've plundered my collection of pillow mints from my room in the B & B up the coast – they will suffice for the sugar-hit I will need in a few miles' time.

The sky's a little heavy, but it is carrying its weight high. I have dressed appropriately (a rare thing), and if the clouds stay at altitude the weather may be kind. The sea is the colour of pewter. It's empty; the fishing boats all landed to the south. Looking north, down the coast, the pebble beach stretches for miles. Aldeburgh looks like the end of the world.

On the map, the coastline is sharp, with clean lines, but here there seems to be hundreds of yards of scumbled shading where the flats of the grassland blend seamlessly with the pebbles and sands of the beach. The flitting strings and rippling woodwinds of Benjamin Britten's first Sea Interlude from *Peter Grimes* pop into my head and for the remainder of the run I can't get them out. (Not really surprising as I later discover that this is the path that he walked every day between fits of composition.)

The opera was adapted from a poem in an unsentimental collection of poetry about Suffolk life called *The Borough* (1810) by George Crabbe. He was a surgeon's apprentice, clergyman, coleopterist, carer and novel-arsonist (three of his own unpublished manuscripts), and he is still underrated as a poet, valued more for the doors he showed others the way to than those he opened. Before Wordsworth and Coleridge, he was writing the poetry of the common man and of the struggle therein to become an uncommon one.

It was on reading an article by E.M. Forster on Crabbe, while Britten was in exile in California in 1941, that he was first alerted to *The Borough*. Forster did the thing that he does in his essays, which is to knit together the art, the artist and the area. 'So remember Aldeburgh when you read this rather odd poet, for he belongs to the grim little place, and through it to England.'[4] It would take an emigrant with a heart of stone to read the essay and not long to feel the shingle of the foreshore at one's feet.

The land is laid flat. And, out of season, it is sparsely peopled: a couple of couples and some dogs. Just over the brow of the shingle the sea gnaws at the beach. The sound hits only my right ear as through a broken set of earphones. The run ahead is clear of any obstacles until I reach the scrubland at the Haven, to the south of Thorpeness. I dodge on to the sand and pebbles and eventually find the path headed north. When I get to Thorpeness, a small coastal village that I am told has charm, I am assaulted by more 'no admittance', 'private road' and 'no way through' signs per square mile than I have ever encountered. As I test the validity of each sign, I discover the lie – there is always a way through. The inhabitants must find themselves under siege from visitors in the summer months, but I am not sure this is the way to deal with those who come in earnest to breathe some sea air. Perhaps the golf club could be persuaded to give up one of its holes to car parking? It already occupies more space here than the entire village. I zigzag through the village and have lost all sight of a coastal footpath, but I know that if I keep working north I will soon find my way.

Back on the tight loam of the path at the other end of the town and I feel the first pulse of my rhythm. The patter builds from your toes, through your feet and your heels, the swing of your knees and the rotation of your hips, all the way up the axis of your spine, to your fluttering arms and breath. Today it makes elemental chords with the waves as they break on the foreshore. It takes thousands of steps to build this rhythm, but build it does. It's emboldening and so systematic it leaves you reluctant to stop or divert.

The path is now an eely line of chalk and clay, hard and compacted, but mushy in more sheltered spots. Tall briars that flick at my shoulders and obscure the sea enclose it. They are dense and appear crosshatched with determined ink. They are grey, black, even peacock-blue in the patches of sunlight. They are sharp and bare and so tightly packed that beyond the curves ahead, where the path slithers out of view, it looks like a holloway. Running the path, as it turns this way and that, feels as natural as water running a riverbed, always finding the easiest way, 'burrowing like a root, going deeper./Like sucking 'pon fruit, but sweeter'.[5] Good paths pull us in. They are coercive, as if they possess their own gravity. Because of this, they seem indelible, but here of all places, there is a reminder that these are anything but permanent ways.

As I climb through the briars, the coastline is revealed as a place in an enduring state of review. Noticeboards, warnings of eroding cliffs, danger signs, all have given way and are disappearing into steep landslides.

With falling blood sugar, I keep thinking about the mints that I remember I've left in the car.

The cliffs are as jagged as broken teeth. I know to keep away from the cantilevered edges as they are probably unsupported outcroppings ready to disappear into the sea.

I almost burst with excitement when I finally see Sizewell nuclear plant on the horizon, steadfast: the housing of the Magnox reactor like an enormous and tired breeze-block. I think about the roads I worked to get into the town, and I wonder if they are up to the headlong rush of an emergency evacuation.

Sizewell A was decommissioned about ten years ago at a cost of over £1 billion. (This figure is small fry compared to the cost of decommissioning the Sellafield nuclear plant in Cumbria: the estimate over the next century is £70 billion.[6]) A high percentage of the energy created in a nuclear reactor can be controlled, but the radioactive fragments that are left after the splitting of uranium atoms cannot be simply turned off and so need to be maintained in a safe state by constant cooling. This is why the decommissioning process is expensive and slow: once fission has begun it cannot be stopped.

Neither is the safety record of nuclear sites particularly reassuring. During the decommissioning of Sizewell A, a contractor who had decided to wash some of his clothes discovered a water leak. A 15-foot crack had opened in one of the pipes connected to the cooling ponds which contained the reactor's highly radioactive waste. Forty thousand gallons of the water had leaked, some into the North Sea. The water level in the cooling pond had dropped by over a foot, yet none of the alarms had been triggered. If the water had continued leaking until the next inspection was due, the waste could have overheated, melted its casings, caught fire and been distributed into the air. The decay heat from spent fuel is so intense that it can raise the temperature of rock strata for tens of thousands of years.

The Windscale fire of 1957 (which scored a five on the seven-point International Nuclear Event Scale) spread radioactive contamination across the UK and Europe. In 2005, the Sellafield disaster saw the leak of 160kg of plutonium and 20 tonnes of uranium (scoring a three on the INES). The 1979 Three Mile Island incident in Pennsylvania in the US scored a five, and was also a coolant-leak failure. Both the Chernobyl and Fukushima disasters were sevens. Chernobyl is still surrounded by a 30-kilometre exclusion zone. The Fukushima disaster was caused by something as unpredictable as a tsunami. Over 600,000 people had to be relocated because of both these accidents.

If we go, we really are going to take the whole planet with us, it seems.

It makes me think of Richard Jefferies. He wrote what is arguably the first piece of speculative apocalyptic science fiction as far back as 1885.

After London is set many years after an unspecified ecological disaster. The action of the novel is a little staid, but the scene-setting is breathtaking. It begins,

> The old men say their fathers told them that soon after the fields were left to themselves a change began to be visible. It became green everywhere in the first spring, after London ended, so that all the country looked alike.
>
> The meadows were green, and so was the rising wheat which had been sown, but which neither had nor would receive any further care. Such arable fields as had not been sown, but where the last stubble had been ploughed up, were overrun with couch-grass, and where the short stubble had not been ploughed, the

weeds hid it. So that there was no place which was not more or less green; the footpaths were the greenest of all, for such is the nature of grass where it has once been trodden on, and by-and-by, as the summer came on, the former roads were thinly covered with the grass that had spread out from the margin.[7]

Jefferies's version of the future is dominated by his belief of what the past was in 1885 when he was writing. What constitutes the past is always historically contingent. For example, chronological bibles that dated the beginning of time to 23 October 4004 BCE were popular throughout the nineteenth century. But once the contrast of a much longer, deeper and darker model of history slowly emerged as a result of geological and biological theory and discovery, a space in the future also opened up wide enough for speculative science fiction to occupy. That the past provides a model for the future is a common thread throughout literary history. We can see it in H.G. Wells's *The Time Machine*, where the deep past becomes a deep future for Wells's Time Traveller to penetrate. There, he finds humans that have degenerated back to uncivilised existences, even to a sort of cannibalism. They have not progressed, but regressed. For much of this sort of fiction the present is a hinge in time. It is the final point of progress before a future of inevitable degeneration that looks just like its past.

But the proliferation of nuclear power throughout the UK and the rest of the world is putting an end to this idea of the future as a return to a more natural state. Without stable government, or without people, the unmanaged radioactive waste at these sites (which are springing up all over the world) will leave an indelible mark on the planet. If these reactors had been built at the same time as Stonehenge the nuclear waste from them would still have to be managed for many more thousands of years before they were safe.

John Ruskin fretted about the longevity of the great buildings of the world, but his sentiments are just as meaningful in the context of the long-term environmental cost of things like nuclear power. With regard to the world's great ruins, Ruskin said, 'We have no right whatever to touch them. They are not ours. They belong . . . to all generations of mankind who are to follow us.'[8] It seems like an insurmountable responsibility to have taken on, showing a stratospheric faith in the stability of the future. The chance of there being a nuclear accident today is so minuscule as to be immeasurable. But sufficient time need only be added into that equation for it to become a certainty.

I was wrong about Thorpeness having the densest concentration of warnings against trespass: it is Sizewell. As I get closer, the signs come into focus, and the multiple fences look like something from *The Great Escape*, and I suppose that is as we would wish it. So, after admiring Sizewell B's impressive architecture (it looks like a giant blue Lego brick wearing half a ping-pong ball), I dawdle a bit with a playful Labrador, but I know I've reached the outward hinge of this journey and degenerate back through the evolution of this run.

The coastline here is still littered with reinforced anti-invasion defences from the Second World War. Like little concrete beach huts with apertures for gun emplacements, these defences are now liminal and littoral spaces where one can go to shoot up in peace and quiet. It reminds me of a lovely bit in a Chekhov short story, 'Lights' (1888), about graffiti:

> You know that when a man in a melancholy mood is left tête-à-tête with the sea, or any landscape which seems to him grandiose, there is always, for some reason, mixed with melancholy, a conviction that he will live and die in obscurity, and he reflectively snatches up a pencil and hastens to write his name on the first thing that comes handy. And that, I suppose, is why all convenient solitary nooks like my summer-house are always scrawled over in pencil or carved with penknives.[9]

The story is about a doctor who while travelling in a desolate landscape comes across a hut in which to rest where he finds two men who see no value in life or any kind of attainment because we are all headed for the same fate. They spend the night there exchanging their rather bleak stories of loves lost, found, then dumped.

The people who frequent this emplacement hut do not share Chekhov's sentiments. In some neighbourhoods, graffiti can be a sign that suppressed whispers are being given voice; the politically disempowered speak through the rattle and hiss of a spray can. But here? I doubt these tagsters were in the throes of some existential crisis in their moment of creativity. The hut is decorated with spray-painted swastikas, illegible tags, and images of women being penetrated by disembodied genitals with prickly scrotums that resemble the chin of Desperate Dan. Quite who is speaking, or what is being said, I'm not sure. Odd to think the emplacements were put here precisely to keep the Nazis out, yet they have found their way in, nonetheless.

At points, the pathway back is unnavigable because of the landslips. I make my way down to the beach, but the shingle is too fine and my feet disappear into it and I have to suck them out as if it is quicksand. The foreshore is obscured by the incoming tide, there is nothing solid to run on, so I break my stride and walk until I can find solid ground.

The sun is beginning to set. It's with great relief that I reach the shaded, grass-sand-shingle outside Aldeburgh. It's really too early in the year to run barefoot, but a couple of miles out, that's what I do. Because I was carrying so much sand and grit, when I put my feet onto the mossy grass it's like running on a bath sponge. I'm rasp-thirsty, and am convinced that the grass is quenching me through the soles of my feet. My steps are short, my knees a bit sore, and ignoring the waders on the wetland to my right, I can think of nothing but the B & B mints on the passenger seat of my car, and the Aldeburgh Bookshop, which is going to close before I can reach it if I'm not quick on these numb feet.

Ted Hughes (in a review of Max Nicholson's *The Environmental Revolution*) argued that our relationship with the earth in the West derives from an essentially Christian model. (Christianity is after all one of the most anthropocentric religions of the world.) Nature was not entrusted to us, but gifted by God.[10] And now that God has retreated from the world we are left to find meaning, value and fulfilment in plundering the planet in an all-out race towards progress and material comfort.

In that review, and indeed throughout most of his work, Hughes worried for our physical and spiritual disconnection from nature. The issue, though, runs deeper than that. Even the term 'nature' is problematic: Raymond Williams thought it the most complex word in the English language.[11] And because there is no nature that we are not already of, some have questioned its existence as a distinguishable entity in itself. The word is just a means of describing certain phenomena that we experience in the world (such as particular kinds of growth, reproduction or decay). Just one of the many wonderful things about Charles Darwin was that he understood this. But from the 1860s onwards, his Theory of Evolution has been too often misread as having an endpoint or an intention. Namely, that evolution is a progress towards the hominin. Or that through some act of will or education we are able to alter the course of nature's plan. How can something that does not exist have a plan?

We are learning more about our disconnection from the natural world through all manner of environmental crises. Swine flu, DDT and the foot-and-mouth crisis all have their roots in the hare-brained drive to profit and ever-cheaper food. Cheap additives (sugars and corn syrups, for example) are driving an obesity epidemic and are surely connected to the explosion in type-2 diabetes that is going to cost us billions in long-term healthcare. Couple this with the cost of physical inactivity, which has been rather cautiously estimated at around £1 billion.[12] Add to this the associated costs to the economy of things like lost productivity and funding the obesity problem, and the figure pushes past £10 billion.[13] Living cheaply has never been so absurdly expensive, and it seems far from sustainable.

Is the idea of sustainability even sustainable? Current estimates suggest that in the history of the planet there have lived a total of around 60 billion people. A staggering 11 per cent of earth's human inhabitants over the last 2 million years are alive as you read this.

I live in south-east London. Here the population density is about 10,000 people per square kilometre. For the whole of

England it is around 400 people for the same space. In the US it is around 33. And in Australia just a little less than 3. The weight of it all seems too much to bear; little wonder millions of us run, walk and cycle out onto the hills and into the woods to escape into some space.

When I made it back to the car, the little pain I had in my knees subsided. I opened the car door, wrestled the sweets from their wrappers and chewed my way through them. Few things in my life have tasted and felt so good.

At the end of the Chekhov story, the main character, a doctor, leaves the graffitied hut and sets off again on his journey into the stark landscape.

> And when I lashed my horse and galloped along the line, and when a little later I saw nothing before me but the endless gloomy plain and the cold overcast sky, I recalled the questions which were discussed in the night. I pondered while the sun-scorched plain, the immense sky, the oak forest, dark on the horizon and the hazy distance, seemed saying to me:
> 'Yes, there's no understanding anything in this world!'

But the beauty of it is that we don't have to. We can't live life if we are always seeking to understand it. Better to go out and play, use the body, pique curiosity. The fact that there is no point to it is what makes it all so very special.

'KEEP SANTA CRUZ WEIRD', FOREST BATHING AND ENVIRONMENTAL EMPATHY

There are lions in the woods here. At least that's what the notices say. I am in a forest of redwoods. Their ludicrous, neck-straining height make me feel like Tom Thumb or Rumplestiltskin (whose peculiar name I have sympathy for). Being alone in the woods like this has a sort of enchantment. The magic of them is that they cannot be seen. If you're lucky, you can distinguish about

50 yards in any direction; beyond that may be pasture or the edge of the world for all you know. Even though I know the sun is gleaming, not much heat seems to make it down from the canopy a mile above my head. There are occasional columns of light so harsh that they might denote the point of an alien abduction.

I travelled by starlight to California. I caught the train in Seattle and we rattled all the way down the Pacific coast for a day and a night. The train was roomy, a little shabby, but it had a couple of glass-roofed cars where by night with the lights dimmed I was able to look at the stars as the train snaked its way through the mountainous Cascade Range (part of the Pacific's Ring of Fire) that reaches from Canada all the way down to California. I watched, bleary-eyed, as the landscape sweeping by slowly turned from the deep blue of Washington state to the snow white of the mountains, to the lush green of Oregon. Finally, as dawn broke over seemingly endless farmland, it changed again to a tired and arid yellow.

Alighting inland, I hired a ride to take me via San Francisco down the coast to Santa Cruz. The hire guy called me 'Mr . . . *what's that?*' He walked me to the car, showed me round the controls and I was off.

Later, as I approached San Francisco, I tuned the radio to a classic rock station (I simply had to) and was so overwhelmed when the playing of 'For What it's Worth' by Buffalo Springfield coincided with my crossing the Bay Bridge into the city, that I thumped the roof of the car in celebration as if Mandela had just been released. I knew that I was coming back in a week-or-so, so after browsing the streets, I set off down the coast en route to Santa Cruz.

If you've seen Joel Schumacher's *The Lost Boys* (1987) you will have seen a fictionalised version of Santa Cruz. In that film it was populated by crazies, hippies, loners, rockers, drifters, bikers, losers and vampires that looked like rejects from Twisted Sister. In the real city, there were signs in cars that said 'Keep Santa Cruz Weird', as if its weirdness was somehow under threat. That night, I ate at a lesbian vegan diner.

I had come to the city to teach at the interstellar academy of the Dickens Universe, and of course, to run the fir and redwood forests of California.

'The Universe' is an annual meeting of Dickens scholars and enthusiasts from all over the world. One of the conditions of our attendance was that we generously agreed to teach the Universe's subjects unpaid. One of the reciprocal perks was that the scholars didn't have to pay for alcohol at the late-night bar run by the 'Cruz directors'.

There would be a small handful of friends there, but it would mostly be hundreds of new faces.

My heart sank when I arrived and saw that I was scheduled to take the 8am class the next day.

The novel of the week was *Bleak House*. So there were lectures on *Bleak House*, seminars on *Bleak House*, screenings of *Bleak House*, readings of *Bleak House*, talks on *Bleak House*, presentations on *Bleak House*, book panels on *Bleak House*, workshops on the seminars on *Bleak House*, seminars on the lectures on *Bleak House*. At coffee, we discussed the seminars on *Bleak House*, at lunch we discussed the lecture on *Bleak House*, at drinks we talked about *Bleak House*, and that evening instead of the nightly screening of *Bleak House*, there was a play about *Bleak House*. Everywhere there were dog-eared copies of *Bleak House*, like a tornado had struck the Penguin Classics factory and rained them all down here. Some of the attendees wore *Bleak House* T-shirts.

At breakfast on our first morning (served at an eye-watering 7am), I met my friends Olivia and Jess. We took out our lists and compared pupils. They were older hands at this game and so we began collating names. Olivia and I laughed at Jess, who had one of the world's most eminent Victorian scholars as a pupil. Then Jess laughed at Olivia who had star of stage and screen Miriam Margolyes in her class.[14] She had recently been on a Friday-night chat show back in the UK where her wildcat wit was uncontainable by the show's usually edgy and flamboyant host. She was a force of nature. What chance did Olivia have, teaching structuralism, sexuality and psychoanalysis?

The names on my list looked reassuringly anonymous, so naturally I belly-laughed at both their misfortunes.

Coffees downed, breakfast trays stowed, and fleet-of-foot with chin stuck up, I walked into my class of unknowns to discover both stars had jumped ship to my group because of old alliances with fellow pupils.

There were 30 of us in all, and with one exception, I was the youngest in the room. They had all come to talk about *Bleak House*. I was co-teaching with a committed Freudian who thought the novel was all about sex (which it probably is), and he annoyed the group when he said that the character we think of as Charles Dickens didn't really exist as a person (he probably didn't). The pupils throughout the week reveal themselves to be an extraordinary bunch. They have PhDs. They are corporate lawyers, judges, doctors, actors and teachers, and they have deep pockets of knowledge. (One of them shamed me with her carefully laid-out explanation of the nuances of the British class system – she was American.) On the second day, when we were working from the book, I realised that Miriam Margoyles (who has read most of Dickens unabridged for audio books) could read a passage for us. As she did, I had a sort of out-of-body experience when I realised 'My God! I've got Babe doing Mr Guppy's proposal!' All through the week, I can't remember her interrupting a single person, and by the third day I was completely in love with her.

I hate nothing more than being presented with a timetable and the pushy expectation 'to attend', even if – absurdly – I have travelled thousands of miles to do just that; so feeling dehydrated, overly regimented, and in need of escape from the claustrophobia of the dirty fog of *Bleak House*, I decided to go hunting in search of some forest shade. I wanted freedom. I wanted to go to the place of outlaws' hideouts and get lost for a bit.

The meringue-white fog (as expected) lifted after breakfast, which made it inevitable that I would dodge the scheduled two-hour talk on theatrical adaptations of *Bleak House* – I just couldn't take any more of the claustrophobic fug, the bleak bleakness of *Bleak House*. Neither could I wait for Wednesday's scheduled 'free afternoon', overselling itself somewhat, squeezed as it was between 4 and 5pm. (That's not an 'afternoon' that's coffee and a decent loo-break.)

I unravel my trainers and head north, away from campus, away from the city of the holy cross, into the forest. Or at least I think I do. I keep following paths that lead momentarily into the wild only to find myself teleported to another part of campus: the engineering block, then the library (housing the university's Grateful Dead research archive). After a mile or so I lose the forest altogether, pass the sports block, and there is a wide green belt of meadows between the university and the city below – surrounded as it is by the Pacific. The university's eco-friendly gym has glass walls so that the treadmillers can bathe in the irony of this view while they stamp energy-guzzling two-kilowatt machines in a building that ruins the view for all but those in it.

Five and a half thousand miles from London by plane, and I have been followed here by that tree so familiar from London's streets: the plane! Why is it that the place where you live only comes sharply into focus when you are away? Aspects of London's character, its trees and its world-leading levels of pollution, seem more present to me here than they do at home. And why, with the Santa Cruz campus surrounded by beautiful wild forests, are there so many plane trees?

Developers and local authorities love them at home because they are tough, hardy and tolerate root compaction. The particular idiocy of their selection by developers is that the trees get by in polluted environments because of an ever-renewable bark (much easier, too, for planners to choose a single tree that tolerates pollution and ignore the fact that the capital is so polluted that only one tree can flourish in it).[15] The fallen scabs of bark are horrid to step on while running barefoot, as are the armoured fruit that falls from their branches. At certain times of year the skin of the tree resembles a crocodile's. And the pollen that I warred through on Peckham Rye is the final part of an arsenal that it uses as if to battle the entire city. On the wrong day of the year it is like running through turmeric. (I later discovered that the schoolboys of this world used to grind up the seed balls to be used as itching powder.)

Almost any British tree has a glut of poems dedicated to it. There are poems about pine trees, pear trees, apple trees, cherry trees, oaks, birches, beeches, even ones concerning rose trees are easy to find. But nobody ever lost their mind over a plane tree. While Amy Levy's 'A London Plane-Tree', written in the 1880s, before her suicide, expresses respect for the only tree that can cut it in the big smoke, even it is hardly a 'love' poem: 'Others the country take for choice,/And hold the town in scorn;/But she has listened to the voice/On city breezes borne.' And while she listened to the city's voice, she squirted her junk into the eyes of Londoners like it was tear gas.

Despite this, I feel for our forests and our use of them. There are woods near me, in Downe in Kent, where Charles Darwin lived most of his adult life. I was running there recently, marvelling at the silver birches that had seeded themselves so tightly they looked like what a lawn must look like to a beetle. As I went round a few times, zigzagging and path-crossing, I stopped now and again to explore uprooted trees, to see what their decay was giving back to the forest, or to listen in on the birdsong, or to climb to the canopy on the laddery branches of the Macedonian Pines. I passed about thirty or forty people in ones and twos. Every single one of them had dogs with them. There were no children. No one was in the forest for its own sake. And, as a runner, I suppose I wasn't either.

The idea that woodland should be used *for* something has a long, long history. The etymology of the word 'forest' is telling. Just as a weed is not a distinct 'thing' but a plant in the wrong place, the word 'forest' began as a functional term. The word comes from '*foris*', which means 'outside'. Legal writer John Manwood explains in his 1598 eye-drooper on forest law that they are territories, 'of wooddy grounds & fruitfull pastures, priuiledged for wild beasts and foules of Forrest, Chase and Warren, to rest and abide in, in the safe protection of the King, for his princely delight and pleasure.'[16] Forest law was a foreign import that arrived with the Normans, after which 'forest' land quickly spread.

The revelation is that 'forest' is actually a legal term, not a geographical one. It denotes a special area, outside the common law, for the preservation of the monarch's hunting rights. Forests may have taken on a more democratic identity, as places of reflection, play, refreshment and recreation, but they are still being *used* – most commonly, now, to escape the city and its *Bleak House*, fuggy atmosphere.

While I'm here in California, the air quality is reaching crisis point back home. Just before I left there were reports that, late at night, the streets were having to be hosed down. Only they weren't using water, but a kind of glue (calcium magnesium acetate). Pollution levels aren't so much being tackled, as dodged. The glue turns London's streets into black-carbon flypaper. Once the black carbon lands on it, it sticks to it so it can't redisperse. Some reports noticed that the areas where the acetate was used coincided with the placement of the EU's mandatory pollution sensors.

Black carbon is harmful stuff. Our lungs can cope much better with biomass fuels and wood smoke because we've evolved with them for hundreds of thousands of years, but tiny black carbon will penetrate any commuter mask on its way into your body. And once there, it is reluctant to leave. Run by the Hammersmith flyover on a bad day and you may as well do it smoking a fag, for all the health benefits you garner.

Why would any sane person want to have an immersive environmental experience in such a place?

A recent report from King's College London pegged Oxford Street as the most polluted thoroughfare on the entire planet (with levels of nitrogen dioxide that are higher than even massive polluters like Mexico City or Linfen). That said, research published in the *British Medical Journal* suggests that it is still 77 times better for someone to cycle than not.[17] Even running by a polluted highway will expose you to five times less air pollution than car drivers on that same road (and this is a conservative estimate). Car drivers are at risk not only because of their proximity to the exhaust of the vehicle in front of them, but once black carbon enters the vehicle cabin, it has nowhere to disperse. Exercise and mobility still win.

The city of Santa Cruz, though, is not large. Its proximity to the ocean on one side and the forest on the other helps to keep its pollution levels far below that of most cities.

The university's rise coincided with the countercultural revolution of the 1960s, which to an extent explains the design of the campus, which is not so much built on its surroundings as interleaved with it. Where we would find neat, lawned quads, Santa Cruz's buildings are separated by fir bridges which cross deep ravines out of which 200-foot redwoods climb for a flash of the sun. I have already seen five black-tailed deer wandering between the peripheries of campus and coppice.

I reach one of the meadows and decide to work my way round it to see if I can make it to the forest. As I start to climb back up the fields, away from the city, there is a sign hung on some blackened barbed wire that warns me about mountain lions – despite having spoken to one of the college staff about this, who with a dismissive wave of the hand told me not to worry because no one ever sees one, I am concerned to see that the sign says the last sighting was yesterday. I'm all for the wild when there are flowers to sniff, but I really would prefer not to be eaten.

The corollary of London's drenching in the jet stream is that there has been no rain here for months. I watched from the train the northern part of the continent turn from green to yellow, thinking this was normal as we approached the equator – but California is experiencing a Saharan drought. The grass is so dry it scrunches like newspaper beneath my feet and I worry that a flicked fag butt could burn up the whole county.

In this no-man's-land between town and gown I have to switch between concrete and grassland. And everything is so dry. Butterflies on the breeze look like blown shreds of torn paper. Up across the meadow I can see the beginning of the fir-green of the redwood forests. The sun, and therefore the ground, is so hot that I have to put my shoes back on if I want to save my feet for a run tomorrow.

Despite the trees being different, almost all forests smell the same. Processes of growth and decomposition are often identical, and the chemicals released by such processes can be similar, too.

Between the wars in Soviet Russia, a biochemist called Boris Tokin began to look into the activity of plants' immune systems. He found that some plants and trees give off volatile organic compounds (phytoncides) that protect them against attacking organisms such as bacteria or fungi. There are thousands of different phytoncides. More recently, research in Japan has begun to snowball around this idea, and it is producing some eye-goggling results. Tree hugging is for the hippies; it's all about tree-sniffing, now.

In Japan it is called *Shinrin-yoku*, or 'forest bathing'. There have been a number of studies which aim accurately to measure the various health benefits to be derived from spending a little time breathing the air of the forest. The neuropsychological effects bring about real changes in our nervous and immune systems. My decision to bunk off and go for a quiet run in the forest could promote long-lasting immunological responses such as increases in white blood-cells and natural killer cells (the latter play a special role in the rejection of tumours and virally infected cells). In one of the trials, this immune-boost was measured at significant levels up to a month later.[18]

A review paper in 2010 was able to conclude that 'forest environments promote lower concentrations of cortisol, lower pulse rate, lower blood pressure, greater parasympathetic nerve activity, and lower sympathetic nerve activity than do city environments'.[19] A follow-up trial confirmed that forest time 'significantly reduced blood pressure and urinary noradrenaline [which causes raised heart-rate] and dopamine levels [a mood regulator which is elevated by things like cocaine and amphetamines]'.[20] And a more recent study showed that forest time 'improved nocturnal sleep conditions for individuals with sleep complaints'.[21] Is it any wonder that so many bedtime stories seem to take place in a forest?

The redwoods grow so well here because it is just far enough from the coast for there to be little salt in the air, while the morning fog provides moisture and temporary respite from the burning sun. Their red pelty bark comes from the high tannic-acid content, which also provides some resistance to forest fires. If the tree dies, the forest creates a marvellous spectacle: a cathedral tree. Nine or so new trees grow around the nutrient-rich remains of the dead tree in a kind of horseshoe shape so regular and ornate as to look intentional. There is even a gap in the canopy created by the dead tree for the new trees to grow into, so each grows perfectly vertical, hundreds of feet straight up like giant prison bars.

The forest feels strong, deep and still – its size, fabulous. When I was a child, even though we were not a bookish household, I remember marvelling with wonder at the pictures of redwoods in an old encyclopaedia we had. One had its trunk carved out so a car could drive through it, and I loved this Lilliputian inversion of what should have been big and what should have been small.

There are tonsures of clearings in the forest, with gravel paths that wind through the scorched grass, which is already the colour of wood shavings. My heart pulses like sonar, while I wait for something to come back from the depths of the forest. Although I can feel the increase in elevation in my legs and lungs, the thickness of the trees is so disorientating that I have no idea how high I've climbed so far.

There's a lovely bit in Roger Deakin's *Wildwood* where he says that negotiating a forest is a little like walking a riverbed and looking up and through the life in the water. I like the image because it puts us *in* rather than *on* the landscape. It connects us to it in ways that can create a desire to accept it and see it for what it is. I am convinced that the woods create in us a kind of empathy with the landscape, which cannot exist elsewhere. This is part of what Deakin's book is about, of course – but there are other aspects to it, too.

The term empathy originated from the German *einfühlen* (literally 'to feel in'). It did not begin its life referring to other people, but to things. The writer, philosopher and author of early German Romanticism, Novalis, said that an understanding of nature comes out of those who are able to mix their thoughts and reflections with all things, creating through their sensations and emotions an intimate and multifaceted sense of the world by feeling themselves into it.[22] This ability is the means by which we connect ourselves to the world, and there is no form, *animal, vegetable, mineral,* so steely, fibrous or wild that our emotions cannot find a way to penetrate it, feeling some of it for what it is. Empathy is not a projection, but a reaching into something else, a burrowing down into it.

Towards the end of Tolstoy's *Anna Karenina,* our hero, Levin, is beginning to learn how he might lead a good life. He lies down to regard the sky and asks himself,

> Don't I know that that is infinite space, and not a rounded vault? But, however I may screw my eyes and strain my sight, I cannot help seeing it round and limited, and despite my knowledge of it as limitless space I am indubitably right when I see a firm blue vault, and more right than when I strain to see beyond it.[23]

Levin is learning to live and see within the limits of his body. He does not follow the fate of his brother Nikolai (the radical thinker, who dies bitter and frustrated). Levin's journey is a process of learning that 'the good life' is an embodied one.

In a redwood forest, there is no getting away from the fact that we do see things in relation to our bodies. The tree trunks are great, muscular legs – their bark is our skin. Their intelligence, even in the close proximity of the cathedral trees, enables them to grow many hundreds of branches, not one of which collides with another. Their height is great, relative to our own (and particularly mine). The fact that hard frosts never seem to gather round the roots of the trees suggests they even have a kind of body temperature. We cannot help but use our bodies and their ephemerality to make sense of our relationship with the world.

Numerous studies have demonstrated that empathy for the environment increases drastically when we actually spend time in natural places, rather than merely thinking or reading about them.[24] The potent presence of the environment impresses itself upon us and forges an empathetic response that is difficult to shake off.[25] Running regularly in natural surroundings may make you green with empathy.

I have long felt that being in certain environments has an empathetic impact on me. For one, they have nurtured an interest in the different characters of trees (from mature beeches whose mossy branches in winter look like the head of the Medusa, to the tightly packed shaving-brush bristles of hornbeams). On so many occasions I've returned from runs desperate to know more, whether it be about the vagaries of nuclear power or the parameters of avian intelligence.

Running on Blackheath, under the constant surveillance of a murder of crows, I wanted to find out about the intelligence behind their eyes. My curiosity, piqued, was rewarded.

In 2008 the first reports appeared about an ongoing study that was being conducted at the Washington School of Forest Resources, in which crows were trapped, banded and released by mask-wearing staff. They discovered two surprising things. First, that after five years and counting, banded crows still remembered the masks and would hound and dive at the staff wearing them. Second, that crows who were not involved in the experiment in any way also joined in the angry mob that jeered the mask-wearing staff, even when they were over a mile away from the original incident. Scientist John Marzluff went so far as to suggest that some of the crows were able to 'make and use tools, forecast future events, understand what other animals know, and – in our [experiment] – learn from individual experience as well as by observing parents and peers'. The birds were capable of 'advanced cognitive tasks shown by only a few animals'.[26] And this only scratches the surface of their abilities: they show evidence of intergenerational memory, and can even outperform 8–10-year-olds in some problem-solving tasks.

It seems logical that a curiosity for something should lead to a knowledge of it, and an empathy for it. But this would be an odd way to motivate the sedentary, or indoor-exercisers, into outside spaces.

Despite our knowledge of the beneficial impacts of being out in the environment, research suggests that the non-runner's default response to the notion of 'going for a run' is that it seems to represent a great deal of effort for worse than no reward. Research, though, is already demonstrating that when we run outside, it is not just about us looking at the environment. The natural world also sends something back to us, through our eyes or the soles of our feet: the effects can be greater feelings of happiness, stress relief, even enhanced levels of creativity.

Happiness is in fact one of the key determinable outcomes of a subjective connection with nature, but despite this runners and non-runners alike are inexpert at forecasting affect.[27] We are not very good at knowing how things might make us feel. I have, countless times, not wanted to go out running in the rain, but I have never had my personal forecast of a grim, damp, cold and wet run confirmed by my experience of it. If I am honest, I think the rain may even heighten my enjoyment of running. This experience has been confirmed for me hundreds of times. Perhaps it is something to do with the dynamics of anticipated misery offset against that congenial hearth of the body's warmth (once it gets going), and the empty streets and parks. But still, every time it rains, I have to prise myself, sulking like an adolescent, out the door.

A recent study tested the comparative hedonic effect of walks outside and in, and although the outside 'natural' walks produced a greater happiness quotient in the subjects, those subjects also demonstrated that same inability to forecast that happiness. The investigators concluded that their subjects failed to maximise the benefits provided by exercising in natural environments, and therefore closed with the suggestion that not only were the subjects missing out on the beneficial effects of their surroundings, but that as a result the natural world too would fail to benefit, as the opportunity to create empathy was lost.[28] I don't think it is possible to overstate the fact that without environmental empathy, we are doomed.[29]

These studies suggest anything but a unidirectional transaction. The benefits that move back and forth resemble more of a feedback loop between us and the environment.

Neither do the empathetic benefits to be derived from time spent in nature end there. A recent review enquired as to whether nature could make us more caring. The review, which considered four studies, concluded that 'participants immersed in natural environments reported higher valuing of intrinsic aspirations and lower valuing of extrinsic aspirations, whereas those immersed in non-natural environments reported increased valuing of extrinsic aspirations and no change of intrinsic aspirations'. (Is this a nice way of suggesting that gym-goers are less happy and more worried about what people might think of them?)[30]

Intrinsic aspirations (such as the desire for growth, happiness or connectedness) are repeatedly linked with improved mental wellbeing. Extrinsic aspirations (fame, money, respect) rely on external confirmation – Western culture errs on the side of the extrinsic, encouraging us to care about our hair, skin, weight, car, promotion, or how many Twitter followers we have.

I am as extrinsically motivated as anyone. I care about all of these things. Running, though, can be a respite from them.

I was at an event recently where they screened a documentary about running made by Matan Rochlitz and Ivo Gormley.[31] The filmmakers cycled alongside runners while filming and interviewing them. It was as if the fact that they were running made the subjects open up and confess to some unbelievably frank truths about their lives. One of the runners was in his sixties, with long white hair streaming behind him as he jogged in the sunshine. He was rocketing along. I don't think I've ever seen anyone of his age going close to such a pace. But he expressed disappointment with his times and didn't seem to like the fact that he could no longer get so much out of running as a result.[32] Asked how it felt to be getting slower, with a short laugh he replied, 'Terrible.' I wanted to shout at the screen to tell him how fantastic he was. What he was doing was beautiful, and that was something that the filmmakers could obviously see, too. Extrinsic motivation in runners can chase away the very enjoyment and fulfilment that running is supposed to provide.

Lounging around in the arena of the ethereal, the barefoot and the tree-hugging for a little longer, there is also the Earthing movement.

Earthers believe that we are disconnected from the world. We live earthlessly – our daily life spent in glass-and-concrete buildings, sitting in chairs, sleeping off the floor, hanging around TVs and computers, barking into mobile phones, travelling on trains, and walking in shoes. All of these activities create electrical static in our bodies that, because of city design, we are unable to find an outlet for. They believe that we literally need to earth our bodies for electrical realignment with the gently negative charge of the planet. The Earthers believe that the positive charge we receive from modern life makes us more vulnerable to illness, stress and depression, symptoms that we might associate with modern life. Our body's electrophysiology, which has been a constant for millennia, may be at root the cause of our malaises, they believe. We need to be exchanging our electrons with the earth more often. It all seems a bit 'California' to me, which, as it turns out, it is.[33]

Neither does it help that it is quite heavily merchandised: available for purchase are Earthing books, Earthing sheets, Earthing mattresses, Earthing shoes and Earthing mousemats. The movement's website's banner has the sort of golden sunsets that you might see adorning the covers of motivational works of devotion stacked among the crêpe paper in the windows of Christian bookshops. My little moan over, there is evidence that earthing our bodies – by being outside barefoot or sleeping on earthed bedsheets – does have an impact on our wellbeing. It is early days for the studies, and they lack the mature robustness of, say, the experiments around environmental psychology, but that doesn't make them meaningless.[34] In time, the Earthers may find that their work dovetails with existing research quite nicely.

The connection between our bodies and the natural world is anything but passive. Being in it makes us more empathetic to what is happening around us. It has beneficial effects for us that are as yet incalculable. And the effects recur cyclically. The fact that a green place may give us something means that we in turn are also able to give something back to it. It ensures a more thoughtful engagement with it. Kinetic empathy: feeling the world *at* your feet is likely to encourage you to feel *for* the world at your feet, maybe even going so far as to feel it feeling you. The empathy that this kind of experience creates seems to me one of the most potent weapons that we have against things like deforestation and green-belt development.

As if I needed any more evidence that natural places have an impact on us, on my way back from Santa Cruz I stopped over for a couple of days in San Francisco. For years I had wanted to go there. I imagined running up and down the streets, being overtaken by trams and tourists, heading to the coastline to see Alcatraz and the Golden Gate. But I made two terrible mistakes. Another lecturer was in town, but only for the day. Having bought a site-seeing ticket that lasted for 72 hours, he gave it to me, so that I could use the remaining time. Accepting his ticket was my first mistake, because doing so all but wrecked my time in the city, as I had to rush to see everything within the allotted period: I spent most of my stay hopping on and off buses, seeing everything from the outside, just driving by. I even have blurred and illegible photos, snapped as we sped by significant places of which I have no memory.

The second mistake was that I went out on my first evening without a map. The sun was setting; it was a beautiful evening. On my walk, a couple of people berated me as they wheeled their tottering towers of trash, their life's belongings so precarious that they would lose everything if they hit a kerb. Someone else ran up to me and shouted something into my face while looking straight through me. A little later, feeling a bit more cautious, I was walking a sidewalk with cars parked to one side. There weren't many people around, just one guy about ten yards in front of me. Then he stopped walking, and with that familiar hip shuffle that accompanies a pair of trousers coming down, he hunkered into a squat. Ignoring the shelter of the parked cars three feet away, he strained and defecated in the middle of the sidewalk. Taking time to finish the job, he gouged some tissues from a jacket pocket, wiped, and dropped them on the concrete, too. I suppose, when you gotta go . . . He had committed what the San Francisco Police might call a '22500ak' – an 'illegal parking'.

I cannot remember what happened next, whether he got up and walked away, or stayed crouched as I walked by. Fortunately it's a blank. Places make us behave in certain ways, and from that moment on I wanted to leave. I never ran in San Francisco. Imagine being a runner and not running in San Francisco? Imagine writing a book about running, and not running in San Francisco?

It is not only those few plants that respond to the electrophysiology of touch that know we are here. Some respond differently to the colours we wear when we stand near them (blue affects a process called phototropism – growing towards the light; red may change what time of year the plant thinks it is – a sensitivity called photoperiodism). And when trees and plants release scents, tannins, gases and hormones, they are, at the simplest level, responding to their environment, and as we move through it, that means they are responding to us, too.

Forests clearly have more to offer us than we can understand or explain. Sure, some of the benefits are measurable, but there will be other benefits that do not fit so easily into the parameters of a randomised trial, or do not receive such willing research-funding from universities or corporations. However much they have to offer us, we pose the greatest threat to these places. The forest was, is, and will remain a magical place, and we need it more than we know.

6.
WILDE TIMES ON TREADMILLS: RUNNING INSIDE AND OUT

GREENWICH, LONDON; SEASALTER, KENT; AND NORTH CORNWALL

'Are there no prisons?' asked Scrooge.

'Plenty of prisons,' said the gentleman, laying down the pen again.

'And the Union workhouses?' demanded Scrooge. 'Are they still in operation?'

'They are. Still,' returned the gentleman, 'I wish I could say they were not.'

'The Treadmill and the Poor Law are in full vigour, then?' said Scrooge.

– Charles Dickens, *A Christmas Carol*, 1843

Esther's term of imprisonment was ended. She received a good character in the governor's books; she had picked her daily quantity of oakum, had never deserved the extra punishment of the treadmill, and had been civil and decorous in her language.

– Elizabeth Gaskell, *Mary Barton*, 1848

GREENWICH

Back in London, and it is my third run in the rain this week. When I set out this morning I was dressed for an Indian summer, but met an English one. The clouds were high and motionless, and I never saw them coursing behind me until I was on the heath. As I crossed the upland into Greenwich Park, clouds mustered and with a friendly chuckle a shower began. Then, a cloudburst and within seconds shards of rain were falling so hard that they stung like bees through my T-shirt. The beeches, chestnuts, sycamores, elms, alders, hornbeams and planes would usually provide ample shelter; some of the numerous pollarded oaks in the park are so aged that they date back to the Tudors. The canopies of others reach up to 60 feet and today they bowed so much I could not even duck under them for shelter. Pendulous with the water's weight, my T-shirt drooped to my knees; then there was the lightning.

As the rain poured and I marvelled at the detonating pins of water exploding as they hit the tarmac, thoughts and conversations sprung into my consciousness, fulgurant as the blue-white flashes in the sky. *Why put up with this? – you do not have to run in such dangerous surroundings – a spell inside might be just what you need – surely it is weather like this that modern conveniences like the treadmill are made for – what is it that can repeatedly drive someone out the door and into such Old Testament scenes?* But I knew that I loved this. Not the cold, the wet, the blisters that I would probably get, but *something*; it was as if the electric charge of the lightning was resonating through the loam and into my veins. Today, I knew, would be seared in my memory for life.

Running has a way of shunting together ideas for you that at first glance do not seem connected. As the rain fell, I had a glancing thought about running indoors, and from there I gibbon-swung straight to a bit of Rosa Luxemburg, writing from her prison cell to a friend: 'My home is in the entire world, where there are clouds and birds and human tears.'[1] Was it just coincidence that the particular bit that had risen up to my consciousness was a piece of prison writing? It was so much more invigorating being here than in the manufactured space of a gym.

I was recently contacted by some anthropology doctoral students who were studying territoriality and etiquette in these most private of public spaces. My relationship with gyms is ambivalent at best. They always seem like a nicer idea when I am not in them. For years I have joined, left and joined them again. In the past I have used them because I am always in an embattled state with my weight, or because I had some injury, or because it was raining, or because I liked playing on the machines.[2] But I could never keep attending beyond a few months, because for me they always became synonymous with that modern epidemic: boredom.[3] Going 'inside' made me feel bored and trapped. Where do these feelings come from, and how could it make sense that I was happier drenched and dodging bolts of lightning? It is not just about plunging into the outdoor experience, with the resulting enhanced levels of arousal in the hippocampus and the cortex; there was something 'not right' about the gym.

Real places are capable of creating an empathy within us that, whether through the media or education, is hard-won elsewhere. The fact that so many of us go to gyms might tell us how easily we are becoming disconnected from our surroundings. And while they play an important role in remedying the global pandemic of inactivity, they are far from the answer. There is an old Seinfeld joke, along the lines of: 'What is it with all the security around health clubs: the photo IDs, the signing in? People with memberships only go twice a year. Who's breakin' in?' The gym is great for people who go, but the vast majority of us with membership don't.

I remember a crisp March day, a few months before the storm run, which was very sunny and filled with the tensile promise of a summer about to arrive. I had set out on an eight-miler. This is probably my favourite distance: short enough to not have to carry water, long enough for the normal beta-wave activity of your brain (16–25Hz) to slow to something more resembling the alpha waves that precede sleep (8–12Hz).[4] For weeks previously, I had been pacing the cell of a minor injury, stretching and strengthening, taking it slow. But it was too spruce a day to stay in. So I did a nice run around a haunting and decrepit council estate in Kidbrooke, where I watched in wonder as claw-diggers gnawed at the buildings like giant stop-motion tyrannosaurs. As the blocks were ripped open, they revealed the insides of the deserted flats, still curtained and carpeted, like doll's houses gone wrong. The buildings together looked like a jaw of rotten and broken teeth. I called in at the gym on my way home. It was not a nice one. So unpleasant, in fact, that they knocked it down a few weeks later and built a block of flats atop its corpse. But I always admired its honesty and simplicity. There were never any alpha males pumping iron, just us omegas. It didn't even have a sound system, only a battered little ghetto blaster that sat on the floor in the corner of the room. It couldn't play CDs because the lid to the drive had been broken off, so its radio was always turned up to 10 on the volume dial. That corner of the gym was always unoccupied.

On that day, all five treadmills were in use, but no one else was in the room. The treadmillers were in a neat line, facing floor-to-ceiling windows that looked out onto the busy high street. I thought perhaps these people were like me, nursing some injury or training for something; or here to enhance some activity that took place elsewhere.

I sat down and strapped myself into a rowing machine. I was flanked by my fellow inmates, all walking their mills. The radio was frequently interrupted by aggressive signal loss that sounded like an old smoker trying to clear their throat. I played, imagining I was pulling all the treadmill belts as I rowed. None of us broke pace. None of us spoke, and none of them jogged, either – they kept steadily to their strolling pace. It was odd that they had come to such a grubby place to pay to walk nowhere. Then, one by one, they left. And when I left, too, all that remained was the disembodied echo of the radio, motivating an empty room.

The contrast of experience was so memorable to me. Even an average terra-run (the kind with your real feet on real ground) can be food for all senses, creating fresh new brain cells. It seemed strange to me that when I went to the gym it was as though my senses were numbed in some way. There was something about treadmills that always ended in my feeling uneasy. It was not that terra-runs were always good and 'treadmilling' bad, but I had noticed that one tended to dispel gloom while the other only suspended it – one invigorated while the other conciliated. It also seemed like they were both part of something much larger, to do with our relationship with the environment, consumption, our bodies and psychologies. I wanted to know why a feeling of freedom that I thought was physiological and hormonal did not transfer inside. I wanted to know where these thoughts and feelings came from . . . History, I suspected.

Philosophies and technologies of all kinds, for imprisoning, punishing and exercising the body, exploded around the time of the Enlightenment and the Industrial Revolution.

I started plaiting some historical strands together, a kind of dialectical family tree, because I wanted to see exactly what made up the genetic DNA of the treadmill. I was amazed with what I found.

From what kind of soil did the treadmill grow?

Around the eighteenth century, with the European Enlightenment in full sway, there was a proliferation of all kinds of philosophical and technological investigation. There was a huge rise in mechanisation, and growth in the sciences, and this shone new light on theories of education, government and law, bringing about all manner of change.

If philosophy is the hare, then real reform is the tortoise. Some of Thomas Paine's recommendations from the eighteenth century – poor relief, pensions, free education for the poor, and child benefit, which did not see sunlight until the 1942 Beveridge Report – influenced the plans for the emergence of the welfare state after the Second World War. One contemporary of Paine's was Cesare Beccaria, who worked in the field of prison reform.

Born in 1738, Beccaria was part of the Milanese aristocracy. He studied law, and showed an early interest in mathematics and economics, but fell under the sway of French Enlightenment thinkers like Montesquieu and Voltaire. With his friends he formed his own literary talking shop, the 'Academy of Fists' and out of that came a philosophical and literary magazine, the *Coffeehouse*. In this atmosphere, Beccaria produced the first tract in a completely new field of enquiry: penology.

On Crimes and Punishments (1764) is an empirical and sociological analysis of the death penalty.[5] In it, Beccaria argues for a new kind of legal system: one where punishment should be seen as a deterrent, and not retribution. He asks what use is a death penalty for theft when such a punishment predetermines that a thief may commit many more serious crimes to escape capture? Rather than protecting them, severe punishments like torture or hanging put citizens' lives in greater danger. He suggests that because society's punishment can progress no further than the life of the criminal, it would make reasonable sense to have a more measured legal system, one supple enough to deal with the nuances of crime. He argues that most important of all is that the criminal believes they will be caught. Society's punishment of crime should be effective, open, public, visibly fair and swift.

In England, shortly afterwards, John Howard (influenced by Beccaria) was instrumental in bringing about many changes to British crime and punishment. In 1777 he produced his first edition of *The State of the Prisons in England and Wales*. The book is replete with numerous statistics of the transported and the condemned. It details, too, the levels of fees for imprisonment and exposes the idiocy of a system that requires its prisoners to pay for their imprisonment, yet imprisons them for non-payment. The book concluded with a call for a parliamentary enquiry into prison reform; which in time led to new laws being passed.

It was still too early in history for the treadmill, but its reasons for coming into being were slowly beginning to emerge.

In 1779 the Penitentiary Act was co-drafted by Howard and the famous jurist William Blackstone.[6] The act sought to nationalise prisons by creating a network of state-run facilities. The prisons were meant to function as a real alternative to the other two options of the death penalty or American transportation (the latter was no longer an easy option after the Declaration of Independence in 1776). Prisoners could be put to 'hard labour' instead of languishing in restful confinement. The 1778 Hard Labour Bill had provided the philosophical structure for the Penitentiary Act in recommending the construction, all over the country, of Houses of Hard Labour. Chapter XXXII stated that in these houses prisoners should undergo toil of 'the hardest and most servile kind, in which drudgery is chiefly required, and where the work is little liable to be spoiled by ignorance, neglect, or obstinacy'.[7] They were to be fed 'inferior food, and Water, or Small Beer'.[8] Their clothes should be designed 'to humiliate the Wearers' and 'to facilitate Discovery in case of Escapes'.[9]

Humiliation is quite a different form of punishment from hanging, thumb-screwing or flogging. It is mental, not corporeal. For philosopher and historian Michel Foucault in *Discipline and Punish*, this period represents one of the major turns in modernity, where punishment no longer addressed itself to the body of the criminal, but to the soul.[10] The criminal was more likely to be permitted to live, but would be moulded into a more passive and conforming individual. Foucault argues that the 'enlightened' penal reforms that ran throughout the nineteenth century were not driven by ethical or humanitarian concerns, but an ever-deepening expansion of state and institutional dominion over the individual's interior life.

Throughout the Victorian period, the accentuation of the servile and useless aspect of the prisoners' labour became more focussed. In 1817, Sir William Cubitt, a civil engineer from Norfolk, proposed a solution to the Penitentiary Act's requirements. One of the principal difficulties was that prison labour at the time could not be seen to be taking work from the innocent and the free. 'Hard Labour' had to be found, but of a kind that no free person would willingly subject themselves to. William Cubitt's invention was called the treadwheel, some called it the 'Discipline Mill', but soon after it came to be known as it is today: the treadmill.[11]

In the effervescence of invention during this period, the *Monthly Magazine* announced in 1797 a new patent for Francis Lowndes's Gymnasticon, the earliest of static exercise machines.[12] The magazine explained that it may be of use,

> when peculiar or sedentary occupations enforce confinement to the house, it promises to be equally useful to the healthy as to the sick . . . The merchant, without withdrawing his attention from his accounts, and the student, while occupied in writing or reading, may have his lower limbs kept in constant motion by the slightest exertion, or, the assistance of a child.[13]

The handle on the lower spindle was so that, if desired, a child might be employed to turn the wheel so that the user benefitted from the movement without having the distraction of the exertion.

Though it would not look completely out of place in the many thousands of gyms throughout the world today, the Gymnasticon was a commercial disaster. Unsurprisingly, it disappeared from history until the invention of electricity could bring it back as the cross-trainer. But surely its existence went some way to contributing to the technological refinements that the treadwheel would undergo in the nineteenth century.

Something was clearly in the air. Anxieties over movement and the body abound in the period. That early Romantic writer and philosopher Jean-Jacques Rousseau worried for the state of the bodies of civilised men in his *Discourse on Inequality* (1753):

> Since the savage man's body is the only instrument he knows, he employs it for a variety of purposes that, for lack of practice, ours are incapable of serving. And our industry deprives us of the force and agility that necessity obliges him to acquire . . .

The Gymnasticon, from the 1798 Patent.

Give a civilized man time to gather all his machines around him, and undoubtedly he will easily overcome a savage man. But if you want to see an even more unequal fight, pit them against each other naked and disarmed, and you will soon realize the advantage of constantly having all of one's forces at one's disposal, of always being ready for any event, and of always carrying one's entire self, as it were, with one.[14]

Throughout the nineteenth century, prisoners of Her Majesty (for they had moved out of the private sector) who had committed the most serious of crimes were put to 'Hard Labour'. There were comparatively few crimes that warranted the death penalty (in the earlier part of the century the national murder-rate rarely reached beyond double figures – about the same number as for the London borough in which I now live); numerous Hard Labourers were put to work on the treadwheel. Cubitt's early design resembled a large cylinder that ten to twenty men could climb on together to operate like a widened water wheel in cooperation with on another. In Foucauldian terms, the treadwheel punished the body by the hard nature of the endless and, importantly, useless climb.

The treadmill made frequent appearances in the literature of the nineteenth century. It features in Dickens's work; in his letters, his essays, his short fiction, and many of his novels (*The Pickwick Papers*, *Oliver Twist*, *The Old Curiosity Shop*, *A Christmas Carol*, *Dombey and Son*, *Bleak House*, *Little Dorrit*). In Anthony Trollope's *The Eustace Diamonds*, Mrs Carbuncle explains to our heroine, 'it is my belief that they can keep you upon the treadmill and bread and water for months and months, if not for years'.[15] But, as the century progressed, the treadwheel was fine-tuned and weaponised to encompass more directed forms of psychological punishment beyond that of the prisoners' humiliating clothes. Several refinements were made; what had begun the century as a gruelling physical experience became one that tortured the prisoner, body and soul, leaving many destroyed by their feat of endurance.

In 1885, when the Criminal Law Amendment Act was passed by Parliament, the main goal was to raise the age of consent for girls from 13 to 16 to clamp down on London's epidemic of child prostitution. It also outlawed sexual acts of unspecified 'gross indecency' between men. Its most famous victim was Oscar Wilde.

He underwent three trials in 1895: the first brought by Wilde himself – a libel action against the Marquess of Queensberry, his lover's father; the second a criminal trial that ended in a hung jury; the third another trial, this time resulting in a conviction. In sentencing, Justice Wills remarked: 'I shall, under the circumstances, be expected to pass the severest sentence that the law allows. In my judgement it is totally inadequate for a case such as this. The sentence of the Court is that . . . you be imprisoned and kept to hard labour for two years.'[16]

In his essay 'The Soul of Man Under Socialism', written four years earlier, Wilde could not have been more tragically wrong in his assessment of the imprisoned life, where he believed, 'a man can be quite free. His soul can be free. His personality can be untroubled. He can be at peace.'[17]

Wilde was sent first to Pentonville Prison, then to Wandsworth, and finally Reading. His health declined swiftly when put to hard labour. In his first year he collapsed and spent two months in the infirmary. In his biography, Richard Ellmann explains that Wilde was unfortunate in that his spell inside just preceded a wave of penal reforms at the end of the century. He worked the treadmill for as much as six hours a day.[18] Documented by the prison's chaplain, the account of Wilde's punishment makes for harrowing reading:

> When he first came down here . . . he was in an excited flurried condition, and seemed as if he wished to face his punishment without flinching. But all this has passed away. As soon as the excitement aroused by the trial subsided . . . his fortitude began to give way and rapidly collapsed altogether. He is now quite crushed and broken . . . and I fear from what I hear and see that perverse sexual practices are again getting the mastery over him . . . The odour of his cell is now so bad that the officer in charge of him has to use carbolic acid in it every day . . . I need hardly tell you that he is a man of decidedly morbid disposition . . . In fact some of our most experienced officers openly say that they don't think he will be able to go through the two years.[19]

The chaplain and officers were not far wrong: Wilde's time on the treadmill all but destroyed him. If the chaplain is to be believed, it led first to depression, then to addictive masturbation, and finally to life-threatening exhaustion. He was later transferred to Reading Gaol, and there conditions for him improved. He was given access to pen and paper and the regimen was not so severe. During this time, he drafted *The Ballad of Reading Gaol* (published under the anonymous cell-door number 'C.3.3.').

> We sewed the sacks, we broke the stones,
>> We turned the dusty drill:
> We banged the tins, and bawled the hymns,
>> And sweated on the mill:
> But in the heart of every man
>> Terror was lying still.[20]

Wilde did make it through his two years, but only just. He never fully recovered and died in exile and infamy only a couple of years after his release at the age of 46.

How could it be possible to feel good about the treadmill?

It was, after all, once the principal tool of punishment in Her Majesty's prisons; now we pay for the privilege of running on them.

I can see that they have their uses. Many people, especially women, feel safer in a controlled, indoor environment. Others like the consistency of experience that they offer. Without environmental variation, the runner can just get on with their exercise; no plans, or clothing or footwear decisions, are necessary, because it's the same every time. It never rains on a treadmill.

Some like to be entertained on their runs. And this doesn't just apply to treadmills; one of the most attractive aspects of a running club is its social dimension.

My friend, Scarlett, the enthusiastic exerciser, was once fond of treadmills. She said, and she's not alone in this, that they gave her control when she was recovering from an injury. At the time (and I suspect she's not alone in this, either) she enjoyed the playful merging of biology and technology: 'I felt a bit SF on them, which was kind of cool; like a cyborg.' She's right: step on, play some Daniel Avery, and you will see what she means. But that was years ago and now even she runs regularly outdoors.

At my gym, the treadmills have a programme that will allow you to choose an environment, like a New Zealand coastline, and this will play on the TV screen as you pound away in front of it. The screens are really quite large, with a bewildering number of options, none of which is 'off'.

In most of the other gyms that I have been to, machines are aimed – like a crossbow to a bullseye – at a TV. Many have lines of screens tuned to different channels, and there are cables, pastel walls, double-glazing, giant bouncy balls, mirrors, adverts, techno, Lycra, tired yoga mats, and loads of noise. Gym users seem oddly infantilised as they suck on the teats of their water bottles. It's all so easy to dismiss.

Yet P.G. Wodehouse was right in his first Blandings novel, *Something New* (1915), where he explained that anyone who wished to exercise outdoors in London had a choice: either give up, 'or else defy London's unwritten law and brave London's mockery'.[21] But most of us are not as brave as Wodehouse's hero, Ashe Marson, so we retreat to a gym, because you can't do battle rope in a hail storm; I've tried and it's absolutely awful.

Yet I am happy running in a storm, and staying off the treadmill. Despite what Scarlett said, I still didn't understand its popularity at all. So I went to meet someone whom I thought might. Dr Russell Hitchings, an expert in human geography at University College London.

When I get there, a short walk from Euston Station, the building looks like it was designed by the architect of Senate House down the road (the building which Hitler had earmarked as Nazi headquarters after the invasion). As I push through heavy glass doors, the security guard at reception looks suspicious of me at first, but his face is botoxed of any emotion by boredom. He directs me. All university buildings are alike. They have their own logic, which is never mastered in a single visit, and there is always something a little alimentary about working your way to someone's office in them. We have a building at the University of Kent designed by a prizewinning prison architect, and still, after working there for eight years, I get lost navigating to class.

Finally, I arrive at Russell's room. Unlike most faculty offices, his looks out onto a busy London street, which seems perfect given what he works on. He is interested in the changing aspects of everyday life and how they affect the populace. He has been involved in all sorts of projects from winter mortality rates among OAPs to dirt management at music festivals. And I am here to talk to him about another of his interests: the difference between indoor and outdoor running.

He and his colleague, Dr Alan Latham, wanted to find out what worked for recreational runners, so that public-health policy could encourage adherence to exercise regimes, and the best outcome for those exercising.[22] Their idea is that government may be better placed to promote such activity if it knows exactly what the qualities of that activity are. Russell tells me that he and his colleagues are interested in running because 'It's good for us, in lots of ways. Though quite a few people are getting into it, there is always scope for more to join them, in view of the associated health benefits. And it's the easiest sport to do in the context of having difficult schedules to coordinate.'

And while we chat about gyms, I explain that my own experience of them is common to many people, in that I've never been able to keep going to them beyond a couple of months.

'But if you kept going to the gym, you'd probably become someone that goes to a gym. It's about developing a habit.' If you want to keep going, you'll have to keep going.

Russell and his colleagues wanted to get away from the idea that only one thing is good: outdoor running in natural environments. 'We wanted to know what worked. And if running on a treadmill in front of a big screen with nice images on it was the thing, then that was fine.' I admired his willingness to suspend judgement, his desire to wait and see what worked best, but I just couldn't believe that millions of years of evolution had brought us to this: lab-rats in front of TV screens.

The trial that Latham and he organised was constructed to investigate people's habits, choices and motivations for running where they did. The resulting article explains that 'part of the appeal of seeing everyday life as a battleground of social practices competing for our time is that it helps us to recognise people as not always so in charge of their actions as we might otherwise assume'.

He tells me that their trial subjects were split between treadmill and outdoor runners. I ask why treadmill runners seemed to like that kind of running.

'Well, you might be asking the wrong question. We found that runners don't seem particularly keen to actively reflect on their practice, so none felt devoted to the treadmill. They would go and exercise on a treadmill, and because exercise is a good thing, perhaps didn't feel the need to reflect on it afterwards.

'In the trial that we ran,' he explains, 'the subjects all agreed on what the ideal environment was for running (the park or by the Thames, etc.) but because of other thought-processes, the runners were quite good at removing their own practice from any consideration of what the right environment was. And it was working for them so we didn't want to mess with that.

'Because we are academics, constantly analysing and thinking, we project that on to others, who are not always reflecting. But we found that many of the runners we spoke to on the trial only reflected on their practice when they were not able to run because they were injured. When they could run, they just wanted to get on with it.'

In the essay itself, it becomes much clearer that the subjects tried to talk around their motivations for running where they did – as reluctant to reflect on their practice as we might expect a longstanding addict to be.

On chatting to Russell, I think I have a much less scientific attitude to all this, a bit more old-fashioned and Reithian; I want people to know what they are doing, and understand how they might get the very most out of their practice; to be best informed, then make a decision. I worry that the treadmill runners may be left ignorant of the other forms of exercise and psychological improvement that they are missing out on.

I ask why he and Latham chose these particular trial subjects. He explains that they wanted to use runners that were not athletes or members of a running club (as many other trials have done).

'We suspect running is a lot less social than other studies have suggested. Most runners don't join a club. And those that do are self-selecting as social runners.

'It's too easy to critique the gym, to set yourself up as an outsider and say they are neoliberal, expensive, or an unnecessary use of resources, but in doing so, you'll blind yourself to all the good that they do for many people.' I like the sentiment, and he is right, they do serve the members who actually attend quite well – but that is only a very small percentage of the population. It's clearly a practice that does not work for most people. But those for whom it does work seem to be busy people who do not have the time to think about things differently, or do not want to.

'In other words, it is precisely because many recreational runners are busy that otherwise considered individuals now both persist with and enjoy relatively unthinking exercise in a range of environments.'

Hitchings's work is so interesting, we end up talking for hours as the world, in a headlong rush to nowhere, eagerly crashes by outside. We decompress by chatting about our own running habits. I hope he doesn't mind me saying that he looks super-fit in the way that certain runners I could mention do not. So I ask him what he does. He tells me that he treadmills during the week and runs outside at the weekends. He is an outdoor-running agnostic.

We talk a little more about going to the gym, how he sees exercise as part of his working day; and just when he thinks he's finally got rid of me, I go off on one about the length of a worker's day and how technology seems not to make life easier, but rather makes it so that we now have to be experts at everything. A travel agent was once the only one who had to know how to book a flight – how to negotiate that process which seems booby-trapped to the uninitiated. Similarly an insurance-broker was the only one who had to spend hours comparing quotes. Technology has added all this labour to our day, and even exercise (traditionally an outcome of our work) is now additional to it. It is little wonder that gym adherence is such a problem when the capital required is not only membership fees, but the available time and energy; all are inaccessible assets to those on low incomes or working two or three jobs.[23]

I want to get around the idea of exercise, with all of its uncomfortable associations with social responsibility, body-capital and symbolic status, to something more immanent: movement and real experiences.

The killer for me is that I suffer extreme treadmill amnesia. Time spent on a treadmill is lost to me. I can rarely remember doing treadmill runs, just that I've done them.

For the creation of long-term memory there has to be a process of encoding where, at a neuronal level, usually in our sleep, memories are mapped and associated, consolidated and biologically stored.[24] The problem with treadmill runs is that they are too similar to one another to function effectively in this process; they have no emotional burrs to allow them to adhere to other memories.

I have done something in the region of a hundred runs on treadmills. I can remember a couple of them. There is one from about eight years ago where I did a mile in under six minutes. And even then I only remember having done it, not the doing – and I cannot remember the gym that I did it in. And there was one in the Lewisham gym where I ran barefoot. It was awful, I got heat blisters from the rubber belt and as an extra 'fuck you' got a fierce static shock when I stepped off the platform.

Perhaps I don't really know how to run on a treadmill yet; it is all too new.

As a species we have been running indoors for only 30 of the many millions of years of our history (that's about 0.000015 per cent of our time on earth). When I put this theory to Scarlett, she thought it was a bit much. I was ranting and being unfair. Even though she gave up on them, she had known 'moments of great joy' on treadmills. Not least, in her eye-line had been views of 'hot guys lifting weights'. I promised her that I had not known any such joy (meaning the treadmill, not the guys lifting weights).

Not that he would, but if Oscar Wilde strolled into a gym today, what would he make of the lines of runners and walkers? 'Exercise is the name people give to an inability to imagine doing something worthwhile'; *Mens sana in corpore sano* I prefer the immoral mind in the sound body.' But then, maybe Oscar is not our ideal role model for public health, fitness and exercise.

Ever since the period around the Industrial Revolution, the relationship between human and machine has been at the forefront of many philosophies. In the nineteenth century particularly, much ink was spilt by, among others, Wilde, Dickens, Gaskell, Carlyle and Mill – all of whom worried about the consequences of the mechanisation of the individual.

Walter Pater's *Studies in the History of the Renaissance* (1873) was the work that influenced Wilde's aestheticism probably more than any other. The 'Conclusion' to the study proved to be the book's rallying call to an increasingly atomised century at risk of forgetting its biological imperative. Pater countered the materialist philosophies of the century's greats, Comte and Hegel, and instead urged his readers to pay greater attention to their senses. Time is always slipping from our grasp, he warned. And 'not to discriminate every moment some passionate attitude in those about us, and in the very brilliancy of their gifts some tragic dividing of forces on their ways is, on this short day of frost and sun, to sleep before evening'.[25]

As the years have gone on, I have realised that my treadmill experiences are like Pater's 'sleep', where moments of passion or brilliance are rare, and real experience struggles for oxygen in my memory. Without any particularly refined mnemonic skill, I can remember nearly every outdoors run I have done in the last 12 months – probably even further back than that. In most cases I can remember: how the ground felt, the weather, the time of day, the side of each street I ran on; and in many cases I can remember what I was thinking about (when I was thinking). I can recall a considerable number of the runs in detail: running on Blackheath in a blizzard; my first barefoot runs round Lewisham; running up what felt like a vertical cliff to the Tennyson monument near Freshwater on the Isle of Wight (twice); or a barefooter at Seasalter on the northern shoreline of Kent – a beautifully stressed, post-apocalyptic run of coast, where the staff in a deserted pub gave me a free bag of crisps because I had missed lunch and they had closed the tills – I was so hungry I ate them with the grace of the Cookie Monster.

In the case of the Seasalter run, for example, I had no knowledge of the coastline so began the run shod. About a third of a mile into it, I decided to remove my shoes and lay them on the grass. I could collect them on the way back. The ground was thick with lichens, like dimpled layers of dried orange skin and flattened pistachios. (These are among the oldest living organisms on the planet, some specimens still going at 8,600 years old.[26]) The topsoil was hard and dry, but softened by a cool pelt of grass. It was bliss to run on. The road felt miles away and I hardly needed to share the deserted path. There were a few kissing gates that had waist-high nettles corralled in them, so I climbed onto the sandpaper of the concrete sea wall and shuffled round them instead. My feet rustled along with only my shallow breath and the soft exhalation of a wave now and then.

Just about the only person I saw on the run appeared after I had done my few miles for the day. I was returning to collect my shoes. From a hundred yards away, I could see them nestled in the grass, as conspicuous as a discarded Coke can on a college lawn. One shoe was fire-engine red; the other custard-yellow (though they were a pair). The man who had stopped nearby was a little older than me. He leaned over to get a closer look at the shoes; if he had been a dog he would have barked at them. He glanced up and saw me a good many yards off. His gaze fell to my feet and, 'Ah!', all was explained. He began to move on and gave me a smile as I passed him to collect my shoes. I slipped them back on and, suddenly hungry, went in search of food.

This run was well over a year ago and still I remember: the Essex skippers; the crisp sun and the light breeze; the vapour trails in the sky like broad wet brush strokes; the marble patina of the topsoil; the empty caravan site; the serious-looking, fat, topless man on the white bike who would not look at me as we crossed paths; the toffee-coloured sea; the industrial buildings on the skyline that looked abandoned. It may sound like a special run, but it wasn't even a particularly memorable one – I didn't have a trespassing adventure, I was not chased by man or animal, I was not snapped at by an adder, there were no special sites to visit, no particular moments when my perspective in the landscape suddenly found a balance of shape, depth and colour and was transformed into arresting beauty. One thing it was: it was a real and a lived moment. And it is clear in my memory, whereas I cannot get away from the notion that if John F. Kennedy had been shot while I was running on a treadmill, I would be unable to say where I was when I heard the news.

During the nineteenth century the design of the prisoners' treadmill changed. To refine the effect of sensory limitation, panels were installed between the prisoners so that their stalls resembled a voting booth. They could no longer see or talk to one another, so they could contemplate their crimes in bare isolation, and without distraction. With this small change, the process of working a treadmill became one that was about absolute institutional power being brought to bear upon the psychology of a prisoner. While the modern treadmill may seem much more like an activity characterised by fun and freedom rather than imprisonment, the two things are only as different as, say, a bike and a motorbike.

In the gyms I have been to (excluding the scratty Lewisham one), with their lines of TVs screens, they usually played a selection of news, sports, advertisements and soap operas. The screens were usually muted, but you could plug in your headphones if you wanted to. In the past, as a consumer of this experience, was I quite innocently being provided with a bit of entertainment for my run, or might something else have been going on?

Sociologists, ethnographers and anthropologists are interested in gyms because they are a sandpit for the peculiarities of our social engagement. We behave so oddly in them: whether it is the eccentricities of membership structures, changing-room etiquette (I witnessed the amazing sight of a man counting the muscles in his six-pack last week), responses to arbitrary rules and regulations, or the ways in which privacy works. Erving Goffman, in *Behaviour in Public Places*, asks why it is that when we are walking down the street and meet a stranger's eyes, we immediately feel the need to avert our gaze. He suggests the reason we look away with such rapidity is that we instinctively want to be complicit in creating an illusion: when we are in public, we like to pretend we are in private.

As a species, we mostly live in the discordant environment of the city, a place that presents us with more faces than we are built to register. Neither, it seems, are we particularly attuned to being in places where we do not know other people. And treadmills and gyms are tied up with all these complexes.

What I think is that treadmills, and their organisation in these gyms, have a similar effect that the separator panels did for the prisoners of Her Majesty.

In the complex public space of the gym, if Goffman is correct, it would be unusual to catch someone else's eye. I am sure that somewhere, love has blossomed between the rushing rubber belts, and strong friendships have been forged on those stain-proof carpets, but while it took me a while to learn, the etiquette is identical to the rules of social engagement at men's urinals: eyes forward, concentrated silence, always choose the vacant space farthest away from the one that is occupied. No talking. No farting. And no looking.

Gyms are public places, they have to be to generate profit, but when I am in them, I feel strongly like they want me to feel like I am somewhere private.

Businesses, institutions and other structures constantly try to predetermine and shape our behaviour as consumers, subjects or citizens. And I believe that gyms are no different. I feel persuaded into thinking that privacy is my right in such places.

I also feel that it presumes I want to avoid social engagement, but even hard-labour prisoners of the eighteenth and nineteenth centuries were permitted to think while they worked their mills. The gantry of TVs and the music of the modern gym assume that thought is not desired.

It reminds me of a George Orwell essay from 1946, in which he attacks with horror the idea of the new 'pleasure resort'. Orwell was suspicious of the fact that the modern construction of 'pleasure' involved never being alone, never doing things yourself, never seeing or hearing anything natural, being in artificially temperate surroundings, and never being out of earshot of music.[27] It was difficult for him not to conclude that such environments functioned as a return to the womb – being without daylight, with a regulated temperature, without work, and where thought, if it were possible, would be drowned among the thuds and thumps of the mother's body. The gym's pulsating techno seems a poor substitution for the maternal heartbeat.

Yet even with so many reasons to avoid treadmills, for years I used them, and paid a high price. For me it was the drive-thru window of exercise: fast, forgettable, futile. And I think William Cubitt's invention is such an enduring success because it continues to do what it was always designed to do: to block out experience.

ST JULIOT, THE NORTH ATLANTIC COAST AND THE POETRY OF OPEN SPACE

Having already discovered that terra-running is one of the most profoundly blissful ways of doing nothing, I should also add that it can be a tricky skill to refine. Our culture is not great at letting us bunk off. Like quite a few academics, I mainly work from home. Some think this a luxury, and when I first started doing it, it certainly was, but it also has drawbacks. No one, for example, tells you about the guilt, or just how often you end up working because books, emails and materials are constantly accessible to you and not locked away in a distant office at evenings and weekends. Working-from-home guilt is the quiet little housemate who seemed lovely and ideal when you interviewed them, but once they have rented a room from you never, ever, ever go out. They are always there, reminding you that you could always be doing more than you are.

One guaranteed escape from guilt is running. I can disappear for an hour or two, return, express mild surprise at the time passed, rinse the salt from my face, and get back to work. It is an escape in other ways, too.

Much of my job is spent looking at a screen or reading; it can seem like life is spent in front of a tiny glimmering square of the world. This kind of forward focus seems not so far from the prisoners' treadmill of concentrated, unidirectional effort. The effect can be claustrophobic, and a run represents a necessary change of life's aspect ratio, from close-up to wide angle.

So, heading out, there is always the barely conscious desire to find empty space. The body needs it; space is what it's for. Not merely a glimpse of Blackheath or Regent's Park, but the highest and broadest and deepest and emptiest place possible. To counter life's tunnelscape, you need to see a landscape, lyrical, articulate and broad; so wide it pulls at the elastic of peripheral vision like a deep stretch. The greater the space, the greater the likelihood of your believing that you have been transported to a weird afterlife where the sun has long since set on humanity and you have been stranded. The more deserted the square-mileage of land, the more bare earth you can see, the more convinced you will become that you have entered such a place. The best runs are a search for the possibility of, as Jo the crossing-sweeper in *Bleak House* puts it, 'nothink'.[28] Not-thinking, huddling down into the body's experience, is a kind of mental repose, a Pilates for the brain. It is different to the mental numbing of the gym, because there it seems we have to work to block so many things out. Here we can let them in. It is like a blissful sort of 'little death', from the French, *petit mort*, for orgasm. It is for this reason that I think that the runner's high is as much spatial as it is hormonal, as much connected to being outside, in wide-open spaces, as it is to do with neurotransmitter release in the brain.

Ninety minutes into a run recently, I found myself in a wood. I lost my head and floated free. I dodged between the ash trees, jackdaws barked as I slipped and slid on the sticky mud, but I was in a haze, not really there, even though my body seemed to know what it was doing. I felt more naked than the ploughed-up fields. (Over the years, I've also mulled over how similar running can be to something like reading, from the physiology of the horizontal eye-scan – where the fixations are footfalls, the saccades are the flight – to the similar levels of focus and absorption and the marsupial collection and organisation of knowledge, to the syntaxes and story-arcs of a good run.)

The experience of 'nothink' (a state of mental arousal crossed with something like sleep) brings with it a kind of attention to the details and aspects of the world that are seemingly imperceptible at other times. 'Nothink' creates a kind of high-definition recollection coupled with a creative ability to identify points of connection between the inside and the outside.

Our man Thomas Hardy was always pioneering new ways of letting the outside in; of bringing the natural world to our attention and imagination. He knew the impact of the environment, and he spent a life in writing trying to make sense of it, and to understand how it is tied up with our emotions, and our wellbeing.

It may seem odd to bring Hardy together with 'running' in this way, and it is something I've struggled to explain in the past, but as I slip and stumble along the cliff-paths that he walked, hundreds of feet above the crashing Atlantic, I am about to discover that in his writing – so unyielding and real in the way it brings the world into focus – there is only a mole's whisker between what's on the page and what's in the world. The frictive immediacy of the engagement with the environment that I derive from real running, as I grab at tussocks to stop myself slipping into an inlet, is matched on the page by Hardy's instinct to notice, reframe or describe the world. Running has the potential to be a deeply immersive activity, and of all the poets and novelists I've ever read, Hardy's writing is the most similar in its immersive qualities.

It is not surprising that the places that he loved are such impressive environments. They are places that, once experienced, become impossible to forget.

I have come to one of those places today. I have meandered along the roads of north Cornwall to find a tiny hamlet called St Juliot, so remote that I don't remember having seen a single road sign for it. I have parked under the outreaching branches of an old oak tree, probably 'springing from a seed/Dropped by some bird a hundred years ago'.[29] Here there are a few houses, outbuildings and a 1,000-year-old church.

It's an English summer day: rain feels possible, there is a slight chill in the air, and the wind is bouncing everything around, back and forth like wild deely-boppers.

The young Hardy came here in 1870. He had been a bright boy growing up in rural Dorset, where his mother did not want his intelligence wasted by his becoming a bricklayer like his father (and later, his brother). So the young Tom trained as an architect and was shipped off to London, where he worked just off Trafalgar Square. He read, wrote, went to plays, and attended the National Gallery every day, where he would stare for 20 minutes at a single picture; he had a few dalliances, even travelled on the tube when the Metropolitan Line opened in 1863; but London was a filthy place. It stank.[30] The whites of the wash would stain brown if they were hung out on the line at the wrong time of day. As it has many others, the mother city made Hardy ill. In a matter of years, he went from country immigrant to metropolitan emigrant when he returned to Dorset to take up work once again at the architect's that he had left a few years before. How hard it must have been to return to the town from London without the kind of success for which he must have hoped.

Shattered by his five years in London, Hardy accepted the invitation to work on a church restoration in north Cornwall. It was an escape for the as yet unpublished and unmarried young writer; an escape from failure.

I have driven over from Devon today, where I have left behind the lush bracken and fernland that seem to breathe as they radiate so much moist heat. But Hardy, travelling from Dorset in March 1870, would have set off in the dark to catch the first of four chugging trains, at the end of which he would still have been 16 miles from his destination. St Juliot, it seems, was even less accessible in the nineteenth century than it is now.

At the rectory nearby, he arrived intending to meet the vicar, but was instead greeted by the vicar's sister-in-law. She was called Emma Gifford. In a staid brown dress she welcomed him and explained that the vicar was indisposed with suspected gout and her sister was busy taking care of him.

I walk up past the church to the rectory (it is now a B & B) and imagine the young man, standing there, anxious at meeting 'a lady' but giving nothing of his own humbler background away, unsure of how to conduct himself. I think of her, too – living the quietest of rural lives with her sister and her brother-in-law. Hardy didn't know it to look at her, but she was, as 'Victorian ladies' go, a thrill-seeker.

The wild remoteness of the environment at St Juliot summoned an equal wildness in her. She loved to ride side-saddle: fearless of the cloud-high cliffs, she galloped along those hills with rain running down her back, her wet hair trailing behind her in the wind, the Atlantic waves all the time crashing on the strand of the beach below. Such excitement would have provided necessary respite to escape a contented, but cosseted life.[31] Up here the ruggedness of the landscape seems to conjure the very possibility of such adventuring, and this must have been especially true for a Victorian lady whose nearest neighbours lived nine miles away.[32]

Over 40 years later, after an overwhelmingly unhappy marriage for both of them, it is one of the oddities of literary history that Hardy immortalised her and their wild courtship in a cycle of 18 poems published shortly after her death that are as breathtaking in their technical ingenuity as they are heartfelt in their lyricism.[33] The longlived tragedy of what his own marriage would turn out to be could have come straight from the plot of one of his own novels.

The rectory is round the corner from the isolated church which overlooks a valley running down to the Valency River. At the other end of his life, Hardy was still, in 1925, mythologising this first visit in a poem that celebrated a trip to a quarry that he and Emma made on his second day at St Juliot (examining slate for the church restoration).[34] He was never able to let go of this place and those few days he spent here.

I walk round to the church, and imagine that the view from the graveyard down the meadows and into the valley looks just as it must have 150 years ago.

I have my car key, some water and my phone (unknown territory ahead), so I set off north to find the Cornish coastline that was to become the backdrop to this intense love affair which produced some of the finest poetry of the twentieth century.

What would have been mud-filled, ankle-breaker lanes in 1870 are now tarmac tracks, and although there must be footpaths, I haven't a map to find them. The hedgerows are mature and tall and there is no room for myself and a car, if one comes by, but one doesn't.

At a fork in the road, neither way offers any clues as to which I should take, so I guess. (Losing your way means giving in to the idea that the world is far greater than our consciousness is comfortable with. That feeling of anxiety is tinged with the bliss that there is always more to experience. It means we open ourselves up to the possibility of true discovery and surprise. The comfort is that, in space, unlike in life, we can almost always turn back.)

Straight ahead the air looks clearer and the sky bigger, but I have to choose left or right. I'm now on a much faster B-road that doesn't have a millimetre of pavement – HEDGEroadroadroadHEDGE. After a couple of unfulfilling minutes, I am certain I've gone the wrong way, so I about-face in the hope that I will be able to escape this danger.

I am stuck on the road for over a mile. I have to flatten myself against the hedge as an orange tractor clatters by, leaving fumes of hay floating into the traffic piled up behind it. An Audi's wing mirror brushes against me, thrusting me into nettles, the driver's view obstructed by the van in front and possibly by the phone the car driver is thumbing. I hear the passenger shout something to the driver, but whatever it was is taken by the wind. Stuck on this road, I am definitively not feeling the freedom of north Cornwall.

It seems that great runs need to have the dynamic of a terrible beginning to give them that cold-air blast of meaning and energy. I need to have faith that this one will come good. I have miles in my bank, I reckon that I can comfortably manage about fifteen, of which these are only the first two. Then an unmarked seabound trackway gestures, and at last I leave the road behind.

With open ground in front of me I can cut through it like a razor. Within a couple of hundred yards I am on the South West Coastal Path overlooking the Atlantic, watching waves crashing wildly on the shore hundreds of feet below me. They rage hard at a deep inlet. The height of the cliffs is daunting, so great that I cannot work out how far down the water actually is. I look across to the parallel cliff face and I can just make out a couple of ramblers, but their progress on the path looks fiddly, antlike.

The hundreds of feet of shale cliff in comparison look uncanny. Their colour is a purple grey, like dried blood. Shale is the chameleon of English rock, it borrows its tints from its surroundings and its alien tendencies are only enhanced by the fact that outcroppings of it have even been found on Mars.

The ocean has eaten hungrily, cutting a deep cleft into the hillside, and it sounds unsatiated still. I turn south and can see Bactrian humps of black slate rolling off into the distance.

In one of his early novels, *A Pair of Blue Eyes,* Hardy filched scenes from his experiences here. There is a scene so memorably tense that the term 'cliffhanger' is said to have been named for it. It is one of the most thrilling turns in nineteenth-century fiction and takes place here, on these cliffs.

Two lovers (Henry Knight and Elfride Swancourt) are on a romantic afternoon stroll when Henry finds himself stuck, and after losing his footing is suddenly clinging for his life hundreds of feet above the hungry monster of the Atlantic. Elfride (the thrill-seeker in part responsible for the slip) offers to run for help – at which point the episode ends, leaving the reader to wait for the next periodical instalment.

We return to Henry, trapped and alone, contemplating death while he hopes to be saved. With his grip weakening, he has only minutes to live. His eyes come to focus on something in front of him in the rock: 'It was one of the early crustaceans called Trilobites. Separated by millions of years in their lives, Knight and this underling seemed to have met in their death.'[35] Elfride returns, without help. Instead, she sassily rips at her underwear, tying the bits together to make a rope. I won't plot-spoil it for you.

Hardy and Emma's relationship was born up here. They travelled unchaperoned and explored as they pleased. Their passion was not just something that emerged between them, but was also a communion between them and their environment.

'Beeny Cliff', a poem written by Hardy 43 years later, goes back to this day in the early March of 1870, and uses the landscape to frame and make sense of their entire marriage. This isn't just writerly indulgence. Being here, in this unchanged place, one can see that their passion for one another comes out of the crags, rock and earth of this coastline. It was the woman riding on horseback on these cliff tops whom he fell in love with, not the one who greeted him in the porch of a rectory.[36]

Hardy left St Juliot after his three-day visit feeling himself engaged, but he had no career, no future and no means to marry. Within four years, though, he established himself as a nature writer of particular power.

As I head south, clambering up and down cliff paths, making appalling progress, my lungs burn and the wind makes me shiver like heather. My heart-rate rises and falls with my altitude. The intensity of the landscape, of my experience of its sharpness through my shoes, only heightens the otherworldly sense of the run. Like the stones crumbling and tumbling off the cliff path, life falls away in moments like these and the possibilities seem endless. Shards pinch my feet, and because of the stone's fissility I slip and stumble on the scrape, rattle and roll of dusty descents, but the hazy sense of disordered coping with the terrain never distracts me from the wonderful intensity of the run. It's an experience that I can't make sense of: ragged, tired, ecstatic, and oddly sweet, like I have had a jug of syrup tipped over my head.

After only four miles, my legs are in orgasm-spasm from exhaustion. They are used to spirit-level London pavements, not this constant negotiation and elevation. The fact that I am so tired reminds me of how strange and wonderful this is.

On another ascent, there is a bench and I start to doubt that I can make the return journey. The same small group of us that had holidayed together in the Cotswolds (my partner Adam as well as Elle and her dog, The Captain) are here in the West Country, though 40 miles away, over the county border. I dial Elle's mobile, the only one that works where we are staying.

'Any chance you fancy a coffee?' I ask Elle.

'Oh yes. Are you nearly back?'

'No. Er, I think I'm near Tintagel.'

'Oh.'

'And I think I need a lift back to my car.'

'Oh.' There is some mumbling in the background, and then I am sure I hear a little laughter.

'I think I'm about 40 minutes away from Tintagel.'

'OK. We'll meet you there.'

Pause.

'And make sure you bring money,' I say. What a dear friend I am.

By the time I arrive in Tintagel my legs are shaking. I know how twenty miles feels, and I am shocked to see that I've covered only eight. I later work out that I have been running 12-minute miles – these are the sorts of times politicians manage in marathons. The rugged passion of the place has defeated me completely.

It all seems so very, very far from the treadmill.

Many figures have questioned the real cost of modern life, from the Romantics through to the postmodernists, and Thomas Hardy is certainly one of the most consistent sceptics. But Hardy is not simply a soppy Romanticist who believes that we can return to nature. His work frequently reminds us of the embodiedness of being, that our consciousness is not a by-product of our body, but is in it and entwined with it.

His lyric poetry frequently saunters a similarly Romantic path: how the moral and social order of society exhausts us because it is so unnaturally organised around social institutions (it is what most of his tragic fiction is about). For the last 200 years, thinkers have had a go at the sort of idealism that wants to get around this problem. You can't go back to nature, they say. Where would that be? When would it be? Does it even exist?

But you don't have to go back in time.

After you run a long distance, usually the first thing you want is a big glass of water. The pleasure and satisfaction this brings is short-lived. Once you feel your stomach start to bloat with all the water, then the gratification begins to diminish. But this is not the end of the water. It is about to go to work, in every cell of your body, helping it to repair, and get your system back online. The benefits have far greater longevity than the initial quenching of a thirst.

And just as the effects of that glass of water go on long after the last gulp, so authors such as Woolf, Edward Thomas, Coleridge, Wordsworth, Clare and countless others have understood that the benefits of spending time in a natural environment persist even when one is back in the city.

We cannot attain freedom from cities, work, responsibilities and civilisation, but for Hardy it is always within touching distance.

This, from his extraordinary 1896 poem 'Wessex Heights':

> There are some heights in Wessex, shaped as if by a kindly
>   hand
> For thinking, dreaming, dying on, and at crises when I stand,
> Say, on Ingpen Beacon eastward, or on Wylls-Neck westwardly,
> I seem where I was before my birth, and after death may be . . .
>
> Down there I seem to be false to myself, my simple self that
>   was,
> And is not now, and I see him watching, wondering what crass
>   cause
> Can have merged him into such a strange continuator as this,
> Who yet has something in common with himself, my
>   chrysalis.[37]

Hardy's spidery long lines ramble on so extensively that they rarely fit a standard page-width. These are thoughts, permitted space to roam free. If Edward Thomas was a shark that needed to stay in constant motion, Hardy was a whale, that climbed the heights to come up for a blast of air, and then returned, renewed, to the depths of civilisation. Hardy's Heights become for him a place of rapturous emptiness, of 'nothink'. Hardy succeeded in dragging himself from his enclosed confines – out of the tunnel and onto the hilltop; out of the prison of civilisation and language to become something animal and new.

With words long gone, barriers begin to break down and the biology of the body comes into its own, reminding you that it is a soft machine. It is the thing that you're running with and through. Words and names only seem to get in the way. Indeed, one of the problems with the way that we relate to nature is that we insist on calling it that. Nature is something 'out there'; our identity and our relationship to it dictates to some extent our inability to see through it, to it. The nineteenth-century Sussex labouring poet, Simeon Brough, writes in 'Nature' (1882):

> The word hangs like a frame.
> Below the land, up there the sky,
> A rippled pane lies between all It and I.
> A fine Web once It was,
> With Methuselan threads 'twixt It and us.
> Now it's seen as from afar;
> A gift once given - lightning lit, rent apart.
> And so the pane endures.
> No stone may score nor sun may scorch
> This scrub-land that stands 'twixt a word and its thought.
> All to the Web we fly,
> And lost to Time, like sense, the pane
> Dissolves as vapours weep,
> And lost are the words, full fathoms deep.[38]

By the end of the poem, both what he is trying to say and the rhythm of saying it have dissolved into a haze. Where the poem suggests that it is perhaps death that provides the way back through the woods, I think that solitary distance-running is a way through, too.

On that long run in the woods when I lost my head, the hypnotic spell of the endless rhythm of my feet and my breath pared away at me until, like the smooth steps at some holy shrine worn down by the passing thousands, I had gone completely, and only my body was left. Clipped observations occasionally broke in:

> If the soil weren't so wet it would look seared . . .
> It folds and rolls away toward a leaden sky . . .
> The cut wheat like greying stubble
> slowly dying on the sagging jaw of a corpse.

But soon even those thoughts sunk and I floated out of life into my little death: a place where you find peace and can drop out of the world, and live for a time with the sentience of an animal. Breath comes in, goes out, in, out; hundreds, thousands, all the same. The sun shines. Air warms and chills. Leaves fall. Breath comes in, and out. The sky, the scored canopy of the wood, the jackdaws in the field, the mud underfoot, breath in and out . . .

Language is no use when there is no one to speak to, or signs to read. As Hardy says of his Wessex Heights, 'mind chains do not clank where one's next neighbour is the sky'.

In the conclusion to that poem, Hardy saw these moments as forms of escape from a life he found hard. All of what he is trying to say is there, in the last five words of the poem:

> So I am found on Ingpen Beacon, or on Wylls-Neck to the
>   west,
> Or else on homely Bulbarrow, or little Pilsdon Crest,
> Where men have never cared to haunt, nor women have
>   walked with me,
> And ghosts then keep their distance; and I know some
>   liberty.[39]

The gym and the treadmill seem from a different planet. Real, long runs in these sorts of wild, open spaces, have a potent, even hallucinatory, appeal that can provide escape from sense, logic, everything. They are a rest from life itself. They can be like the gym on acid.

Running puts us unquestionably here, emphatically now.

The treadmill is running enframed; an experience that's pared back, removed from its meaning and context. It is the paper coffee cup of running. Years ago, when I first blogged about the treadmill, I said that I wasn't at all sure what I was doing when I got on one. Now I'm more confident and think that if you exercise on a treadmill you are effectively minimising, shrinking and refining all the benefits that you might otherwise gain from running. It is the junk-food of exercise. If you want to rescue some of your life from oblivion, stay off the treadmill, so that you may remember some of what you would otherwise forget.

PART IV
ROAMING

7.
THE ANTIQUE ART OF TRESPASSING: HOW TO RUN WILD

NORWOOD AND SHOOTER'S HILL; HARROW; FAVERSHAM; WALDEN POND, MASSACHUSETTS; AND PARIS

Please Stay on the Trails
Restricted Access Restoration Zone
Violators are subject to fines

> – Trespass warning sign at Walden Pond,
> Massachusetts

The soul of a journey is liberty, perfect liberty, to think, feel, do just as one pleases.

> – William Hazlitt,
> 'On Going a Journey', 1822

There are few concepts as tricky for philosophers as freedom. Like slavery, pornography or art, it is difficult to define, but most of us know it when we see it. It may have more to do with how someone feels than with the concrete conditions of a life (or indeed, the concrete conditions of an urban life). For runners (and for all of us, in different ways) freedom is bound up with the body and its liberty, autonomy and self-governance, its ability to experience, and its motility. It is as much physiological as it is psychological. Inevitably, there is also a political aspect to it.

While I don't think running is particularly rebellious or revolutionary (if it was, I'm sure we wouldn't be allowed to do it), I can't help but think that this aimless motion does contain within it at least a questioning of the waves of economic utilitarianism that we are daily subject to.

Is movement political? The relationship between politics and movement is so close that defined factions of like-minded folk are called just that: a movement.

Leaving behind the electrical static of modern life is essential to our wellbeing. We may not be able to escape the city, but we are still free, when running, to revel in the fact that we are basically highly mobile stone-agers ripping down the lanes, byways and boulevards of our cities. Running can satisfy our ancient appetite for novelty, and also our need to extend our mental maps concerning where and how we might live. Freedom like this, to forage for experience, should be an inalienable right for anyone. So what can you do to get off the rails and treadmills of life? Explore, forage, trespass and roam.

PRESCRIBED PATHWAYS IN SOUTH LONDON, HARROW AND FAVERSHAM

I am on my way out of London. Most people tear the plaster off in one eye-watering rip, so to speak, choosing to go somewhere entirely new when leaving the city. Not me, I am peeling it off hair by hair.

In a bid for freedom, we moved house in midsummer, after a spring spent among the crazed prospectors hunting for the perfect fixer-upper – anything that needed half a day's decorating was marketed as possessing potential. In an eagerness to escape the fray, we found ourselves in the nowhere asteroid-belt of suburbia, not quite able to gather the exit velocity to shoot beyond the event horizon of London. We had failed to leave.

A couple of days after we moved in, I suddenly realised that I had forgotten something. We had been living in Lewisham before (a few miles from the centre), so I was spoilt for places to run: the bald upland of Blackheath, the oak- and alder-filled Greenwich Park, and 184 miles of Thames Path – on which I could go east or west on either the north or south side of the river. And there were multiple routes for getting to my routes, through pin-drop-quiet Victorian suburbs, a daisy chain of miniature parks, or the dirty bustle of the high street. It was also possible to take a tenner and a door key and run the entire way into the centre of town, parade around Green Park, Regent's Park or Hyde Park, buy a falafel in Soho and ride the train home, happy, if a little salty.

Now I was in a new area and was cut off from all this by millions and millions of little houses. Neither in nor out of the city, if I wanted to run it must be meticulously planned. I had to avoid traffic, people and estates (because they are no fun when you can't find your way out). There had to be the reward of pleasant space somewhere along the route.

When I look at the map, there is a blob of green near the end of our road, and it reticulates with other blobs in quite a complex jigsaw, but I decide to make do with only the first one. I should be grateful.

I riffle through some boxes to find some running kit (including shoes), change and head out into the sun. There is a territorial aspect to running in a new place. It's not that you take ownership of it, but that you announce yourself as a dweller on the land, or a browser of the local businesses.

At the corner is a steep, climbing 'B' road and in the distance I can see the Crystal Palace transmitter. There are lines of cyclists heading in both directions, running their weekend training routes, by the look of their lyrca and the whizz-click speed they are all going.

I run by hundreds of metres of wire fence, looking for the entrance to my very own green blob, then there's an opening, completely unsigned, and so understated that I can't believe I'm here.

The pathway is compressed loam with some stones (I take my shoes off but it is absolutely horrible to run on, so after ten steps I have to wipe the soles of my feet against my shins and put them back on again). As I turn south again, the park opens up. But there is no play area, no goalposts. It's not a park, but a nature reserve, South Norwood Country Park. The path has become compacted chalk, so there is still no possibility of going barefoot, unless I dodge on and off the path onto the grass, where there is a medium chance of encountering some organic dog matter. To the west are bulrushes, grown so high I can barely see over them. To the east is a lake with moorhens, mallards and Canada geese – none of which I can see because I'm not actually on one of the prepared viewing platforms.

It was as dull as it sounds. My momentary relief at finding somewhere that looked like a good place for a regular browse and forage quickly revealed itself as a glorified mono-path, a runner's equivalent of the tube, which I could circumambulate either clockwise or anticlockwise, confined to wearing shoes because the pathway was so unforgiving.

Later, on other runs when I explored further, venturing into new territories, I found more of the same: smaller parks and forests that were literally tens of feet wide, poorly demarcated golf driving-ranges, and scalped playing fields that were featureless or lay within a few yards of heavy traffic.

These roaming runs got me thinking about how important our freedom is, and how we can exercise that which is available to us in ways we may not have previously considered.

We live in three dimensions (of course we do), but we don't regularly make as much use of them as we might. When I went to New York recently, it struck me for the first time how very flat our lives can be. Being shown to my hotel room I had to equalise in the lift, and then decompress on my flight back down to the lobby, just like when on a plane. Throughout the few days of the stay, I was always moving across, along, high up and all the way back down again. New York is the only place where I ever really noticed this; elsewhere we just seem to exploit two dimensions.

There is a book about this, Edwin A. Abbott's satirical novel *Flatland*.[1] It is a post-Euclidian fantasy of interdimensional travel where beings (shapes) who live in the two dimensions of Flatland struggle to understand the possibility of a third. The hero, called Square, meets the Sphere who tries to explain the third dimension. They travel to one-dimensional Lineland, and no-dimensional Pointland, where they appear as an idea in the head of its only inhabitant. *Flatland* is also about our inability to see beyond the dimensions of our own comprehension. The 2D and 3D dimensional-tourists do actually appear to the inhabitants of Lineland, for example, but only as one-dimensional lines (not the squares and spheres of their 'real' bodies). Ultimately, the novel is a satire that exposes our inability to perceive that which we are not equipped to see.

On a run recently, I had stepped out to do ten-or-so miles. If you are going to do that much, the fact of having to do a certain number of miles creates a wonderful kind of freedom to roam.

I had begun a regular route, but a few miles in, when I turned one of my regular corners, right beside me was a passageway that I had never noticed before. A wormhole. I still had at least seven or eight miles on the clock, so I could turn in any direction I liked. The new pathway could take me anywhere. It would not matter where. I could run it for four miles and, if I was lost, easily retrace my steps back. I had strayed a couple of metres past it, but I was already within the event horizon, so to speak; I turned sharply and entered the passage.

I have done this before, seen a passageway, turned and explored it. The effect is uncanny, much more so than one might imagine. You leave one part of London, follow a trail and find yourself in quite another. The path has created a new connection between two places, like a topographical synapse.

There is a corner that I turn on a quiet road in south-east Blackheath. On a satellite map I am only a couple of hundred feet away from Kidbrooke (what a beautiful name for a place). I could vault a few fences, dodge some guard dogs, climb a tree or two and I would be there. If I wanted to get to Kidbrooke by established routes, however, it would be at least a two-mile walk between those two practically adjacent points on the map.

Our experience of the space around us is not purely two-dimensional, because all sorts of legal boundaries circumscribe it. In such circumstances, it is much closer to the one-dimensional travel that Abbott fictionalises in his Lineland.

What about the fourth dimension? 'That which hath been is now' (Ecclesiastes 3:15). My wormhole recently brought me out in another suburban sprawl. Once out of the passage, the sun in the sky was clear and I could easily read my heading if I needed to turn back. I still had a couple of miles to borrow from the bank if I was going to follow the same route back, so I persevered. Masses of twentieth-century housing, bright red brick, white panelling, tower blocks, scruffy veterinary practices, and 'that roar'. That roar could only be the A2, the main road between Kent and London (Bond has car-chases along it in the Ian Fleming novels, and it is the road that Dickens's young hero, David Copperfield, sets out upon to find his only living relative in the world). Vibrant new places, even ones that may not appear immediately pleasing to the eye or ear, possess a kind of power that can be overwhelmingly impressive. And this is one such place, Shooter's Hill.

I first heard of it many years ago when I was reading another Dickens novel, *A Tale of Two Cities*. Set in the eighteenth century, the book's dramatic beginning has a mail coach lumbering up Shooter's Hill on a dark and stormy night, and a man is chasing it on horseback. The passengers in the coach know well why it is called 'Shooter's Hill', because it belongs to the highwaymen. (But it was already called Shooter's Hill, long before the daring Turpins of the eighteenth century. The name is first recorded in 1226, the road having acquired it at some point before then – so presumably roadside robberies have been a tradition here for over a millennium, dating back to a time when the shooters would have been firing from a quiver full of arrows.)

I run down a ramp and find myself at the still centre of a roaring vortex of traffic travelling north, south, east and west. It is a concrete crucible with beds of flowering lavender, but the smell is not of flowers: it makes me wonder who could possibly want to come here for a piss. Many it seems, for the stench crowds out nearly everything else.

Time folds, here. I remember the irony of being stuck here in a traffic jam for nearly three hours, late for my very first lecture the previous year. A lecture on time, history and *A Tale of Two Cities*. The confluence of geography and circumstance few would sanely believe: jammed as I was in my steel cage at precisely the spot where the novel begins. Time folds again and it takes us from Dickens's writing of the novel in 1859, to its setting in the 1790s. This was also known as the Dover Road – the mainline in and out of Revolutionary France. Again the strata folds, and the hanged highwaymen are here, strung up in the eighteenth century and before to deter robberies, when surely the effect must have been to scare the bejeezus out of the passengers on the mail coaches. Deeper, and we can see the marauders hidden among the trees of the Dark Ages, when this place must first have gained its name.

It folds forward, too, to the very beginnings of the internal combustion engine. The earliest cars were tried out here. Alexander Gordon, in *A Treatise Upon Elemental Locomotion and*

Interior Communication (1834), recalls, 'In 1826, Mr Samuel Brown applied his gas-vacuum engine to a carriage, and ascended Shooter's-hill to the satisfaction of numerous spectators. The great expense, however, which attended the working of a gas-vacuum engine, prevented its adoption.' But here there is a great deal of growling sensory evidence of its world domination.

I left the sunken roundabout via a subway that funnelled the noise of the road to an unbearable level, making it sound like I was trapped in a wind tunnel during some aerodynamics experiment. I made my way back to the A2, then looped my way back through Blackheath and Greenwich Park. I had discovered the joys of four-dimensional travel, the right to roam in space-time. Suddenly atop centuries of history I found as deep a freedom as any reader knows. Brushing up against these other worlds I never knew existed, in times and realms forgotten, inhabiting other minds, and ways of being, felt the same as being released from the limits of the present.

But there is fun to be had in three dimensions, too. One of my favourite runs of recent years was done in a place not unlike the South Norwood Country Park, but its rules of access were a little different. It taught me that getting off the path is not just fun, but necessary.

After two consecutive days of wedding attendance, I'm a little the worse for wear. I am staying with Adam's relatives in South Harrow. The whole houseful has a hangover. Even though I am returning to south-east London later in the day, it seems a shame to miss the opportunity to tramp unfamiliar ground. I look at the map. Foolishly refusing to take a phone or water, I set out for Harrow-on-the-Hill and the school where the poet Lord Byron led a rebellion against the new headmaster in 1805, and which the novelist Anthony Trollope attended as a 'free day-boy'.

The pavement decoration of my childhood was sweet wrappers, fag butts, and white dogshit. In adulthood, it is gnawed and discarded chicken bones. They punctuate the pavement like commas strewn across a page of the *New Yorker*. This street is busy. It is lunchtime on a Sunday afternoon and there are people everywhere. There are a few recognisable shops. My favourite is the gall of 'Hollywood Pizza – Kebabs and Burger's'. I have never been to Hollywood. Maybe it is just like this there. After a mile of heavy traffic, I turn off the main street and head up the hill. Nowhere else in the world does geography work in the same way as in London. One moment you are slipping on takeaway wrappers, the next you may as well be in a quiet village in the Cotswolds, for all the Elizabethan architecture and carless streets.

I struggle to the top of the hill – it's about a 300-foot climb – and head where the traffic is not going. On the right, a mews falls away from the road. I laugh when I see the road sign for it: Obadiah Slope – the most unctuous of villains from Trollope's 'The Chronicles of Barsetshire'. The whole street is like turning down one of those alleys in Cambridge and finding yourself in the fifteenth century.

I have crowned the top of Harrow's Hill and the road begins to slant and curl away. An old couple are crowding the pavement coming up the other way. And as if she's featuring in her own Edwardian drama, she has a parasol. She falls behind her gentleman friend to let me pass. I do the most unaccountable thing. I have never done this before. I find that I am also featuring in the same Edwardian drama. I salute her. She smiles.

The sun is hard on my face and I am starting to feel a little thirsty. I am not willing to give up all this hard-won altitude so quickly. I turn back the way I came, but I cross the street so as not to alarm the Edwardian couple. Through a narrow crack between two of the school buildings, I catch a miniature portrait of a stunning view. The structures I can see are like letters in an anagram. All the characters are there. You know the word, but it looks different. I am so used to seeing this view from four o'clock on a map that looking at it from ten seems unreal, as if it's been drawn incorrectly from memory. I want to see more but there's no way through.

Then, a few yards further, there is a gate. It has a big sign that says 'PRIVATE', but unfortunately I don't see it. I squeak my way through.

There is no chance of a stealthy look at the view because I am now running on a gravel path that coughs 'stop!', 'get out!' and 'private property' with every step. The TV-screen version of London spreads to a super-wide Cinemascope. Wedges of green field spread out beneath me. I stand for a moment, breathless. But I am not alone – someone is here, and he is looking up from his open book and watching me. I try to act like I am supposed to be here. I bid him good afternoon and ask him the quickest way down to the fields. Without missing a beat, he tells me and I'm off again, crunching down the gravel path. Working my way between the folds of the buildings. Some kids are photographing some others who are wearing what look like dunce's caps.

It looks like Sussex, not London. It is so green and deep it's like you could swim in it.

Then another corner, and straight ahead of me is a running track. I can't not. This is my first time on a track since school, perhaps the first since, aged 13, I did a catastrophically poor 'mile' in a house match and came in last by minutes (I'd like to say asthma got the better of me on the day, but I think it was probably hubris). I slip off my shoes. I go round once. There are hundreds of windows overlooking me and people are playing tennis in the next field. Surely I can't get away with this. I go round again.

As I turn one of the bends, I see someone walking fast in my direction from the car park. At the next arc of the track I peel off, burrowing deeper into the green. I don't look behind me – why would I? I am supposed to be here.

I branch off onto a rugby pitch, still heading for the London skyline, but preventing my escape is a ha-ha where the ground dips steeply into a shoreline of breaking nettles. And, 'ha ha!', there is a surreptitious couple here lying on the grass. Who are they hiding from? They certainly are not schoolchildren and they are not happy to see me. I keep moving, doing a sting-avoidance dance of *pliés* and *fouettés* to work my way through the nettles, and I am into another field which looks like farmland.

The sun is high. My throat burns for water. I am at least three miles from base. And still, there are more people. Walkers, this time: a family? I pretend to myself that I am brave in these situations, but I am uncomfortable. I run straight towards them – of course I do, I am supposed to be here. I smile a welcome but they are oblivious to me.

Over a stile, a field, over another stile, another field, a push through a gate. Then I find a thicket of wild berries that no one has picked – it is full of inky black fruit. I drop my shoes to the ground, and pull at one of the berries to taste. It is like honey. Within seconds I am grabbing at them, adeptly feeding myself with both hands like a crazed switchboard-operator from the 1930s. Each one bursts in my mouth – water! Only this way can you get the full flavour of the fruit: with the traces of grit and cobweb that seem to accentuate the deep, deep, sweetness. They are warm, still, from the heat of the sun. I eat 50 or so. The bloody juice goes straight to my head and I'm ready to go again, leaving the hills and the school behind me.

I've eaten the forbidden fruit and am bound for the future. Through another field, over another stile and I am suddenly back in the white buildings and ambient noise of suburbia. In only a few more yards I am on a dual carriageway, like the fields and their fruit were a dream.

I am lost. I can't go back, it's too far, it's uphill and while the risk of being caught on the school grounds was worth it for a first look, I'm not prepared to take the chance again. I run to the lights, dodging in and out of traffic, riding the waves of cars like a surfer, squinting against the glare. I become convinced that there is a mathematical sequence to the cars' movement through space, as it feels like I could do this with my eyes closed, that my balance and the movement of my limbs are processes that are independent of thought.

I hope that one of the junctions will look familiar. They don't. The place names are all recognisable, but I can't situate myself in relation to them. The traffic stops. The car windows are open in the heat. With my shoes still rolled up in my hand I ask a couple in a glimmering Merc for directions. The driver's voice is absolutely London, but his manner is not. He is prolix and careful in his response. I had expected him with his eyes forward to wind up his window at the approach of a barefoot wrong'un. Instead, he explains the landmarks that I must look out for. He can see that I am tired and hot. He apologises for sending me up a different steep hill. 'Are you sure you will be OK?' he asks. His car is facing the opposite direction but his intonation is clearly offering me a lift. In the hot sun, on the run, the normal rules don't apply, it seems. I feel like he would have opened his wallet if I'd asked.

'I'll be all right. Thank you.' The lights change and the cars are on their way again. And I am on mine.

I make my second climb up Harrow's Hill. I hit a bend in the road that at last I recognise. I run faster and faster and faster, giddy with the excitement of the run – or is it just the crimson sugar of the wild berries hitting my bloodstream?

When I returned to the house that day, there were eager enquiries about where I had been, and although I could obviously describe the run, with the school, the track, the nettles and brambles, I couldn't explain it. It is years later, now, and I can see the run because the magic of GPS has superimposed it in red on a digital map for me, like arterial tracks in the landscape. But I have realised that my runs are not the lifeblood of these places. It is the other way round: it is of course these places that now run in my veins.

The joy of that run was to do with the confluence of a number of things. It was a morsel of life devoutly rescued from the oblivion of the everyday. It was mostly barefoot, so I could feel the warmth of the place rising up through the roots. And there was an aspect of escape to it. I escaped 'being caught' (though the worst that would have happened was that I would be asked to leave). It had all the ingredients that a circular tramp around my local nature reserve lacks.

One of the earliest writers about leisurely exercise of this sort is the essayist, philosopher, journalist, art critic and painter William Hazlitt. Born in Maidstone in Kent, he was educated and brought up in all manner of places in the UK, Ireland and the States. He went on to become one of the most important writers of the Romantic period; he knew all the doers and sayers of the time. He was always writing to the moment, on any issue of the day, sensitive to circumstance, like an exposed nerve.

One of his most overlooked pieces concerns the importance of walking and exercise, and it could have been written for runners.

'On Going a Journey' was first published in 1822, and surprisingly, given the number of insights that he captures perfectly in a series of small turns of phrase, it's an essay often ignored by Hazlitt scholars (it goes practically unmentioned in the major biographies,[2] and isn't included in modern editions of his essays).[3]

He covers many aspects of what solitary running might be: 'When I am in the country, I wish to vegetate like the country . . . I go out of town to forget the town and all that is in it.' He doesn't like to socialise while he exercises, because he likes either to be 'entirely myself, or entirely at the disposal of others; to talk, or be silent, to walk or sit still, to be sociable or solitary', and not do either in half measures. Those who confuse walking with socialising may think they are doing the same 'walking' that Hazlitt is talking about, but they are not. He argues that 'In setting out on a party of pleasure, the first consideration is always where shall we go to: in taking a solitary ramble, the question is what shall we meet by the way.' Here, the wonderful aimlessness of the best runs is captured.

I once set out from my home in Lewisham to run to Walter de la Mare's birthplace in Charlton, simply because I like his ghost stories, and I felt the urgent need to outrun the perimeters of my knowledge. It was a 15-mile run that took in numerous parks and suburbs, as well as the weird interstellar stillness and silence of the Thames Barrier. When I turned the corner on de la Mare's street I saw the typical large Victorian semis. I counted the numbers as I went along, but when I got to his, I discovered that where the house should have been was now a run-down council block. The house must have been bombed in the war. The sheer fun of this became a feature of the run, and it didn't matter at all that the thing I'd set out to see wasn't there, because the thing I'd really intended was to go on a journey and glide by the world.

Hazlitt also proffers a warning against trying to explain one's motivations and experiences. Explaining things only makes a 'toil of pleasure'.

> You cannot read the book of nature, without being perpetually put to the trouble of translating it for the benefit of others. I am for the synthetical method on a journey, rather than the analytical. I am content to lay in a stock of ideas then, and to examine and anatomise them afterwards.

This is all sense-making stuff. Many a solitary runner or rambler would agree with these sentiments. I want him on my team.

But the truth is that when Hazlitt wrote these smart lines he was in the grip of unimaginable turmoil and was desperate for escape.

He was in his early forties and in the sway of an infatuation so extreme that it would bring him to tears as he wrote (as sensitive as an exposed nerve in his personal life, too).

On the 16 August 1820, Hazlitt was staying in a Holborn lodging house and was brought breakfast by a daughter of the house, Sarah Walker. In a matter of days, Hazlitt's life was turned upside down. In the next couple of years, he would seek a divorce (exceptionally rare at the time, because in England only an Act of Parliament could dissolve a marriage). His wife agreed to become a false witness to an act of adultery in Edinburgh, so that divorce could be filed there. A stupendous extremity of emotion drove him to lure, test and stalk the new Sarah. He even got other people to try and sleep with her to test her devotion to him, a depth of devotion that he had all but imagined. He wrote a book about his infatuation.[4] He published it anonymously, but his many political enemies soon identified all parties and criticised them loudly.

At the end of 1821, John Tomkins arrived at the boarding house, and Hazlitt immediately recognised a rival for Sarah's affections. Consumed with petty jealousies (which turned out not to be so petty in the long run, because she went on to live as Tomkins's wife for decades), lurching between misery, frustration, happiness, belief and fulfilment, Hazlitt decamped from the Walkers' boarding house to Winterslow in Wiltshire. And this is where and when he wrote 'On Going a Journey'.

The essay suddenly takes on a completely new hue. The voice belongs to someone desperate for freedom, to get away from the town and all its associated troubles – to escape from himself. Hazlitt emerges from the story chaotic and bruised. He got his divorce, married a woman whom he thought was rich, but turned out not be. He never really recovered from the infamy of the Sarah Walker infatuation and died a few years later in 1830.

No wonder that Hazlitt exercised to escape such worries. For him, it was an essential component of feeling free.

With a careful eye, one can see the reflections of Hazlitt in Virginia Woolf's 'Street Haunting – a London Adventure', her 1930s paean to walking and movement. Under the guise of going out in search of a pencil, Woolf sets off in the full knowledge that what she is really doing is an excuse for an aimless ramble through the city. Like Hazlitt, she talks of the freedom of sloughing off one's repressive identity and plunging into the anonymous mass of London and Londoners. Our houses and homes, with all their belongings and carefully chosen fittings and ornaments, are carapaces. Our possessions are weighed down with the ballast of memories and associations that define us; all this we break free from when we head out into the fray. The great pleasure and adventure that is movement is also freedom and escape.

I would say that these are the best two short pieces on walking and why it matters. But the case for the prosecution might be tempted to retort that Hazlitt's essay was written during what may have been the lowest and most emotionally tumultuous time of his life. And didn't Woolf suffer all her life from crippling depressions, so extreme that she committed suicide? The prosecutor might continue, citing other famous literary walkers who were far from happy, such as John Clare, who spent much of his life in and out of asylums for the insane, or Thomas Hardy, who lived a long life, but spent a good deal of it writing the most depressing novels ever written in any language and the darkest poetry that the world had ever seen. Nature, movement and the environment make you utterly miserable, the prosecutor might say. The evidence speaks for itself.

The defence might say that the evidence is circumstantial: despite the personal lives of these virtuosi, it seems that access to nature provided essential sustenance to their creativity and wellbeing, and that without it they couldn't have written a word or indeed coped with the world at all. They wrote about the environment because it was the cornerstone of their being and of their creative and imaginative lives. Without access to open space, without the taste of freedom that only lungfulls of fresh air can provide, they would have stagnated – been lost into a dark pit of morbid tendencies. And we would be without the fruits of their work.

Virginia Woolf's father, Leslie Stephen, was also quite the mover. He was a fan of the walking tour, ascended the Matterhorn, and also contributed to the genre of the pedestrian essay. 'In Praise of Walking' (1902), like others in this genre, is about the rather ponderous and serious matter of amusement. He claims that 'walking is the natural recreation for a man who desires not absolutely to suppress his intellect but to turn it out to play for a season'.

Stephen was an esteemed man of letters, a lynchpin of nineteenth-century intellectual thought – his wide circle of friends included George Eliot, Darwin, Henry James, Thomas Huxley and Hardy. He was the founder of the *Dictionary of National Biography*, an essayist, editor and philosopher. He was respected, urbane, smart; he even had a long respectable beard. But he was a bad boy when it came to trespassing. Stephen despised the frumpery of the 'wooden liars' – the notices that proclaim 'Trespassers Will Be Prosecuted'.

When I go out on the tramp, through parks, fields and vales (and yes, school grounds sometimes, too), I know that I am exercising my freedom to do so. Trespassing is by no means an essential component, but it is the fast-forward to feeling like you are roaming free, playing at life, bunking off from the rules.

The adventurous spirit does not always work out for you, though.

I attempted an escape recently, after a long day of meetings and spreadsheets. My head felt like it needed the promised empty space of an unknown landscape or an unopened book. So on the way back to London, I stopped off at the market town of Faversham in Kent.

The sun is the whitest it's been all year. I slip on some spindly 'barefoot' shoes that I keep under my car seat for such emergencies.

The first couple of hundred yards by the creekside are blissful, but the path soon has other ideas. It comes to a dead halt and then I am in an alley which suddenly ends. Next I am dodging some kids playing football on a rectangle of grass by another car park. Concrete-panelled fences and tall white vans are not what I had in mind. Had my glance at the map been insufficient? Just when I am about to turn back to my car to get my GPS unit, I find the footpath. It takes me round the back of some industrial buildings and just as I turn south to rejoin the creek I feel a swoop of disappointment. The path is blocked by a big steel gate with cows and their calves all pouting at me. Can I push it open and shove them aside? I am stepping up to do just this when I notice that I have excited the entire field. Never have I witnessed such bovine sauciness. More of them come running from all angles. I must possess the kind of looks that cows find irresistible: so keen are they that they start trying to climb over one another to get a piece of me. I am worried that they might cause one another injury, so I back off, into another field and away. At this point I am only half a mile into the run, and the rest of it seems to last for hours.

I pinball around the landscape, coming up against at least eight dead ends, literally running down blind alleys. I give up the run when I accept that I am lost, running north, south, east and west, to work my way back. When I find myself scrabbling on all fours out of someone's clunch pit to be told that 'Trespassers Will Be Prosecuted', I feel like kicking the sign over, but 'barefoot' shoes just aren't up to this.

I give up and follow the sun back to my car.

Trespass is not always the cheeky fun it's cracked up to be.

Laws of trespass and egress vary substantially throughout the world. In the UK, despite what the many signs may tell you, you cannot be prosecuted for trespassing in order to look at a view, pick primroses or cut a corner across a field. You can, however, if you trespass on the railways or land belonging to the Crown, or are after a free pheasant for your dinner. Reasonable force may be used to eject you from someone else's land, but only if you are refusing to leave it.[5]

Since 1623's Limitation Act, trespass in the UK has been a civil matter. Until the last century, all that was necessary was that you disclaim any title to the land, explain that the trespass was involuntary, and tender any appropriate amends for damage caused.

Leslie Stephen's 'Sunday Tramps', a group of byway surfers that he led for 12 years, included figures like the novelist George Meredith. Over the weeks, months and years that the group met, one of the constant topics of conversation, and the subject of consequent actions, were the signs that warned 'Keep Out'. Stephen practically sought them out. When challenged, the group was organised to adhere to the Limitation Act's edicts, proffering a shilling to make amends for any damage caused, leaving the landowners (rather than the walkers) with nowhere to go.

Stephen and his merry men were stalwarts of the establishment. For them, trespass was made easier because of their class, but this didn't apply to all.

In Elizabeth Gaskell's *Mary Barton*, the mill hands are eager with curiosity and the desire to improve themselves:

> There are botanists among them, equally familiar with either the Linnaean or the Natural system, who know the name and habitat of every plant within a day's walk from their dwellings; who steal the holiday of a day or two when any particular plant should be in flower, and tying up their simple food in their

pocket-handkerchiefs, set off with single purpose to fetch home the humble-looking weed.[6]

Despite such warming sentiments, the lower orders were seen less as trespassers, more as poachers. In the early twentieth century, numerous cases were brought against ramblers (not all the plaintiffs won) after they had been roughed up, threatened or in some cases shot at. The spring gun, a contraption that used a trip-wire to set a gun off with the intention of maiming the legs of ramblers, was still in use in the 1950s.[7]

In his recent book on the poet and critic Edward Thomas, Matthew Hollis has suggested that it was a brawl with a gamekeeper that played perhaps the most significant role in sending Thomas to his death in the First World War.[8] One morning, while Thomas was visiting his friend Robert Frost in Gloucestershire, they went strolling in some woods to which Frost believed he had right of access. A bullish gamekeeper saw them off the property, but the pair were angered at being threatened at gunpoint and treated like criminals. Later, they went to track the gamekeeper down, but he was gone, so they sought him out at home. Frost gave the man a dressing down at his front door, and as he walked away, the gamekeeper took down his 12-bore from above the lintel and took aim at Thomas, whose instinct was to back off. This quite normal reaction Thomas saw as a shameful spinelessness that he never recovered from. Although it is more complex than this, part of what sent the poet into the Great War was the driving need to prove to himself that he was not a coward. He died proving it.

It was in a similar climate that the National Parks and Access to the Countryside Act rambled through Parliament at the end of the 1940s, as part of that gamut of legislation that saw the biggest share-out in the history of Britain, with the creation of the National Health Service and the Welfare State, and the nationalisation of the mining industry and the railways. The Act has left us with more footpaths and rights of way than anywhere else in Europe.

Much like John Ruskin before them, Tory backbenchers worried that their countryside would not survive the onslaught from the townsfolk that did not understand it.[9] But this was nothing compared to the waves of political and public support that there were for the proposed opening of 12 National Parks and the recognition of Long Distance Paths. It all seems like a different world from today's parliamentary buffoons who try to sell off our forests to venture capitalists eager to invest in property of any kind as long as it makes money.[10]

In the US, trespass laws change from state to state (contrary to popular belief, Americans can't shoot someone for trespass alone – although in Texan law it is a last resort for those refusing to leave). A trespasser in the UK has to intend to do it in order to be guilty of a civil offence, but not in Australia. In the Philippines you are likely to be fined. In Nordic countries (Estonia, Finland, Iceland, Norway and Sweden), you are able to walk across land, camp (as long as it's temporary), boat on someone else's pond, even pick wildflowers or mushrooms – all as long as no harm is done to the land or the wildlife. These countries have no history of feudalism, and so their use of the land is not hampered by the same historic hierarchy of power and land ownership as the rest of Europe. But Scotland is also blazing a trail. In 2003 the Land Act (Scotland) was passed, and it too permits universal access (including to inland water) for educational and recreational purposes. It is only a shame that this ruling does not extend south of the border, for what is more important than education and recreation?

Trespassing, the right to roam, the bid for freedom, the need to feel mobile and unencumbered, all are where the track-markers between running and politics meet.

NATURAL RESERVE AND THE M25; WALDEN, MASS.

When it comes to trespassing, I'm as lightweight as boiled air, a bit like John Clare, who 'always feared the farmer coming by'.[11] The artist Véronique Chance is in a different class.

The first time I saw a work of art by her was at a gathering called RunFest, held at the Slade College of Art. The organisers had aimed to bring together scholars, artists and practitioners who all use or work on running in some way.

I have been to many conferences, but never one like this. They are usually dry affairs. But even a quick glance around the room told me that we were not in Kansas any more.

For one, the delegates (such a formal word) had the lowest mean weight of any intellectual gathering I've attended. The healthy, rosy-cheeked mien was also unusual for academics. Neither had I ever seen a gratis tray of choc-chip muffins last an entire morning, to be cleared away at lunch, uneaten.

As I moved through the building with its institutional art deco architecture, I climbed flights and flights of stairs graffitied with messages like 'RUN, don't walk'. Then, using all my body-weight to wrestle open a swing door, I arrived. I pointed out my name badge. 'Is that Why-bar?' someone asks.

The programme is packed with a variety of activities, games and performances, more carnival than conference. There are delegates in shirt-and-tie, T-shirt-and-shorts, and full running-garb, and even a couple in what I hope is fancy dress.

When I walk into the foyer, the walls are covered in photos and artworks. One is a huge OS map (probably more than two metres square), denoting in motorway-sign blue an orbital run tracing the M25. There are a few pictures along the route. My first ungenerous thought is 'But didn't Iain Sinclair do the book and the movie of that?'[12]

We are called to gather in a white, sky-lit garret for the first lecture of the day. Paint-stained chairs are scattered about the room. There are skeletons in one corner, a 'history of jogging' exhibit in another, the walls are covered in artworks, photographs, paintings, collages and video installations. In another corner, a speaker is spitting white noise and I wonder if this is part of an installation commemorating the auditory loneliness and isolation or sensory blindness of the long-distance runner, a sound map of the disappearance of the outside world experienced only through endurance. I think this is rather good until I later discover it's just static from the knackered audience-mic.

Throughout the day the variety of talks and presentations is impressive. There is the runner who ran her first 10k over a bet with her brother. Bitten by the bug, she now competes all over the world in ultramarathons and endurance races in the Sahara and the like. There is the Asperger's runner who 'took up sprinting at 32 and no other fucker in the country has done that'. She gives one of the day's most enthusiastic and perfectly delivered presentations, explaining why she doesn't belong with other runners: 'I've got no interest in running a long way. You can't go flat out for 5k, so it's boring.'

There is also a talk by Véronique, who ran and catalogued a remarkable 150 miles around the M25, and I realise what a misjudgement I had made – it was not in the least what Iain Sinclair did. It wasn't the distance she covered, but the gall of it.

A couple of weeks later, in the clatter of a coffee shop, we meet and she tells me about *The Great Orbital Ultra Run*.

Her work often employs video and technology to record her adventures, when she is inclined to step out and confront the world. *A Winter Landscape* (2009) is a six-screen projected-video installation that follows the dual eye view of the runner as she works her way through a harsh Canadian winter. With so many screens, it is at first difficult to work out if the images are all concurrent or compiled. Is the person being chased? Are the cameras even attached to a person? Once the questions settle, the multiple rhythms of the breathing become hypnotic, even somnolent, like certain kinds of music. The effect is a disruptive one that interferes with the idea of viewpoint. After all, it is our whole bodies that move through space when we run, not just our eyes.

For *The Great Orbital Ultra Run*, Chance still pushed the technological and creative potential of using mobile cameras and audio equipment. The cameras that she was wearing not only tracked her on GPS, but took a still image every 30 seconds that was then broadcast live to the Stephen Lawrence Gallery at the University of Greenwich. The cameras went off whether she was striding fields or asking directions at a garden centre.

When she spoke at RunFest, her talk was so mesmerising that I missed most of it. The automatic images flashed up on the screen, superimposed over a slow-tracking GPS animation of her on the M25, and I was wondering, what is the work of art? Is it the run? Is it the presentation? Is it the spectator's experience of watching the live run? Is it those blue marks drawn in the map? Is it the other installation piece, which has all the photographs crowded vertically onto a similarly large map, as a kind of orbital book?

One of the things that I really like about her work is its lack of vanity. The cameras are always looking outwards and away; they focus on the experiences that we all share.

She tells me that she came up against numerous obstacles. She also tells me about sinking into a peat bog as she tried to negotiate something that she thought was a stream. She sank further and further in, past her ankles, up to her knees, her hips and nearly to her waist, when she caught hold of an overhanging branch and was able to lever herself out.

'So, this was towards the end of the nine days?' I ask her.

'No, it happened on the first mile. On the first day.'

Overcoming such a setback so early emboldened her for many days to come. She tells me that the biggest obstacles were not waterways and fences, but the roads. The M25 is not made for pedestrian use or access. On her final day she describes getting to the junction of the A2 and it being so large and bursting with high-velocity metal and glass that she could not even see all the way to the other side of the road. She took a three-mile detour on legs that had already done twenty that day.

I ask her whether there is something about the embodied activity of running that made her bolder, and I wondered if it was something like emotional momentum. 'I think it's that you're always already getting away. But it did change my body. At the end of it, my feet did feel like they needed to run. I couldn't sleep for days afterwards. My legs had developed a muscle memory of running, like a land-sickness after you've been at sea.'

We talk for a while about the range of 'keep out' signs that she had to ignore, and she tells me that although there is the image in the public imagination of the pedestrian warrior, she had to walk a fine line because she did not want to get into a situation where she might have been carted off and detained, leaving her unable to complete the work.

She has an entertaining story about being smuggled through a Tesco distribution depot by a helpful member of staff who was not in the least on message and even gave her a leg up over the fence to help her on her way. But my favourite is when she was running along a byway, a single lane of road, separated from the hard shoulder of the motorway by little more than a grass verge. As she paced along, a car began to follow her. It pulled alongside and its window rolled down to reveal an official-looking man who asked her what she thought she was doing.

Between breaths she replied, 'Er, I'm running.'

Véronique's work is a reminder that we owe it to ourselves to run wild from time to time. Such ideas have a long history.

Wildness, freedom and ideas of trespass have been idealised and argued over since the Romantics, but it was Henry David Thoreau who cornered the market on the subject in the mid-nineteenth century.

Most famous for *Walden*, an account of two years spent living the simplest of lives in a tiny cabin in the woods of Massachusetts, Thoreau's lived philosophy of life was to experience all that it had to offer. An innocent reader of *Walden* may be inclined to think that he lived alone, without contact of any kind from the civilised world for the duration. But I am about to discover that he found the wild not so very far from his local town of Concord.

Thoreau is often berated for the fact that he didn't live in as spartan a manner as the book suggests, but the replica of his hut is there at Walden Pond, and it was not well equipped: small bed, tiny stove, desk, and flute. Even with occasional visits to friends in the diary, this is still a solitary and simple existence.

Concord is a perfect New England town, with its white-panelled churches, Sleepy Hollow Cemetery, and the homes of Nathaniel Hawthorne, Louisa May Alcott and Ralph Waldo Emerson still there on its outskirts.

After a look around its fine bookshop, which detains me for an hour longer than I expected, I set off barefoot on the road to Walden Pond. The air and ground are warm and I'm prepared for a longish run. I'm not sure what I have been expecting, but after only a few minutes, the houses thin out quickly and I reach the Turnpike Road, and a few hundred more yards and I'm at the pond. It's still early, and despite the unseasonably warm weather, there is no one here yet so I cut into the woods. Gnarled twigs and stones take the edge off my enjoyment of the forest, but the strong smell of pine oil, sap, loam and dried leaves more than compensates.

In a late essay on 'Walking', published posthumously, Thoreau explains that real walking is not a directionless amble, and 'the walking of which I speak has nothing in it akin to taking exercise'; instead it is a crusade of thought and rumination.[13]

Thoreau's Walden was thick woodland offset by the light of the glacial pond, but today it has become something quite different.

His notion of Nature was one that could only be sensed briefly: glimmers from another dimension, a Linelander's view of Flatland. Nature was evanescent: momentary flashes of the eternal and transcendent, like the light as it whips and flickers through the black trees I am running between. But the purpose of Walden has changed; or should that be that it has *acquired* one?

In writing *Walden* Thoreau paradoxically tamed the wild place he loved so much. It has become legendary. It brings people like me, not only from miles around, but from other continents, like pilgrims looking for that holy land lost somewhere in the soul. Like me, they hope to find it in the woods, but the woods aren't here.

In the woods, as at Thomas Hardy's house back in Dorset, you can just hear the hum of the road nearby. The bed of the forest is covered in last fall's leaves, dried like brown paper. And therefore beneath them is completely bare loam, because the sun cannot get through to allow grass to grow. Spruce and fir needles elsewhere fall from the canopy and create a soft and springy mattress on the floor that is welcoming to the foot and springs back like firm rubber. Where there is only exposed soil it is like running on a pelt, or skin. I feel microscopic as in my imagination the trees become hairs emerging from the skin of the forest floor, and I am some tiny ectoparasite (which, as a tourist here, is sort of what I am).

On my way back round the pond, the path is forcibly narrowed to less than a metre wide. Rusty iron railings keep me from moving off the path to explore the forest or get down to the water. I am penned like this for hundreds of yards and I am now officially a Linelander, only able to go forward or back. I am on the Walden Pond ride.

Afterwards, I felt like my run was a user error. I understood completely that Walden Pond had to be protected, but in its protection it was being preserved for only one purpose – tourism. A mode of being that demands the one thing that Thoreau despised: obedience. He wrote in his last essay, 'My desire for knowledge is intermittent, but my desire to bathe my head in atmospheres unknown to my feet is perennial and constant.' This cannot happen where there are railings.

A few days later and I meet with Dr Ryan Fong, who is (among other things) a theorist of literary tourism, and we talk about Walden Pond. I ask him about the weird dynamic confluence of past-present-future that exists in such places: what they were, what they are now, and their endowment for future generations. He has written about places like Chatham's theme park Dickens World and 221b Baker Street, a museum commemorating the fictional home of Sherlock Holmes – hyperreal memorials to things that have never existed. So I ask him, 'Is Walden Pond really any different? What's there now would have enraged Thoreau, not that that is such a bad thing. But the place that he was writing about is gone. All that's left is the sunlight, some smells and the feel of it.'

'The lights, the smells and the feel of it, as you say, are precisely the point,' he explains. 'Since the literary tourist is almost always striving to walk, quite literally, into the world of a beloved text. This is an impossible desire to meet, so we capture or make the magic where we can. When we stroll along the places our favourite characters would have walked or stand in the specific locations that inspired our favourite writers, we are seeking out the particular sites where the representational world of the text, the biographical past of the author, and the embodied experience of our own travel all coalesce and meet.'

The blue of the pond that precisely matches the blue of the sky, the noises made by the leaves as they crumple beneath my feet, the bounce of the spruce needles, these are the glimmers of that world where *Walden* and twenty-first-century America congregate.

The end of my run finished with a laugh. The last thing I saw as I made my way back towards the road to Concord was a sign that read: 'Jogging/Running is prohibited'.

Later, when I was flicking through 'Walking' after my run, the irony of the following words was as forceful as a sucker punch: 'At present, in this vicinity, the best part of the land is not private property; the landscape is not owned, and the walker enjoys comparative freedom. But possibly the day will come when it will be partitioned off into so-called pleasure-grounds.'

PARIS

Returning to that hot period for egalitarian legislation, it was in 1948 that the Universal Declaration of Human Rights was first agreed by the United Nations. Commissioned straight after the end of the Second World War, the declaration, consisting of 30 articles (most of which begin with the word 'everyone'), laid out the moral and legal basis by which all countries should treat their citizens. It currently exists in 463 translations and is still hosted on the UN's website.

Freedom is the main concern of the declaration; across its short length, the word is used 14 times. My favourite is clause 13: 'Everyone has the right to freedom of movement and residence within the borders of each state.' And today I am in the city where the Declaration itself was discussed and signed off: Paris.

The banks of the Seine are overflowing. As the tourist boats amble past the Louvre and the Musée d'Orsay, wavelets lap onto the cobblestones, combing the seaweed's emerald hair back and forth in the sunshine. Like the corolla of an eye, Notre Dame's rose window stares me down.

Here on some research business, with a lucky spare ticket I have hitched a ride with my university's summer school, students journeying to spend an intensive fortnight here. Once we reach Paris, we part company – they are off for a lecture at the Pompidou Centre this afternoon, and who knows what other treats in the next fortnight. I wave goodbye, wish them well, and begin my walk across the city.

Hours later, I arrive at my hotel. The last thing I feel like doing is running. Then I go through what is now a process that would be familiar to another lover of Paris, the writer Samuel Beckett: 'I don't want to run', 'I cannot run', 'How can I not run?', 'I shall run'. So I run.

I set out to create my own little *détournement*, the Parisian Situationist term for the mobilisation of one's creativity and movement while mixing that energy with the past and present to make something new.[14]

I step out onto Montparnasse, crumple up my shoes in my hands and start running.

The sun has been hot all day, but underfoot the concrete is quite cool. It is that familiar paving tarmac, with tiny bits of grit in it to give it a foreign twist. The instant I start running, feeling the solid ground beneath, I begin to feel less tired.

I establish a comfortable pace, listen for the right kind of silence from my worn-out feet, and settle into what is going to be a meditative pleasure. I hook round to the Rue du Pot de Fer, where George Orwell stayed in 1928. It is narrow, so no light gets down far enough to warm the grey cobblestones. The dreariness and the poverty that he wrote about while he was here seem long passed.

Dodging into Luxembourg Gardens, I realise my mistake. The pathways are wide and consist of sharp shingle. Few would keep a straight face watching me jiggle in pain on it. I head back for the streets, dancing between couples and kissing-gates.

On the main boulevard, the crowd is thick with amblers, and as I dart between them (all the time trying to eye the unfamiliar ground for dogshit and broken glass), I find myself making snap decisions about which route to take, entirely determined by which lights are on green or red. The optimistic me thinks he's improvising; he's a gay *flâneur*, dancing in the footsteps of Baudelaire; the pessimistic me is not so sure, and the image of a rat in a maze following signals flashes into my head.

On my right, memory is stirred when I look uphill and see the huge-domed Panthéon. In 1851 it housed, among other things, the world's longest Foucault pendulum. These are interesting devices. The original had a weight of 28 kilos attached to a 67 metre-long wire, suspended from the Panthéon's ceiling. When the pendulum swung, it appeared mysteriously to rotate round the horizontal plane (at the rate of approximately 11 degrees an hour). But Foucault's discovery was that the pendulum did not actually change direction. Its rotation was an illusion. It was the floor of the Panthéon that was rotating. As the pendulum slashed back and forth, its fulcrum remained static as the entire world beneath it was turning in space, in a constant state of revolution.

Struck by the magic of this idea, 20 years ago I went to see the pendulum at the Musée des Arts et Métiers. I only started reading in my twenties, so when I got to Umberto Eco's novel about the device, *Foucault's Pendulum*, the number of books I had read was probably still in single figures. The novel cast a spell on me (which I later destroyed when I reread it). I loved the idea of the fulcrum suspended in space-time above our heads, revealing with an atomic honesty the earth's rotation in space. Giddy with the excitement of seeing it, this symbol of constant motion, this miracle of mechanics, I walked into the main room where one of the museum assistants was cupping the pendulum in his hand like a sovereign holding a globus cruciger. With the other hand, he was checking his watch – then he lined up the pendulum with the giant clock face beneath it and set it swinging.

It was my first time in Paris, and I don't know what I was looking for, but if it was a sense of wonder, it was dashed in that moment. The two myths of constant motion and atomic accuracy killed simultaneously. My then partner took a picture of me that lingered in drawers for decades afterwards. In it I was looking at the pendulum, one hand in my pocket, the other hanging awkwardly at my side, with a sort of fixed smile that even a stranger would spot as fake, pretending to a kind of awe at the orb that, only moments before, we had witnessed being lined up and swung. Foucault's pendulum could not even be relied upon to tell the correct time – what could it really tell us about the cosmos and our place in it? I had expected the magic of the universe, and what I got was decidedly small fry and human, a staged experience, a simulacrum.

The UN Declaration reminds us that it is our right to roam free, to *flâneurise* our way around city spaces, exploring the rules of behaviour implied in the complex negotiation of public spaces. But I also wonder if there is something a bit imperious in what the Declaration is trying to achieve and uphold. Its top-down, coercive heavy-handedness surely misses the subtleties of how our freedoms are encroached upon by forces other than state power.

Catching the first scents of the breeze of revolution in the year before the famous Paris student riots of 1968, Guy Debord published *Society of the Spectacle*, a short polemic that worried for our engagement with the everyday, now that the emptiness of modern life was hidden behind consumer commodities and the craving to attain wealth. Our desire for spectacle, he argued, has suppressed the fulfilment that we may find in the everyday. The life of the street has gone indoors to live more privately, and when we need to take to the streets, we take our privacy with us in our shiny cars with secure windows and central locking. Street life becomes a subordinated no-place (or every-place) that always seeks an opportunity to advertise to us in the form of billboards, LCD screens, or the frontages of endless world-brand chain stores, because you are nothing if not a consumer. For these Parisian psychogeographers, wherever the footstep touches the pavement becomes the singularity at the centre of the universe, for in that electrical connection there is life and meaning, time past, present and future.

On the one hand, I'm impressed by Debord's boldness and the way that he and others enabled us to reimagine our relationship with the city; on the other, I am infuriated by their ineptness. For over a decade before 1968, Debord and co. sat about, shoulder-shrugging in their black polo necks, chuffing on Gauloises, theorising away, while the disenfranchised mob idled by their window foraging for meaning. With the streets and boulevards busily spinning beneath the fulcrum of the pendulum, the roar and bustle of the dirty streets and alleys all in constant revolution, why was there so much theorising and so little practice?

Chuck a stone in 1960s Paris and you would hit a so-called psychogeographer, seemingly committed to studying the effects of place on the psychology of the individual.[15] But hunt with a magnifying glass and you would be doing well if you found a work of actual psychogeography from the period. They were all too busy lining up the pendulum, when they should have let it swing. Psychogeography should have been about scraping away at the veneer of the everyday, but at its worst it looked like a pose.

Although I don't have a photograph of the museum assistant's posture, I remember him well, with one eye shut tight like he was aiming a musket. The image of him has stayed with me, I think, because in that moment lies the definition of what tourism is. It is the veneer of travel. A theatrical restaging of something that is always just out of reach. Tourism is travel enframed, and it keeps us away from the reality of places.

George Orwell was deeply suspicious of it. In his essay 'Pleasure Spots', written as the dust settled from the Second World War, he worried for the future of travel. He saw our aspirant ideal of what tourism and luxury should be, and it was one without nature, which denied the present and prevented thought. The ideals of 'pleasure' tourism seemed to be these:

> One is never alone.
> One never does anything for oneself.
> One is never within sight of wild vegetation or natural objects of any kind.
> Light and temperature are always artificially regulated.
> One is never out of the sound of music.[16]

The kitsch of tourism starts to look like the denial of reality itself. In the nineteenth century, writer and art critic John Ruskin had worried about the worker being turned into a machine, but here Orwell's tourist seems less like a machine and more like an empty-headed zombie. Orwell's holidaymakers of the future will find in their leisure hours little to reignite their dulled curiosity: a symptom brought on by their overwork and by so many of the conditions of modern life.

Just as in this essay, Orwell was always committed to meeting the world shoulder to shoulder. Where Ernest Hemingway looked back and reframed his bohemian past in Paris in his memoir *A Moveable Feast* (1960), Orwell's account of low-life in the area that I'm running through, *Down and Out in Paris and London*, seems searingly honest by comparison.[17] Unlike Hemingway, he sought to avoid the stereotypes of the nobility of poverty and wrote the experience of it as it was: grubby, hard, and starved. The newfound energy and metropolitan regeneration in 1920s Paris was not emancipation and wealth-creation for all, but was founded instead upon a bedrock of exploitation that had been around for centuries, Orwell argued.

Hemingway's version of Paris was so romanticised that even he suspected in his 'preface' that the 'book may be regarded as fiction'. Hemingway's time in poverty fed his imagination; it was ink for his pen. The same experience only exhausted, disgusted and fascinated Orwell, who seemed as keen to reach down to the cobblestones to massage their dirt between his fingers. Hemingway, on the other hand, seemed blinded by the romantic moonbeams reflecting off them.

Later in the twentieth century, Debord and friends believed that commodification and commodities became the aspic around real life. I wear shoes nearly all the time, but it is only when I remove them that I realise that when I wear them I touch nothing. Is our resistance to touching the city our way of maintaining a kind of illusion of privacy and disconnection? Perhaps it's being somewhere foreign that makes me so aware that I am feeling the character and texture of the city through the soles of my feet, as much as I am with my eyes. From cobble and concrete to grass and grit, they all feel so new that the ground sparks and tingles. For a second I believe I can feel the neuronal impulses of a netherworld trying to break through the boredom of the everyday.

I had no idea that so many tourists would be drawn to this area. I start taking a long arc of pavement, finding a pathway through the crowd. There are too many people, though. I notice a tunnel of space between the wall and the pavement, and it is only when I step into it that I see it is in fact being used for a public exhibition of cycling photography. I am uneasy doing this, getting in the way of every spectator, trespassing through the complex territoriality of what should be public space, but there's no escape except to keep going – I don't think I could do it if I wasn't running. And then it occurs to me that, unlike practically any other city in the world, Paris is a place where the street is theatre. The cafés that huddle around the corners of the boulevards have seating facing outwards onto the streets, so that even during interval drinks, none of the drama will be missed by the audience.

Uncomfortable at being on show, of getting in people's way, of being so fucking English, I make it to the end of the Parisian tunnel. And in this city of hundreds of exhibitions and things to do, there right in front of me are the students I last saw miles away, across Paris, in the station.

I had figured myself a spectator in this drama, but I was never the one doing the watching; instead I am part of the whole theatre, a recognised bit-part player on the stage, making a cameo appearance in his bare feet. It is a jolt that leaves me in a sort of haze. The only punctuation to this is when I joust by another runner who exchanges a warm smile with me (they don't do this back in London). Her day is getting better, too, it seems.

I later took another Orwellian jaunt to Montmartre (where he worked), and I found that tourism had taken over there, too. The streets were impossible to navigate. The tourists seemed completely undeterred by 'Shop Sex Shop', 'Toys Palace', 'All-In', 'Sexy Shop', 'Cruising' and 'Bistro Cockney'. The pavements were lined with a sort of thick pizza-topping of leaf-mould, so slippery that cyclists' wheels whipped out from beneath them when they tried to steer around the pedestrians, cracking their bones in the muck. The steps to the Sacré-Coeur were so crowded that I jumped onto the concrete banisters and ran up them instead. (I could pretend that I was being an expressive psychogeographer, but it was more play than anything, feeling like Daniel Craig sprinting up crane arms pursuing the bomb-maker, Mollaka, in *Casino Royale*.)

Our time is too valuable and short to be contained within our cubicles and workspaces. To say that movement is political is to rehash what the psychogeographers of the 1960s asserted, but they were correct, it is an inalienable right. We owe it to ourselves to see the world as it can be seen, not to be contained by real or psychological barriers and perimeters. *Carpe diem*, the metaphysical poets of the seventeenth-century said. At the same time, French philosopher René Descartes was famously theorising his '*Cogito ergo sum*' – 'I think, therefore I am.' Well, to me, the truth seems more like '*ergo sum ego sentio moveri*'. While not being quite so catchy, 'I feel and I move, therefore I am' seems much more human.

Touch is political, too. It is when we feel the earth, or even the pavement, beneath our feet that movement becomes desanitised, something dirty and real. It is about engaging with the world as it is, not its shop windows. The very fact that you may get bundled out of a shop if you enter it barefoot is testament to how far you have travelled from being merely a consumer.

Touch, movement, the need to forage, explore and play, these are the things that make us human and make our lives feel real. We do not have a body in the same way that we have a place to live or a bank account. The philosopher Martin Heidegger said, 'We do not "have" a body rather; we "are" bodily . . . we are somebody who is alive.'[18]

At work, manacled to emails, fettered to filing cabinets, there is nothing to lose but your temper, your will, or your marbles. To run is to run against these things; do so and 'you have nothing to lose but your chains', as Marx put it. 'You have nothing to lose but your boredom,' said Situationist Raoul Vaneigem. You have nothing to lose but oblivion, regret and perhaps a little weight.

8.
RUNNING THE STONES OF VENICE: RUNNING, CREATIVITY AND FREEDOM

LONDON AND VENICE

Was the carver happy while he was about it?

> – John Ruskin,
> 'The Seven Lamps of Architecture', 1849

Jog on, jog on, the foot-path way,
And merrily hent the stile-a:
A merry heart goes all the day,
Your sad tires in a mile-a.

> – Shakespeare, *The Winter's Tale*, 1611

Good a thing as long distance running is to a man who is properly trained, it is equally bad for a man who is not trained . . . Take my advice, Chums, and if you would do well on the football field, or win prizes on the running path, begin by doing a bit of running directly the cricket season is over.

> – Running advice from the editor of *Chums*,
> 10 October 1900

Have you ever tried to do something, just to be free of the idea of doing it? Or have you bought something so you wouldn't have to think about buying it any more? Eaten something or had a drink for this same reason? It is a common psychological solution to help control our behaviour. Just taking action quells the cognitive noise created by those unmade decisions that we both want and don't want to make. It reminds me of the conversations I had with environmental psychologists Avik Basu and Jason Duvall, when they told me that our ability to filter out minor distractions (sounds, the flicker of a TV screen, a funny smell) comes at a cognitive price. Like many runners, I had a particular itch to run a marathon, and if I could scratch it, I might be free of it and never have to think about it again.

As I write this, I have just come in from a run round a few miles of South Norwood Country Park at the end of my road. When you run past people, it is like tuning an analogue radio as snippets of conversation fall in and quickly out of focus. A couple of women with some kids on bikes sounded like they were enjoying the rare warmth of spring sunshine, but the only words that I heard were, 'Ten years! And I never knew this was here.' A whole decade had passed by without her or her children exploring her local environment (or at least not this part of it). For me, now, that would be like not having read a particular cherished book or poem, or seen a film, or looked at a painting. It seems unimaginable to me because I am now convinced that running, just like these other things, is an aesthetic experience. It seems bound up with our past selves, those Palaeolithic pioneer-artists that were driven to make figurines or decorative beads, or create cave paintings.

It makes me think of the character Lok from William Golding's *The Inheritors*, a novel which tries to recreate the last days of the Neanderthals, as we see them outwitted and out-performed by their *Homo sapiens* successors. Golding's Neanderthal antihero revels in his body – the first line of the book is about Lok's running. His Neanderthals think with their noses, fingertips and their eyes, and Lok, we are told, has 'clever' feet that he can see and hear with.[1] The very acuteness with which things are described in the novel is indicative of the fact that Lok's world view is gone, and is indescribable to us, whereas the humans in that novel more recognisably see the world as an obstacle to their progress.

I know only too well that distance-running brings out some of the weirdness and the deep history of our bodies. It was this that Golding was trying to get at. The technique he used was to shoot past our species type, and enter the head of a preceding one; by doing this he was able to tell us more about who we are, and how easily we are becoming disconnected from our own lives.

The reason running is such an aesthetic activity is because so much of it happens at the level of the senses. The word 'aesthetic' comes from the Ancient Greek αἰσθητικός (*aisthetikos*): it means 'of or relating to sense perception'. But as far back as Plato the term has always been linked to 'art as experience'.[2] An aesthetic experience is one that fully engages the senses, where your nervous energy *soubresauts* like champagne. Too much of our lives are 'anaesthetic': a psychological numbing to sensory information that the world pitches at us.

In the fifth dimension of cyberspace, we have to compete with hundreds of TV channels, instant news, the torrent of emotional complexity that is routed via social media. Even as we move through the city on the daily commute we are constantly under siege from this clamour for our sensual attention – we live embedded in an ecology of interruptive technologies.[3] So we try to switch off. We do not smile at the strangers we see. We try to avoid the thousands of adverts placed before our eyes. We are so exhausted by it all that in public places we cannot even bear to look up from our phones for fear that someone may talk to us. And the anaesthesia continues as we outsource our memories to our phones, outsource our diet to supermarkets, outsource our friendships to Facebook, and our love lives to dating sites. Each technological revolution brings with it some subtly new form of alienation from what it might mean to be human. But there are other things about us that cannot be outsourced so easily, that we have free access to, once we clear the decks of cognitive noise and distraction.

BLACKHEATH, ETC.

An excited horde is gathered round what the Romans called Watling Street in Blackheath, the road that links London with the Channel ports.[4] They have built up to this for weeks and months and years; this is their big day. Today they will be measured and judged.

I could be talking about the Peasants' Revolt of 1381, when Wat Tyler demanded of the king that 'parks and woods should be common to all'. Blackheath was their rallying point, and although the rebellion failed it was the beginning of the end of serfdom in England.[5] The name of Blackheath is believed to derive from its use as a burial pit in the mid-fourteenth century during the Black Death. It was also the site of Jack Cade's Kent Rebellion of 1450.[6] And shortly after that it was where Cornish rebels camped in readiness for the Battle of Deptford Bridge.[7] In the eighteenth and nineteenth centuries oak trees were felled so that monstrous gibbets could be planted. Instead of today's lampposts that line the road, there would have been the distended corpses of convicted highwaymen, eyes pecked out, swinging in the breeze on their ropes as a warning to their fellow criminals.

But, of course, most of us are familiar with this place because it is the starting point of the London Marathon, and that's why I'm here. But I am not where I am supposed to be.

My motives for running a marathon had changed a lot in the previous few years. They had diminished to curiosity: no longer persistence hunting for a new personal life, I now found myself in the ludicrous position of training for months and raising a few thousand for charity, all because I wanted to see if I could do it.

I had not run in any races, no Parkruns, no fun runs, no 5ks, 10ks, or ks of any description, since school. But, there was something about running the marathon in 2012, the year the Olympics came to town, that seemed special enough to break my long run of not running. Fate, though, had other plans for me.

I applied for a charity place, was accepted, paid my deposit and began fundraising for Asthma UK.

The training was, as everyone tells you, long, hard and time-hungry. Getting up early to prise in runs before commuting and teaching for the day was not easy, but I quickly found that I wanted to run for the charity as much as I did for myself.

At a gathering of runners supporting the same charity we had been told that of all the runners that make it to the start line on the day, over 99 per cent make it to the finish line. The real battle was to make it to that start line.

I always felt anxious when preparing to run a distance that was new to me: but as I clocked up 16-, 18- and 20-mile runs, I began to feel a little more assured that, in a month's time, I might do it.

Towards the end of any distance-training for a race, there is a period called the taper. In that time, the body takes the opportunity, during a lighter training period, to repair and strengthen itself after the battering of those long final runs. For the majority of marathon novices, it is not until the day itself that they get to run 26.2 miles for the first time.

During my taper, I followed my plan, paring the distances back as required.

Then, about four days before the race, my asthma suddenly took a dip. This was the spitting rain before the storm. What would follow was a cold, and because of my asthma, that would probably pass the baton on to a chest infection. I hadn't had a cold all winter, so this was it. Competing while suffering from a cold can lead to all sorts of complications. Even a mild fever that raises your body temperature by less than one degree puts you into a heat deficit before you've even begun the race. Your cooling system is less effective and the result can be heat exhaustion, collapse, or worse.

Perhaps it was just nerves? But the next morning, my asthma sounded like someone was flying a miniature drone nearby. And the morning after that, it sounded like someone dragging a corpse across gravel. I started stacking up on my medication: doubling salbutamol and antihistamines, quadrupling budesonide.

I didn't know this at the time, but our body's natural anti-inflammatory response to heavy exercise and endurance training is to release a small protein called Interleukin-10. The extremity of the body's response leaves the immune system weakened against both viral and bacterial infection. To add to this, the cortisol produced by the intensity of the training is, likewise, a contributing factor in the weakening of one's immune system.

The day before the marathon, I was no better. All I could think about was the number of well-meaning people I had let down. I could cope with telling my family that I had been forced to withdraw, but my colleagues? The students that had sponsored me? My physio, Kev, who had batted me through so many mini crises with a wave of his arm and a 'You can run again tomorrow, don't worry'?

On the day before, I walked up to Blackheath with my mate Huw, a recovering soap-actor. We strolled about in the sun. And I finally admitted to myself that I wasn't doing the race when we went to the pub and Huw bought me a pint of Guinness and we sat down to commiserate. This is not the kind of carb-loading recommended on the day before a marathon.

Later that afternoon, I phoned my mum, my sisters and a few friends. All were kind. Early that evening I went on to the London Marathon website to formally withdraw, but I had missed the deadline that permitted me to pull out with a guaranteed place the following year. I had failed at withdrawing, too.

I went to bed, bitter, sad, and trying to be angry with myself, if only because I needed to blame someone for the utter stupidity of it.

With the sun streaming through the window, I woke before six. I took my inhalers and lay in bed thinking.

'You can do it next year . . .'

'But, you struggled to get this far.'

'What if you get injured earlier in the training?'

'You might never get this close again.'

'If I left the tracker, I could jog along for a couple of miles, very slowly, and enjoy some of the support, so at least there's something to be had from the day. Climb over the barrier after a mile or so, and job done.'

I got up, trying not to disturb Adam, and got ready. I couldn't eat anything so had a coffee and idled about in the flat. I continued planning; I would wear my heart-rate monitor, and run so slowly that I never got over 130 beats per minute.

An hour or so later, Adam came to find me.

I explained my plan, which he thought wasn't a bad one, and he rushed to get ready to walk with me up to the start line. At the time, we lived about a mile away.

He would liaise with another friend, Siân, who would meet me at about the mile-five mark – near the Chunky Chicken takeaway. Adam would make his way to Deptford, and if I got that far, I would meet him there, or call him if I dropped out.

In the park, I take repeated hits of my inhaler before handing it over to Adam. I begin to make my way through the thousands of people, but I don't go to my allotted starting point (it is not fair to make thousands of runners overtake me when it is my deliberate plan to go as slowly as possible). So I lever my way to the back of a queue of about 35,000 people and huddle myself in between the people in rhinoceros costumes and a TARDIS with two little legs popping out of the base. Thirty-five thousand of us, all lined up with our 35,000 excuses ready to account for our not doing well, or doing well despite our excuses (it's a runners' thing, this).

The atmosphere is tremendous and when the gun goes off we all take a step forward and then stop. Then we wait, take another step, then wait, and wait. After a few minutes we take another step and break into a walk. We shuffle along for 20 minutes or more. And by the time I make it to the start line there are nearly 30 minutes on the clock. As I had done on my training runs, I skull half a litre of water in one go and toss the empty to the kerb, where it joins thousands of others.

I had been advised by the charity to emblazon my name onto my shirt. I was reluctant at first, and even considered a pseudonym, but then came round to the idea.

Almost as soon as I cross the start line, someone shouts 'Come on –' there was a pause – 'Veeebarr!' It sounds like a question. I smile and nod but feel guilty knowing that I don't deserve the encouragement.

I eye my Garmin: 131bpm, heart rate is already spiking. *It's the excitement*, I think. We loop out east from Greenwich towards Charlton. The run-traffic is quite thin, and as the three streams that separated the starting-rush join further down the route, we are so far behind that the number of runners barely increases.

At about two miles, I realise how very hungry I am. I didn't eat breakfast because I didn't feel like it. Now I am starving. Some spectators bring treats for the runners, so I start plunging my hands into their bowls of Starburst and thrust them at my mouth, like an Oliver Twist who has been given 'more'.

On the shallow climb towards Charlton, I pass a guy in his twenties. He's completely barefoot, so I wish him good luck, and think *respect!*, as I pass wearing my little shoes. He is going so slowly. His feet don't look hardy, and he doesn't have those fillets of muscle around his lower legs that barefooters often have. Their feet look different, too: their intrinsic muscles develop and, for example, push the big toe away from the others – and their feet get a little shorter and wider as the muscles develop. His look long and thin.

I plunder a few more bowls of Smarties and Haribos and at around mile five, I see Siân, outside the Chunky Chicken, as promised. I have to run up to her, waving my arms about, before she sees me in the wide empty road.

'Tell Adam I'll meet him at Deptford. Get him to bring fooooood!'

My heart rate stays steady in the 130s. People are already walking. I imagine these are charity runners who have found themselves in a similarly unfit situation and are turning out for their organisations and their pride. I pace along feeling fine. We pass through Greenwich and by the *Cutty Sark*. As I run along the route, the noise levels seem slowly to climb.

Overtaking runners, I notice the massive variety of body shapes: short, tall, thin, skinny, podgy, fat; symmetrical runners, linear runners, and those whose gait makes them look like they are whipping up a soufflé. Why don't running-shoe manufacturers celebrate these runners' efforts and achievements?

At around the seven-mile mark in Deptford, against the odds, I see Adam from a distance in the crowd.

'Are you done?' But he can see from my face that I am not, so he continues, 'What about Bermondsey? Shall we meet there, near the tube? Mum and 'Tish [his aunt] are on their way.' This would be about nine miles into the race.

Siân's message never got through – a busy network. 'Food, get me food.'

So off I go, weaving between the shufflers, the chatters and the fancy-dressed. Down the road and into the Rotherhithe curve where more people have spirited goes at my name, and I love them for cheering on strangers like this.

145bpm.

A few miles later I am at Bermondsey and still not quite ready to stop. Adam is there and hands me a roll of sweets.

'I think I'll stop halfway. I'll find a phone box.' (How quaint.) His mum and aunt are just about to arrive, but I can't wait, so I miss them. Now there is no more support from friends, because I've told the people that would have been looking for me that I am not running.

As I turn north onto Tower Bridge, with crowds still roaring, there is no chance of me stopping, yet. With my uncle, my mother and my aunt, I had been here the year previously, and the spectators were five and six deep. My uncle Jim couldn't cope with all the people, so we watched the rest of the race in his hotel room, where he was staying as a guest of the marathon. It was the last time I saw him.

At the end of the bridge the course turns east where the routes kiss. Mile 13 meets mile 23, the runners who are racing 10 miles ahead of us firing off westbound for central London. We must look like a different species to them.

Then I remember that it is only three more miles to Canary Wharf, from where I can get a tube straight home beneath the river.

Through Wapping and Limehouse, the roads narrow, and I get grumpy as I try to overtake people walking four and five abreast. I am not going fast, but it feels like I have overtaken hundreds and hundreds and hundreds of people. Some of the houses are right on the street, and they are hosting support parties.

I start to feel hot. I check my watch: 158bpm. I try not to worry. It's April, but it's sunny, so I wriggle out of the base layer under my vest and roll it up in my hands.

As we turn into Canary Wharf there is a sudden phalanx of support as crowds, several people deep, roar by the roadside. Perhaps it's the height of the buildings but the noise for us slow runners is overwhelming. Then I remember that this bit is a loop within a loop, so in three miles' time I will be back here again and can get the tube then.

It gets a bit quieter again as I work my way south down the Isle of Dogs.

On your first marathon you are advised to do nothing that you haven't done before, except for the distance itself. So you have to get used to the sugary drinks that are served every few miles. You have to be comfortable with your kit, choose only your favourite things. Eat your normal breakfast. You should know how much water you need – learn to recognise the first signs of thirst and respond to them, rather than sticking to a water regimen. This last is a particularly interesting one because more runners are now taken down by hyponatraemia (water intoxication) than by dehydration. The electrolytes in the blood become so diluted that the brain can swell and cause seizures, resulting in blackouts, even death. I'm not over-hydrated to that extent, but I have drunk too much and will need to remedy that soon, or try and hold off.

I look at my watch and am saddened to see that my heart is now in the 160s. I feel like I'm exerting myself, but otherwise I'm OK.

Turning north to go back towards Canary Wharf I pass through a place I know. I think it has the ugliest name in all of London: Mudchute. The crowd is thinner (not surprisingly: 'Hey guys, let's meet at Mudchute!'). I laugh as I see a couple holding a big sign that says 'Because 26.1 would be weird.'

Then, over my shoulder, I hear 'Vybarr!' I never hear my name said correctly out in the wild: they must know me. I have already run past them when I realise that it's Adam, his mum and his aunt. I have to weave back a few yards to them, but my heart nearly bursts with gratitude for their coming all this way. And I suddenly know that I am not going home with them. With only eight miles remaining, I check my heart rate and I tell them, 'I'm going to do it.'

'We knew you were, that's why we came.'

'I'll see you at the finish line.'

In the miles that followed, I do remember thinking, *How could he have known I was going to do the whole thing?* I might not have eaten or drunk properly beforehand, but I suppose the signs were there. I put on all the right garb, I slugged the big bottle of water at the start. I needed fuel; why do that for only a couple of miles?

The crowd support is wonderfully warm. There is an anthropologist (Allen Abramson) who works on running's 'socio-cosmic' potential, its ability to penetrate all levels of class and to insinuate its way into the lives and lifestyles of millions of people throughout the world. And I think of all the money that the runners are raising through this form of mass participation. Since the first race in 1981 it has raised over £750 million – it is the swooping arm of charity reaching deep to help the precariat. Then I realise that what I'm doing is a modern version of classic hunter-gatherer behaviour, using one's fitness as part of a cooperative circle to support and provide.

Going back through Wapping on the other side, I feel for the runners that are still coming through from Tower Bridge. The last miles I remember as being quiet, though I'm sure they were not. I don't remember when it was that my knees began to hurt. I think it was about mile 22. This iliotibial-band problem is what used to take me down after a few miles all those years ago in Brighton – the lateral bend in my knee was unable to take the constant strain and impact of heel-striking. But I know it better now, and I know that the way I run doesn't aggravate it anywhere near as badly as it used to.

I do some emergency gluteal stretches which seem to help. Someone runs over to see if I need assistance. At first I refuse, then I see they have a glob of Vaseline stuck to one of their hands. I take some, and quickly rub it between my toes, then I'm off again. I know that there is no way I am stopping. I have to continue, and if I keep going, it could all be over in half an hour.

'Pain is weakness leaving the body', 'Make pain the fuel for your journey', or 'Pain is temporary, failure lasts forever', the wankers will tell you. No! Pain is not necessary for success, a healthy relationship with failure is. Pain is sometimes just pain and it does not mean anything; it doesn't make you stronger or tougher; sometimes it is just what it is and you do your best to ignore it because you know it will soon be over.

This I manage to do. I know from my Garmin that despite stopping, stretching, and waxing my toes, these are the fastest miles of the race for me, and not just by seconds but by whole minutes. In almost every aspect of my life I have been a slow-starter (reading, education, career, everything), and marathons can now go on that list, too.

Caution drifts behind me like tumbleweed. My heart rate is now in the high 160s, just what I had wanted to avoid, but I've come so far. The quicker I can run, the sooner the pain will stop.

Another bit of advice we were given before the race was that if we saw one of the official course photographers, be sure and smile – it will make all the difference to those mementoes. I mostly succeeded in doing this. But when the photos came through, there was one taken on Birdcage Walk, the last mile, by a photographer that I failed to spot. Neither have I ever seen the look on my face in that photo elsewhere. It is a distorted grimace of pain in which my bottom jaw seems to have collapsed: a cross between Munch's *The Scream* and a surprised Grumpy Cat.[8]

At Buckingham Palace, I turn the corner to complete the final point-2. I pick up my pace (quite how I manage to do this when my knees won't bend, I'm not sure). My lungs are not happy; Pinky and Perky have been squeaking away in my chest for at least five miles.

I see more photographers so try to raise my arms, but I can't even lift my hands to shoulder height, so I look like I'm trying to dance the American Smooth instead of celebrating the end of a long run.

At mile 26.2 I find that, almost by accident, I have run a marathon.

I cross the line, am given my medal and photographed with it. 'Hold it up,' the photographer says. When the photo comes through I look drunk, and am holding the medal the wrong way round. It could be a novelty coaster on a ribbon for all the camera knows.

As I'm processed after the finish line, I have to explain why I've got no tracker, which I'm not quite up to doing. One of the officials feeds me the line that I might have forgotten it, and in defeat, I agree. But then she breaks me the slightly irksome news that I will be timed from when the gun went off, and not when I crossed the start line. My officially registered time is a horrific five hours. (Garmin tells me 4 hours 35 minutes, and 26.93 miles.) It still needles me, even though I know that it shouldn't; after all, part of what took me to the end of the race was the belief that I wasn't actually running a race, and not having the tracker was part of that process. And anyway, I'm not supposed to care about times, but still, I find that I must do – at least a little.

I collect my things, leave a voicemail or two (call-density on the network makes actual connection impossible), and send a couple of texts to my own family telling them I did it after all. Given the communications traffic, I'm not convinced these messages have actually gone, until one comes back from my fellow-asthmatic sister: 'You bloody idiot! [I sort of see where she's coming from.] That's amazing. Well done.'

She was right. By the end, my asthma was really tired of my ignoring its warnings. And although it wasn't an attack, my lungs had clearly had enough. I was too embarrassed to ask for help, given that I was running for Asthma UK, so waited until I got my kit back ('bloody idiot!').

I also know, now, that exercise, through stimulating the hormone VEGF (vascular endothelial growth factor), makes the blood–brain barrier a little more permeable to ease the flow of all the other good hormones released during exercise (BDNF, IGF-1 and FGF-2, for example) – the barrier's job, as we saw in chapter 3, is to keep out the baddies. Exercise when you are ill, and you might be putting yourself at much greater risk than you imagine.

I chugged away at my inhaler, and my asthma calmed again. I was glad that no one I knew was there to witness such stupidity. But I had been so cautious throughout that my watch stats tell me my fastest mile of the race was not the first, but the twenty-fourth.

I climb the steps to the King George VI memorial (very slowly), where I meet Adam and his family and we go and have what I think might be the best pizza of my life, though standing up at the end of the meal was no joke.

As it was during the Olympics, the goodwill in London that day was tremendous. As we made our way home, people smiled and congratulated anyone wearing a marathon number. And years on, when I revisit the less-familiar places that I ran that day, I still find them imbued with the embers of goodwill and support that people shared there.

And it's off my list. One of the first conversations I had at the end of the race was while my legs were being given a rub down by two trainee physical therapists that the charity had provided. 'Will you do it again?' one them asked. Before I had a chance to think about the answer, my mouth said, 'Yes.'

A few years have passed, and I'm not at all sure that I will. I feel free of the curiosity I had about whether or not I could do it. And I'm not sure that the desire for a better time even figures as a motivation. The only thing that might get me back would be the promise of a better experience, a 'personal best'. But I'm not sure that's possible, because nothing could be better than what I experienced that day.

VENICE, CREATIVITY, PLAY AND FREEDOM

When you feel a cliché first take hold it's like the tentacles of an octopus that tangle round you and grip harder than you could possibly have imagined. Well here I am, in the middle of one right now. I am sitting on the southern coastline of Venice overlooking the wide canal of the Guidecca. The sun is setting. I have eaten a fine meal. Sitting outside under an awning, I have watched the world amble by and I have supped at wine that isn't white so much as golden, while I read about the city.

It's a week since the marathon and I'm still not ready to run. When I fold up my book and reach for my wallet there are a few seconds of shuffling before, with a swoop in my gut, I realise that it is in my hotel room, on the other side of city.

I repeat the process of disbelief that I underwent when I locked myself out of my flat in Brighton all those years ago – 'This simply cannot have happened.' Five minutes later, I confess to the waiter, who brings the manager. When I explain, he replies in an internationally understood exclamation: 'Aye, yie yiiiiiie!'

How to make someone believe you when you each share only about 5 per cent of one another's language? I imagine the police being called, and *Midnight Express*, and my family holding vigil at the Foreign Office. But I'm going a bit too fast. In a few minutes we work out that the matter can be dealt with if I leave some security and run back to the hotel for my wallet. That seems a bit more reasonable.

The manager doesn't show much interest in a crusty old copy of Ruskin, but his eyes light up at a camera.

So I'm running through the dusk of Venice because I've handed a £500 camera over to a stranger as imbalanced collateral against a €40 bill. My legs are still really sore.

The three miles or so, there and back, were not my finest running experience. I ran too fast and remember little of it, so focussed was I on getting the business done. But done it was.

My second run was planned a little more carefully.

I had come to Venice as part of an EU teaching-exchange scheme. I'd had to travel just a couple of days after the marathon, and was having trouble making it downstairs (upstairs was fine). When I checked into my room at the liftless hotel I was OK getting to it, but was reluctant to face the stairs again to go out.

For the next few days I taught students about Dickens and the changing conceptions of time in the nineteenth century. I spent the rest of my time chatting to the faculty at Ca' Foscari University about Walter Scott and John Ruskin.

After a few days, I was ready to give the running another go.

Running is underrated as an ethical and efficient mode for *flâneurial* tourism, but many runners on arriving at a new place want to get out there and see what's going on.

I decided that I wanted to run the Lido (where, having stayed too long in the city, the character Aschenbach dies in Thomas Mann's novella *Death in Venice*).

I change into my shorts and pack what I can (phone, hotel keys, travel card), and head out into a crowded noonday sun for the vaporetto (water taxi). I'm wearing VivoBarefoots, very light shoes that will protect me from Venice's unknown pavements. They also have great big holes in the upper so that you can run in water and it just sloshes out again.

The sky looks clear, but the air feels like there's an elemental weight to it. The Frari bells are chiming across the square. It is now that I remember this is a bank holiday. People crowd the alleyways like red blood cells in an artery.

There is no rhythm to find in such a crowd. I've been reading Ruskin and I know it is one of the stonemason's skills, the use of rhythm. It represents the mastery of efficient practice in the use of the worker's energy. But the skiffle rhythm of my own stop-start-dodge-and-run pace is not an easy or efficient one.

Though best known as an art critic, John Ruskin spent a good deal of his profession focussed on the development, happiness, creativity and living conditions of the average worker. At this stage in his career, when he came to Venice, he was particularly interested in the working conditions of the Venetian stonemasons because they played such an important role in the creation of the city's architecture. Unlike the working classes back in Britain who were given mind-numbing labour by their factory owners, he particularly celebrated Venetian stonemasons, not only for their skills as craftsmen, but because they were permitted to enrich the structures of the city's buildings by employing their own creative impulses. The fine and individual detailing, their naturalistic carving, stood as a potent symbol against the mechanisation of British factory workers, whom Ruskin said were simply being 'sent like fuel to feed the factory smoke'.[9]

Over dinner last night I read Daphne du Maurier's short story 'Don't Look Now', and I laugh as one of the people I have to dodge in a tight alleyway is a short old woman wearing a blood-red knee-length thick woollen coat – just as the knife-wielding murderer had done in last night's story. She must be Venetian. Earlier in the week, I was walking with one of the Ca' Foscari lecturers when she stopped to chat to a neighbour of hers. I was dressed like it was the hottest day of the year (which for me, it was). The old fellow gestured at me and joked, 'You must be English, wearing so little.'

Some of the other pathways are quieter, and even in the short time I've been here I know a few routes that are deserted. I don't mind the crowds, though, because I will have to stop for half an hour when I get on to the vaporetto for the island. And besides, while I have no right to feel any different to the thousands here caught up in the trance of tourism, the bloody and sinewy realness of running refuses to let me sleep my way though the alleyways.

Two things create a city, its people and its architecture. For Ruskin, these were one and the same. His love of Gothic architecture is best documented in *The Stones of Venice*, a huge multi-volume work from the 1850s (nearly half a million words). One of the many remarkable things about Ruskin was that he didn't love Venetian Gothic architecture for itself, but for what he saw in it and around it, temporally as well as spatially. Like thinker and historian Thomas Carlyle, the philosopher and social reformer John Stuart Mill, and Charles Dickens, he was wary of the Victorian love of the mechanical. Manual labourers had been reduced to 'hands' that could work in the factory. He was equally wary of 'work'; for workers' happiness the following were necessary: 'They must be fit for it, they must not do too much of it, and they must have a sense of success in it.'[10]

Elizabeth Gaskell's women labourers express the point well. In her novel *North and South*, they proclaim that they have no intention of going into domestic service to be someone else's skivvy. Why would they, when they can sell their labour freely on the open market, in whatever town they choose to live? They are the masters of their own domain: their bodies. The tragedy of this scene is that Gaskell's reader is well aware that these working women have exchanged one kind of servitude for another, as lucrative as it is terrible.[11]

In the increasingly industrialised world of the nineteenth century, Ruskin saw that the worker was being turned into a 'tool', to be beaten and used, blunted, and eventually discarded. Famously, he explains in *The Stones of Venice* that 'you must either make a tool of the creature, or a man of him. You cannot make both. Men were not intended to work with the accuracy of tools, to be precise and perfect in all their actions.'[12] By freeing the worker from his enslavement to the machine, society will yield, with all its imperfections, a productive cell, but more importantly, a contented one.

In his previous work, *The Seven Lamps of Architecture*, in thinking about the rudely ornate aspects of Gothic architecture, Ruskin had explained, 'I believe the right question to ask, respecting all ornament, is simply this: Was it done with enjoyment – was the carver happy while he was about it?'[13]

Medieval 'hand-work' was rustic, rugged, imperfect, unfinished; a signatory expression of the worker's identity, albeit expressed within a specified form. Victorian factory work created, with reliable rapidity, perfectly finished objects, where the mindless machine-operator was merely a faceless conduit towards the means of profit.

The signature had become a stamp.

The other aspect to Ruskin's obsession with Venice was his deployment of the city as a vibrant corrective to Victorian apathy and assumed supremacy. It was a place and a people, both of fading glory. A few years before Ruskin was born, Ludovico Manin, the last doge of Venice, had been forced to step down by Napoleon. The Venetian republic, a thousand years flourishing, was over, and now the city was in decay, too. Like the great Victorian historians, Thomas Babington Macaulay and Carlyle, Ruskin found a parallel for his own times in the past. He hurriedly sketched details from columns, orders and arches, in fear that they would fade and crumble to sand, just as he believed England would. He had already seen it happening in the months and years between his visits to Venice.

Such is the charm of Venice. Its architecture lends itself to melancholy and to death. But its people smile. In the campi the children play, run and scream with a joyful abandon that is much harder to find in the streets of London. For Venetians, the fading buildings are a backdrop to something always beginning.

In later life, Ruskin became obsessed with the damming of a valley in Cumbria called Thirlmere. The reservoir, via a 100-mile aqueduct, would provide water for Manchester's industrial needs. The proposal, and his campaign against it, coincided with those moments when dementia, or at least the loss of his sanity, began to take over. His motives are notoriously difficult to work out: was he conservative or environmentalist? For him, everything had a cost – fiscal, for sure, but other costs could be weighed in the balance, too. So to build a city like Venice, stones must be quarried, woods cut down and energy used, but for Ruskin such a price was worth paying for Venice. Ruskin's anger with the proposed Thirlmere Reservoir was that he felt that Manchester, as it then was, did not justify the cost to his precious Lakes.

In his last years, Coniston was Ruskin's permanent home, so I was curious to see it. But when I went, fate was against me. Some sort of international powerboat time-trial was taking place on Lake Coniston so they coughed, splashed, roared and whistled up and down the lake all day. I went into the house to see the views that Ruskin's household would have seen every day, but invariably blinds were pulled down to protect the furniture. There was a beautiful turret window, though, in one of his bedrooms: a hexagon that jutted out from the room, with one side providing access, and windows forming the other five sides. I went to take a picture of the view, but a woman resembling Mrs Danvers snuck up behind me and said, 'No photographs!' I had hoped to find some clue to Ruskin's manic energy, and his rare empathy for the working men and women of the world, but maybe that is only to be found in his writing. What I mainly felt was guilt at reaching for my camera to take snaps from the very room where he finally lost his mind completely.

The boat ride to the Venice Lido takes about half an hour. I have no map, but I can hardly get lost on an island the shape of a needle. One side faces Venice, the other the Adriatic.

I make my way a few hundred yards to the other side of the island. I see the beach, and a runner doing stretches, but no one else. I smile at him, but I'm a pane of glass. *Ah, I see*, I think to myself, *he's ignoring me, just like London runners*. The pathway is smooth, so the shoes come off.

Onto the sand. I negotiate my way nearer the foreshore where the sand is firmer. There is the soft crunch as shards of shell are ground finer, each step only accelerating the work of time on these flecks' journey to powder. There is no one on the beach. The sun is full in the sky. I must be on the wrong part of the island. I clamber over groynes, making my way slowly along the Adriatic coast. I become convinced that life is elsewhere, that there is something else to see, so after a mile I climb back up the beach, to the road, and to the other side of the island. Is this where everyone is hiding? But no, as I feared, the coast facing the mainland is as empty as the one I started out on.

A yacht whispers into view. It has a few people sunbathing, still as corpses on the dead-calm water, glimmering and silent. Never have I seen the sea so undisturbed, and it is made stranger somehow by the backdrop of Venice in the distance. I turn to make my way back to the vaporetto. I have an idea of how I can continue this run.

I am sort of lost, but I know I'm headed in the right direction – I can see Venice, after all. I feel a sudden urge to record this quietness, made emptier by the sound of my bare feet smooching the concrete. I wrestle my phone from my pocket and turn on the video – but it only records slaps, scene-jerks, and funny breathing. After a mile or so of weaving between beachfront, roads and inlets, I am woken.

Back at the jetty, I run for the vaporetto which is ready to leave.

The first stop is St Elena, on the eastern extremity of the island. On my way in I spied a path that looked like it ran all the way from St Elena to San Marco, the scene of the daily siege of Venice by the tourist horde. Seen from the bell tower of San Giorgio across the Giudecca Canal they look like scarabs attacking a corpse.

There is a game that I have since heard about that some run-commuters play in London: 'Race the Tube'. They exit their train at one station and try to catch it again at the next. I was an early experimenter with a much more middle-class version of this: *Corro la Vaporetto*.

The vaporetto pulls away from the Lido and I am like a dog in the traps wanting to continue my run. The ride back to St Elena is quick. The barrier is lifted and I'm out of the boat. I dodge my way down the landing jetty, take a sharp left and I'm away on the straight while the boat is still taking passengers.

As soon as I begin to run, at a much faster pace, I am immediately reminded of the time when I was eight or so, when on the street I used to see my mother in the passenger seat of our car in her role as driving instructor. The learners, to our amusement, always drove with incredible caution on our empty 1970s streets in south Manchester. I would puff out my chest, straighten my hands to darts like the T-1000, and sprint in an all-out race to the death, leaping over unattended bikes, tightroping garden walls, until either I lost or the car turned off route. It was later explained to me that this wasn't something that the learner driver should have to contend with.

In the first leg of the race I take a clear lead. The vaporetto is slow to shake off its inertia. But then I am suddenly taken off route via an inlet over a bridge, losing at least 40 metres. The vaporetto, with its spluttering wash left behind it, has made good ground and is now out in front, but not by much. I should easily be able to catch it. But then I see another inlet, albeit this time with less diversion. I reach the summit of the arched bridge and see the boat pulling in at Giardini. I keep a good pace and the boat is slow to start again.

My legs have forgotten their marathon last week. We are away. Another bridge to climb towards the Arsenale and each one gets thicker and thicker with tourists whose attention wavers in all directions but mine. Another bridge and my legs feel the climb of this one, but there is a long marbled flat ahead. I let go, pushing hard in the sunlight. As the vaporetto pulls into the stop I pass it again and head towards San Marco. My legs have had enough of this game. Like the crowds, they feel sluggish and inattentive. I pass a thick-haired golden retriever looking very unhappy at being out on a lead in such weather.

The crowd is now so dense, and the canal so busy, that as I glance away and back, I lose the boat in the melee, but I tell myself I've beaten it. I'm sure I will find it again, but there are so many people now that it is difficult to maintain even a walking pace.

I come to a stop outside the hotel where Henry James completed *The Portrait of a Lady* back in 1880. The challenge is over. I wipe the grains of salt and sweat from my face and feel a burning thirst. I remember that I haven't drunk anything for hours. I turn around and retrace my steps to a quieter point at which to catch the boat back. A couple holding hands smile at me, and only then do I realise that it is because I am beaming. I can't quite find the words to say '*Sono felice, non folle.*' (I'm happy, not mad.)

I remember Ruskin's stonemasons who, while they might have had to carve a gargoyle, were at least free to make it one of their own design, and to express their own skills in the process. In the narrow and crowded alleyways, squeezing between pot-bellied walls, and trapped by the ant-colony crowds of Venice, I had not expected to feel almost vertiginously free.

For so long after the marathon, I could not get back into running, and I thought that long run might have killed my interest in it. For years I'd had the nagging desire to do a marathon, and for a while I wondered whether, having satisfied that need, I would now have to find something else. In doing the marathon, had I *done* running? But no, I had listened to the cadence of my feet whispering through the grass for so many hours that it felt as if that rhythm had made its way into my heart.

If the idea of running a marathon was ever a weight, I feel unburdened of it. And I realise that over the years, this is what my running has always been: a gradual process of shedding. My shoes have been getting lighter and thinner to the point where they have practically disappeared. My GPS has gone. I no longer time my runs and I hardly bother to measure the miles any more. And now I have no races to run, either. But there is something else that has changed. The dead weight of unhappiness and disappointment that I carried with me for so long has now receded to nothing.

There is a French word that perfumiers use, one for which there is no English equivalent: *sillage*. It describes the ghostly vapour trail of scent left behind by the wearer. All runners leave an emotional *sillage* behind them, a trail thickly pollinated by whatever it is that they are running away from or towards. Like fingerprints, the runner's *sillage* belongs only to them. But unlike the microscopic whorls, loops and arches of their fingerprints, their *sillage* evolves, slowly and slightly from day to day, and changing altogether over decades. Whatever it was that I was shaking off in my runs has left me.

My running has become something much deeper than a habit or an exercise routine. Now it is part of who I am. It is a part of my personality. I am unsure which came first, or what came from what: am I more self-reliant because of my running, or am I running because I am more self-reliant? The same goes for resilience: I feel like it has taught me how to be in my own company, and continues in helping me to maintain perspective.

As I look back through these pages, I see that the word 'freedom' is used in every chapter. But I am only a little closer to defining it clearly for myself. Many readers will understand that freedom is to be found in the imaginary worlds and ideas that they find in books. That kind of free-range reflection is an essential part of running. And, just like our access to those storybook realms is only temporary, I think that freedom only needs to be fleeting (as it is for Hardy on his 'Wessex Heights'). I can get by for quite a stretch with only the promise of it.

Having spent so much time in the last few days in front of the great Venetian masters, I have realised that, while I have not been freed of my longstanding admiration for Leonardo da Vinci's paintings, I love his drawings even more. Some of the less well-known early designs from the 1480s were not ornithopters, parachutes or war machines, but mechanisms for ripping bars from windows; another could effect escape from within a cell.[14] The invention of these machines looks to be an odd Freudian exercise for da Vinci, suggesting that his greatest fear was imprisonment, and in one of his notebooks he elevated freedom to being 'the supreme gift of Nature'; not elegance, charm, an enigmatic smile, a view, life, the scent of a rose, but 'freedom'.[15] It has no nameable value because it is worth almost everything to us. So I find that in modern life I have to find it where I can. And running's role in providing temporary freedom is that it keeps fresh for me hundreds and hundreds and hundreds of miles of memories, potential and promise, and real, accessible space – wide vistas, long paths, lived lives, and lives yet to be lived. Running has laid down a long open road ahead of me.

The exercising of freedom is part of a promise that we make to ourselves when we feel some sense of what our life is worth. It is a more permanent state than happiness, which is a strange emotion to have as a permanent goal in life. The ancient Greeks didn't even have a word for freedom; instead their closest equivalent was something like *eudaimonia*; it means flourishing.

And for me, these concepts are all part of the same loop: freedom, flourishing and creativity. Just as we can't manufacture happiness, neither can we create creativity, but what I've learned – and this is probably more important than anything else – is that it is within our power to create the environment, the circumstances, the soil in which creativity has an opportunity to flourish.

I think of my dad staring at the telly for hours on end, in his frayed armchair, beside him his TV remote and chessboard, and that felt-lined walnut box of chess pieces whose smell is, in my memory, indistinguishable from him. The highlight of his day was a Fray Bentos pie. His colourful, brilliant, violent and fully lived life was behind him by his mid-fifties. I think of him with no one to play chess with, shorn of wonder and awe, and I know that more than anything, I need running because I want to stay curious. Our curiosity needs to be continually teased out of its shell and into the world. Because it feels like once that goes, everything else follows. Nothing unites us with the world so completely as our curiosity for it.

In an interview recently, crooner Richard Hawley expressed this idea with his typical zeal: 'The minute you close down your radar – not just as a musician but as a human being — you're fucked.'[16] Whatever it is that might keep you curious, hold on to it for dear life. Exercise that capacity, and if that capacity is fructified by exercise, then you're onto a winner.

And I think here is where I shall wish you a farewell, waving at the vaporetto as it chugs away from San Marco, as I turn and flit back into the crowds of Venice, headed I don't know where, breaking into a run.

EPILOGUE

DETROIT

If you want to run, so the myth goes, you only need two things: a body and a place. But we have wandered a long way from the tribes and hunter-gatherers that we used to be, and we don't all have access to the wide open spaces that we once did. Understandably, running remains a hard sell to a populace in the West, of which the majority no longer even know how to stand up straight because modern life has changed our muscles and joints so significantly.

Nevertheless, if marathon attendance and participation is anything to go by, running is on the rise. Sport England have also recently reported a substantial increase in those running at least once a week.[1] More of us doing it can only be a good thing, surely. But there are shadows in the sunshine. Just as with gym attendance and adherence, running is in danger of becoming a luxury, despite it seeming straightforward. It is getting increasingly difficult to enter big-city marathons unless you feel you are capable of raising a few thousand pounds for charity. And the training for a marathon needs time, and time is increasingly one of the indulgences of the better off.

Running is supposedly the most open-access sport activity. It's not that this is a myth, more that running is yet another aspect of our lives that austerity is getting its teeth into.

The health gap is widening as quickly as the wealth one is. In the UK, there are growing inequalities in the levels of physical activity when looked at through the lenses of age, gender, ethnicity and disability. In England, Pakistani, Bangladeshi,

Indian and Chinese men all meet fewer of the recommended weekly physical-activity levels. (As few as 26 per cent of Bangladeshi men and 11 per cent of women from the same ethnic group meet recommended targets.[2]) In parts of Scotland, male life-expectancy ranges from 68 years all the way down to as low 50 in the most deprived areas.[3] In Wales, the bottom 20 per cent of earners are less than half as likely to take exercise when compared with their richer counterparts at the other end of the wage spectrum. The tranche on lower incomes are also twice as likely to suffer obesity.[4]

When I met with Daniel Lieberman at Harvard we chatted about this. He mourned the fact that (perhaps because of absurd farming subsidies) it is 'cheaper to buy unhealthy food than healthy'. He noted that the people who buy running shoes and running gear also have to be fairly well off. 'The average per-capita income of somebody who subscribes to *Runner's World* is pretty high.'

Having seen literally hundreds of runners out on the streets during my time in Boston, I was shocked when I moved on to Detroit. The city has had its problems, and it is without doubt one of the best and most consistently surprising and impressive places I have been to, anywhere in the world. But there were environments in which I was wary of running. Detroiters also strongly advised me against doing so. I thought this might be overly cautious. *I run barefoot in Lewisham*, I thought. So, gingerly I explored some areas, but I never saw a single runner. I know they exist, because I know people there who are in local running groups.

Running should be austerity-free, but it isn't. If you live in those places where people don't run, and you are poor, what are you going to do? Take a train to a place where you can run? But you're poor. Join a gym? But you're poor. Buy some mace (the kind that I was shocked to see available for sale in running stores in the US)? But you're poor. Buy a magazine to learn more about how and where to run? But you're poor. Instead, you could spend less than half the cover price on a soda and a bag of doughnuts.

Running is too important for our bodies and minds, for our sense of identity and self-worth, for our health and wellbeing, and for the environment, for it to be the preserve of a select few. It doesn't have to be this way. We don't need Garmins, Fitbits or Hokas; we are already carrying the technologies we need with us, it's just that the batteries may need a little recharge.

My relationship with technology and running is still changing. I'm not a Luddite, but I'm a bit warier of technology's seductive ways. When I go running I no longer take anything that might interrupt me. My GPS watch has been sat in a drawer for months. It's not just that I don't like being tracked (who does?), but that I don't like feeling aggressively monitored. It's not GCHQ or the NSA that I'm worried about, only that I want to drift when I run, not feel chased by the superego of wearable tech. I don't want to know that I've lost my satellite signal, and that this part of the run in the woods isn't being counted. I don't want my watch to tell me that its battery is getting low, or that I'm in the wrong heart-rate training zone. If freedom is anything, it is surely feeling untethered.

I was recently chatting to someone who works in running technology and he told me that the standard model of consumption with wearable tech is one of constant upscaling. (I suppose he's right – the market for the Apple Watch is only likely to grow.) I did end up with the most expensive and advanced Garmin watch, but I've downscaled back to a pedometer, not because I want to count my steps on the run, but because I live a modern life and am still inclined to inactivity. Because, despite all I've learned, I still sit on chairs, in front of a computer, and watch TV. But I think I do them differently, now. I know better what remedies and rewards I need, and I know too that if I don't want a run, or feel I don't have time for a break, then it is time that I'm short of. If you're too busy to rest, too busy to recharge in the outdoors, too busy to run, then you are *too busy*!

It may deplete you of some muscle glycogen, but outdoor running gives a great deal back to us, and to the places we love. Instead of draining your abilities, running can recharge them by restoring directed attention, by creating new brain cells ready for learning, by releasing all those rewarding neurotransmitters, and by creating a bond between ourselves and the places where we run, bonds that are more complex than anyone can make sense of.

Exercise and knowledge-acquisition are linked at an evolutionary level. Our mind is little more than an organ (the brain) that has, over millions of years of evolution, internalised and fully realised the significance of movement in our body. All of what makes us human comes to us from movement. The chemistry of our whole bodies, our reward systems, our desires and hungers, our innate curiosity to learn, all this comes to us through movement and the desire to find, forage and know. So we may have Achilles tendons and nuchal ligaments and all manner of corporeal features that adapt us for running, but the way we move is part of what our brains have become, too; and as such our brains are constructed to reward our efforts in the short and long term.

We have intelligence because we move. The raised heart-rate of a run floods our brain with the oxygen and glucose that it needs to function well. It elevates self-esteem. It restores chemical balances that cannot currently be achieved through medication. Haptic memories are easier to recall. Aerobic fitness enhances the speed of cognitive response. It increases neuronal connections and dendritic branching in particular (to capture more impulses produced by other neurons). It lowers that hormonal horror cortisol, and so reduces stress. Even our hearts give us something. A substance called atrial natriuretic peptide (ANP) is released during exercise. The more we exercise, the more ANP is released by the heart's muscle tissues. ANP is a powerful dilator, able to penetrate the blood–brain barrier; in animal and human studies it has been proven to have a calming effect. Oh, and it's fun! Running barefoot is more fun than when wearing shoes.

I think the most important thing I've learned in writing this book is that running cannot be enumerated, measured and weighed so easily. What it does for us, what it is, is always something more than what the neuroscientists, palaeontologists, environmental psychologists, biologists, philosophers and poets can say. Long before our senses of sight, smell, audition, touch and taste evolved, it was our ability to respond to space through movement that first developed. It is our oldest sense. Our ability to link motion to reward predates even the limbic system and locates our abilities with those of the very simplest of life forms from over a billion years ago.

The world has much to give us, and all we risk as barefoot runners is encountering a thorn or picking up a blister. Yet it is all too easy to let life pass by in a blur from a car window. There is a busy chemical and hormonal conversation going on out there in the wild. The scents of life we pick up as we glide by are part of a complex communication system between all manner of plants and animals that we can briefly listen in on, if we are prepared to go out on a limb to find them.

It takes me back to that run I did on the mountaintops in the Lakes, where I thought poetry was my guide, but found something else there in the freezing winds, and the drenching rain, and the warmth of my heart. And it is something that I cannot wear, or download, or even write – but we all have it.

NOTES

Introduction

1 Virginia Woolf, 'A Sketch of the Past' (1939), in *Moments of Being: Autobiographical Writings,* ed. Jeanne Schulkind (London: Pimlico, 2002), p. 89.

2 Alexander Gilchrist, *The Life of William Blake* (London, 1863), pp. 6–7. The street is now called Broadwick Street. Blake's family lived at 28a.

3 Muriel Spark, *The Ballad of Peckham Rye* (London: Macmillan, 1960).

4 We are all so plagued by tilting pelvises, contracted hip flexors, hunched shoulders and truncated pectorals from sitting down and bending over a desk that we are no longer able to 'straighten up'. These behaviours have a long-lasting effect. The hip flexors, for example, spend so much of their time contracted when in a sitting position that they actually shorten, preventing full extension when upright and forcing the pelvis to tilt downwards, having the concomitant effect of pulling on the lower back.

5 Guy Debord, 'Introduction to a Critique of Urban Geography', in *Situationist International: Anthology*, ed. Ken Knabb (Berkeley: Bureau of Public Secrets, 1981), p. 8.

6 'Letter to Richard Woodhouse', 27 October 1818.

7 William Wordsworth, *The Prelude*, Book VI, ll. 526–9.

Chapter 1

1 Gilbert White, *The Natural History of Selbourne* (Edinburgh, 1829), p. 199.

2 Quoted in Michael McCarthy, 'The wild, serene Downs fight against protection', *Independent* (10 November 2003).

3   Charlotte Smith, 'To the South Downs', in *Elegiac Sonnets and Other Poems* (London, 1797), p. 5.

4   Thomas Hardy, 'I Look into My Glass', in *Thomas Hardy: The Complete Poems*, ed. James Gibson (London: Palgrave, 2001), p. 81.

5   Virginia Woolf, 'Evening Over Sussex: Reflections in a Motor Car', in *The Essays of Virginia Woolf*, ed. Andrew McNeillie (London: Hogarth Press, 1986).

6   V. Lun et al., 'Relation Between Running Injury and Static Lower Limb Alignment in Recreational Runners', *British Journal of Sports Medicine* (2004, 38), pp. 576–580.

7   *See* Ian Griffiths, 'Overpronation: Accurate or Parachronistic Terminology?', *SportEX Dynamics* (April 2012, 32), pp. 10–13.

8   Daniel Lieberman, 'Strike Type Variation Among Tarahumara Indians in Minimal Sandals Versus Conventional Running Shoes', *Journal of Sport and Health Science* (June 2014, 3:2), pp. 86–94.

9   *See* Allison H. Grubera et al., 'Footfall Patterns During Barefoot Running on Harder and Softer Surfaces', *Footwear Science* (2013, 5:1), pp. 39–44.

10 At the turn of the twentieth century, even Rupert Brooke and his Grantchester Neo-Pagans had the good manners to avoid the trappings of modernity while propounding their commitment to barefoot living. *See* Paul Delany, *The Neo-Pagans: Friendship and Love in the Rupert Brooke Circle* (London: Macmillan, 1987). Virginia Woolf was particularly irritated by the influence of Rupert Brooke over the young men and women walking barefoot in the countryside around Cambridge. She was annoyed by the proclamations 'that there was something deep and wonderful in the man who brought the milk and in the woman who watched the cows.' *See* Virginia Woolf, *The Essays of Virginia Woolf*, 6 vols (London: Hogarth Press, 1986), vol. 2, p. 279.

11 *See* Richard Steele, '*Talia monstrabat relegens errata retrorsum*', *The Englishman* (3 December 1713; 26), pp. 168–74.

12 Daniel Defoe, *Robinson Crusoe* (London: Wordsworth, 1995), p. 126.

13 'Private Correspondence', in *Caledonian Mercury* (17 June 1822). *See also, Bury and Norwich Post: Or, Suffolk, Norfolk, Essex, Cambridge, and Ely Advertiser* (31 July 1811); *Freeman's Journal and Daily Commercial Advertiser* (20 November 1821); and the *Standard* (27 November 1834).

14 He stayed on Abebe Bikila's shoulder throughout the race, but dropped out with heat exhaustion and dehydration. He didn't know about drinking water before a race. He would have won silver if he'd stayed back a little. Bikila ran a phenomenal 2 hours 12 minutes.

15 'Fogo and His Fat Goose', *Bell's Life in London and Sporting Chronicle* (9 January 1831).

16 *Bell's Life in London and Sporting Chronicle* (7 November 1863), p. 7.

17 Ibid. (3 June 1865), p. 7.

18 Ibid. (10 June 1860), p. 6; (31 December 1864), p. 6.

19 Ibid. (28 March 1874), p. 5.

20 'Correspondence: The Best Things to Run in Are Properly Made Running Shoes, Not Boots, Which You Get from Special Makers.' *See Boy's Own Paper* (2 July 1881), p. 648.

21 *The Fishing Gazette: Devoted to Angling, River, Lake and Sea Fishing and Fish Culture* (17 December 1881), p. 624.

22 W. Mattieu Williams, 'The Philosophy of Clothing XVIII', in *Knowledge . . .: A Monthly Record of Science* (date unknown, 8), pp. 242–3. I have Pete Larson to thank for digging out this reference.

23 *The County Gentleman: Sporting Gazette, Agricultural Journal and 'The Man About Town'* (4 October 1890), p. 1402.

24 *Cycling* (11 February 1893), p. 6.

25 The average salary in 1893 was approximately £85. Today's mean salary is £26k. So this comes in at around £100.

26 'The Ring', *The Era* (Sunday, 11 June 1848). The piece recounts a boxer's weigh-in and one of the competitors proffers his running shoes to balance a weight.

27 *See* S.E. Robbins and G.J. Gouw, 'Athletic Footwear: Unsafe Due to Perceptual Illusions', *Medicine and Science in Sports and Exercise* (February 1991, 23:2), pp. 217–24; Steven

E. Robbins, 'Hazard of Deceptive Advertising of Athletic Footwear', *British Journal of Sports Medicine* (1997, 31), pp. 299–303.

28 There is some fascinating work going on in the field of proprioception, and the ways that our ability to perceive the placement of our limbs in space (and in relation to one another) may be disrupted by external as well as internal factors. *See* M. Tersteeg et al. 'Cautious Gait in Relation to Knowledge and Vision of Height: Is Altered Visual Information the Dominant Influence?', *Journal of Neurophysiology* (2012).

29 Robin H. Crompton et al., 'The Evolution of Compliance in the Human Lateral Mid-foot', *Proceedings Biological Science* (22 October 2013, 280:1769).

30 Charles Darwin, *The Descent of Man, and Selection in Relation to Sex* (London: Penguin, 2004), p. 71. For this Darwin lead, I am indebted to Tim Ingold's brilliant paper 'Culture on the Ground: The World Perceived Through the Feet', *Journal of Material Culture* (2004, 9:3), pp. 315–40.

31 Thomas Hardy, *The Return of the Native* (Oxford: Oxford University Press, 2008), p. 57.

32 When I was there, Samuel reported ITB pain within about two minutes. Ten weeks later, he was running barefoot for up to 35 minutes without pain.

33 The company got into trouble because they advertised certain benefits to using their footwear, but without having available scientific evidence for doing so. But they didn't lose the lawsuit; they never went through the expense of a trial and settled it (*see* www.fivefingerssettlement.com).

34 Einstiein's theory of general relativity was put to the test by scientists recently at the National Institute of Standards and Technology in Boulder, Colorado. They wanted to find out if time travelled faster at altitude. With the help of some atomic clocks, they calculated that by getting 12 inches further away from the earth, we would lose 90 billionths of a second off an average 79-year lifespan – so not very significant, then.

35 I walked past a running shop only last night near Parliament Square. A guy was pacing up and down outside the store, trying out a pair of ultra-cushioned shoes as the shop assistant looked on. Ungraciously, I wanted to say, 'If that is the only way that you can run, with these Baby-Spice platform pumps on your feet, then there's something seriously wrong with the way you're doing it. And you're not going to last long.' In that moment, I got close to being the Blackheath lout.

36 Maurice Merleau-Ponty, *Phenomenology of Perception* (London: Routledge, 2012).

37 In the UK, the majority of drugs prescribed are statins, beta-blockers and painkillers. More worrying is the amount of antidepressants that are prescribed: as many as one in five women on a low income is prescribed the drugs. *See* 'Health Survey for England: 2013' (10 December 2014), www.hscic.gov.uk/catalogue/PUB16076.

38 *Exercise: The Miracle Cure and the Role of the Doctor in Promoting it* (London: Academy of Medical Royal Colleges, February 2015).

39 D. Carnall, 'Cycling and Health Promotion: A Safer, Slower Urban Road Environment Is the Key', *British Medical Journal* (2000, 320:888). *See also* House of Commons Library (M. Keep), 'Road Cycling: Statistics' (Standard Note: SN/SG/06224).

40 *See* www.sportandrecreation.org.uk/lobbying-and-campaigning/sport-research/UK-fact-figures.

41 Daniel Lieberman, 'Effects of food processing on masticatory strain and craniofacial growth in a retrognathic face', *Journal of Human Evolution* (2004, 46), pp. 655–77; see also Daniel Lieberman, *The Story of the Human Body* (London: Allen Lane, 2014).

42 One of things often misunderstood about evolutionary debates is that we have not evolved to be healthy, but to have lots of children. So our innate desires are not geared towards a healthy lifestyle, but towards staying alive long enough to mate. Neither is there any such thing as Palaeo

'exercise'. Exercise is only needed in a time and place that lacks an environmental coercion for movement. Modern runners may say that they 'love' doing it, that it means everything to them, but that is only because they do it in a very particular context and environment that doesn't force them to run for the rest of the day on an endurance hunt after their jolly around the park.

43 Dennis M. Bramble and Daniel E. Lieberman, 'Endurance running and the evolution of Homo', in *Nature* (18 November 2004, 432), pp. 345–52.

44 Campbell Rolian, D. Lieberman, J. Hamill et al., 'Walking, running and the evolution of short toes in humans', *Journal of Experimental Biology* (2009, 215), pp. 713–21.

45 Daniel E. Lieberman, Madhusudhan Venkadesan et al., 'Foot Strike Patterns and Collision Forces in Habitually Barefoot Versus Shod Runners', *Nature* (2010, 463), pp. 531–5.

46 W.J. Sanders, 'Comparative Morphometric Study of the Australopithecine Vertebral Series', *Journal of Human Evolution* (March 1998, 34:3), pp. 249–302.

47 D. Lieberman, D.A. Raichlen et al., 'The Human Gluteus Maximus and Its Role in Running', *Journal of Experimental Biology* (2006, 209:11), pp. 2,143–55; and, D. Lieberman, E. Herman Pontzer, E. Cutright-Smith, D.A. Raichlen, 'Why is the human gluteus so maximus?', *American Journal of Physical Anthropology* (2005, 126).

48 Tom F. Novacheck, 'The Biomechanics of Running', *Gait and Posture* (1998, 7), pp. 77–95.

49 Kevin D. Hunt, 'The Evolution of Human Bipedality: Ecology and Functional Morphology', *Journal of Human Evolution* (March 1994, 26:3), pp. 183–202; I.S. Curthoys, R.H. Blanks and C.H. Markham, 'Semicircular Canal Radii of Curvature (R) in Cat, Guinea Pig and Man', *Journal of Morphology* (1977, 151), pp. 1–15; F. Spoor, B. Wood and F. Zonneveld, 'Implications of Early Hominid Labyrinthine Morphology for Evolution of Human Bipedal Locomotion', *Nature* (1994, 369), pp. 645–8.

50 M. Bianchi, 'The Thickness, Shape and Arrangement of the Elastic Fibres within the Nuchal Ligament from Various Animal Species', *Anatomischer Anzeiger* (1989, 169), pp. 53–66.

51 Peter Wheeler, 'The Thermoregulatory Advantages of Hominid Bipedalism in Open Equatorial Environments: The Contribution of Increased Convective Heat Loss and Cutaneous Evaporative Cooling', *Journal of Human Evolution* (1991, 21), pp. 107–15. *See also* Leslie C. Aiello and Peter Wheeler, 'The Expensive Tissue Hypothesis: The Brain and Digestive System in Human and Primate Evolution', *Current Anthropology* (1995, 36:2), pp. 199–221.

52 *See also* M. Cabanac and M. Caputa, 'Natural Selective Cooling of the Human Brain: Evidence of its Occurrence and Magnitude', *Journal of Physiology* (1979, 286), pp. 255–64; and D. Falk, 'Brain Evolution of *Homo*: The Radiator Theory', *Behavioural Brain Science* (1990, 13), pp. 333–81.

53 Leo Tolstoy, *War and Peace*, trans. Louise and Aylmer Maude (Oxford: Oxford University Press, 2010), p. 1392.

54 Tolstoy's later novel, *Anna Karenina,* followed precisely this theme of harmonious and integrated living. The novel is a paean to finding ways of being that are compatible with the world. The novel's hero, Levin, fights to understand what happiness might mean, and what it might be.

Chapter 2

1 This is Wordsworth's famous epithet from his preface to *Lyrical Ballads*, about what new poetry ought to be. Wordsworth's ability to memorise his own poetry is legendary. The 160 lines of 'Tintern Abbey' were composed on a ramble with his sister. He is said to have held the entire poem in his head until he and Dorothy arrived back in Bristol that evening. *See* Adam Sisman, *The Friendship: Wordsworth and Coleridge* (London: Harper Press, 2006), p. 250.

2   Of Wordsworth, Coleridge wrote: 'He is a great, a true
     Poet – I am only a kind of Metaphysician'. *See* Samuel Taylor
     Coleridge, *Collected Letters of Samuel Taylor Coleridge,* 6
     vols, ed. E.L. Griggs (Oxford: Oxford University Press,
     1956), vol. I, p. 658. Perhaps Coleridge's most well-known
     poem, 'Kubla Khan', was famously unfinished when he was
     interrupted by 'the man from Porlock', who was supposedly
     responsible for disrupting the creative trance in which
     Coleridge was composing.

3   *See* Norman Fruman, *Coleridge, the Damaged Archangel*
     (London: Allen and Unwin, 1972); Molly Lefebure, *Samuel
     Taylor Coleridge, a Bondage of Opium* (London: Quartet
     Books, 1977); Geoffrey Yarlott, *Coleridge and the Abyssinian
     Maid* (London: Methuen, 1967).

4   William Hazlitt, 'My First Acquaintance with the Poets', in
     The Spirit of the Age (Grasmere: Wordsworth Trust, 2007),
     pp. 61–84.

5   *See* Coleridge's notebooks from this period: Samuel Taylor
     Coleridge, *The Notebooks of Samuel Taylor Coleridge: Volume
     1, 1794–1804, Text* (London: Routledge & Kegan Paul,
     1957), n. 1190–235.

6   'To Sara Hutchinson, Greta Hall, Keswick, 25 August
     1802', in *Coleridge Among the Lakes and Mountains – from
     his Notebooks, Letters and Poems* (London: Folio Society,
     1991), p. 161. *See also* Richard Holmes, *Coleridge: Early
     Visions* (London: Hodder & Stoughton, 1989), pp. 279–81.

7   Even the famously obscure and incomprehensible Thomas
     Carlyle thought Coleridge obscure and incomprehensible.
     Around 1850, he complained of Coleridge's way
     with words, and his 'confused, unintelligible flood of
     utterance, threatening to submerge all known landmarks
     of thought'. *He's one to talk*, I thought. *See* Thomas
     Carlyle, *The Life of John Stirling* (London: Chapman &
     Hall, 1851), p. 69.

8   'Once again/Do I behold these steep and lofty cliffs,/That
     on a wild secluded scene impress/Thoughts of more deep
     seclusion; and connect/The landscape with the quiet of

the sky.' From 'Lines Written a Few Miles Above Tintern Abbey, on Revisiting the Banks of the Wye During a Tour, July 13 1798', in William Wordsworth and Samuel Taylor Coleridge, *Lyrical Ballads, 1798 and 1802*, ed. Fiona Stafford (Oxford: Oxford University Press, 2013), ll. 4–8.

9 Samuel Johnson and James Boswell, *A Journey to the Western Isles of Scotland and The Journal of a Tour to the Hebrides*, ed. Peter Levi (London: Penguin, 1984), p. 86.

10 Walter Scott, *The Heart of Midlothian* (Oxford: Oxford University Press, 1999), p. 271.

11 Daniel Defoe, *A Tour Through the Whole Island of Great Britain* (London: Penguin, 1986), p. 550.

12 Thomas Gray, *Correspondence of Thomas Gray*, ed. Paget Toynbee and Leonard Whibley, with corrections and additions by H.W. Starr, 3 vols (Oxford: Oxford University Press, 1971), vol. III, p. 1090.

13 *See* japantoday.com/category/national/view/no-of-accidents-involving-people-using-phones-while-walking-increases. And researchnews.osu.edu/archive/distract walk.htm.

14 Gray, *Correspondence of Thomas Gray* vol. III, p. 1079.

15 Coleridge, *The Notebooks of Samuel Taylor Coleridge*, n. 1227.

16 Ibid., n. 1236.

17 Xenophon recounts Socrates's chastisement of his junior, Epigenes, for being out of shape, telling him that fitness makes the body more readied for war, but also for any challenge, physical or mental. *See* 'Memoirs of Socrates' in Xenophon, *Conversations of Socrates*, trans. Robin Waterfield and Hugh Tredennick (London: Penguin, 1990), pp. 171–2.

18 'The Other Boat', in E. M. Forster, *The Life to Come and Other Stories*, ed. Oliver Stallybrass (Harmondsworth: Penguin, 1975), p. 228.

19 Preface to 'A Protest against the Extension of Railways in the Lake District', compiled by Robert Somervell (London: Simpkin, Marshall & Co., 1876).

20 Ibid.

21 *See The Reshaping of British Railways Part One – Report* (London: Her Majesty's Stationery Office, 1963).

22 Coleridge, in *Collected Letters of Samuel Taylor Coleridge,* vol. I, p. 612.

23 Daniel Defoe, *A Tour Through the Whole Island of Great Britain* (London: Penguin, 1986), p. 549.

24 *Rhizocarpon Geographicum* has recently been sent out of the earth's atmosphere as part of an experiment to establish the robustness of the lichen to withstand adverse conditions. It survived its ten-day sojourn. *See* Rosa de la Torre, Leopoldo G. Sancho et al., 'Survival of Lichens and Bacteria Exposed to Outer-space Conditions – Results of the Lithopanspermia Experiments', *Icarus* (August 2010, 208:2), pp. 735–48. The species is also the key component in the relatively new science of lichenometry, where lichens are used to determine the age of rocks exposed to the elements.

25 Kubrick was surely inspired by a similar jump-cut in Powell and Pressburger's *A Canterbury Tale* (1944), where by means of a falcon becoming a spitfire we are taken from the medieval period to the Second World War in the space of a frame.

26 Alexander Pope, 'Windsor Forest', in *The Works* (London, 1736), vol. l, p. 220.

27 It was Alcmaeon of Croton who first suggested that the eye was made of fire and water. The basic idea of Empedocles's theory of perception (told to us by Theophrastus) was that elements in us commune with those outside to create a sense-experience. *See* Plato, *Timaeus and Critias,* trans. Desmond Lee (Harmondsworth: Penguin, 1971).

28 Merleau-Ponty, *Phenomenology of Perception*, p. 127.

29 Ibid., 157.

30 One of the clearest ways of explaining the difference between sense-data and perception is with optical illusions, such as the cartoon by William Ely Hill, 'My Wife and My Mother-in-Law'. In one image there are two pictures (one

of each woman from different aspects). What is seen by the viewer depends on what they focus on. The sense-data (the lines on the page) remain static, but the perception of what those lines represent changes drastically.

31 In one of his letters to Lady Ottoline Morell, D.H. Lawrence referred to history in a similar manner: 'the blue distance – the past, the great past'. *See* D.H. Lawrence, *Letters: Volume 2, June 1913–October 1916*, ed. George J. Zytaruk and James T. Boulton (Cambridge: Cambridge University Press, 1981), p. 431.

32 Merleau-Ponty, *Phenomenology of Perception*, p. xv. Wordsworth said something not dissimilar in his preface to *Lyrical Ballads*: we may see the world clearly 'by awakening the mind's attention from the lethargy of custom, and directing it to the loveliness and the wonders of the world before us; an inexhaustible treasure, but for which in consequence of the film of familiarity and selfish solicitude we have eyes, yet see not, ears that hear not, and hearts that neither feel nor understand.'

33 John Keats, 'To Benjamin Robert Haydon, 8 April 1818', *Selected Letters*, ed. Robert Gittings (Oxford: Oxford University Press, 2002), pp. 78–9. Thanks to Professor Simon Bainbridge for bringing this letter to my attention.

34 J.G. Ballard, *The Complete Short Stories: Volume 1* (London: Harper Press, 2006).

Chapter 3

1 H. van Praag, T. Shubert, C. Zhao and F.H. Gage, 'Exercise Enhances Learning and Hippocampal Neurogenesis in Aged Mice', *Journal of Neuroscience* (September 2005, 25:38), pp. 8680–5.

2 Karen Danna and Ricky W. Griffin, 'Health and Well-Being in the Workplace: A Review and Synthesis of the Literature', *Journal of Management* (1999, 25:3), pp. 357–84; *see especially* p. 378, where they discuss the positive impact of regular exercise. *See also* Rachel Kaplan, 'The Role of Nature

in the Context of the Workplace', *Landscape and Urban Planning* (1993, 26:1), pp. 193–201.

3 (This paper, as of 2013, is currently in press.) 'The Role of Running Involvement in Creating Self-sufficiency for Homeless Individuals through a Community-Based Running Program.' The authors (Yuhei Inoue, Daniel Funk and Jeremy S. Jordan) found that, by means of a regression analysis, involvement in sport, and particularly running, showed measurable psychological benefits (especially self-sufficiency) for those involved in the trials. The study is due to appear in the *Journal of Sport Management*.

4 In this trial runners were found to exhibit decreases in tension and anxiety, especially those who thought about relationships with partners, friends and family. *See* K.T Goode and D.L. Roth, 'Factor Analysis of Cognitions During Running: Association with Mood Change', *Journal of Sport and Exercise Psychology* (1993, 15:4), pp. 375–89.

5 Terry Hartig et al., 'Psychological Restoration in Nature as a Positive Motivation for Ecological Behavior', *Environment and Behavior* (July 2001, 33), pp. 590–607; Patricia A. Hansen-Ketchum and Elizabeth A. Halpenny, 'Engaging with Nature to Promote Health: Bridging Research Silos to Examine the Evidence', *Health Promotion International* (2011, 26:1), pp. 100–8.

6 R.H. Matsuoka, 'Student Performance and High School Landscapes: Examining the Links', *Landscape and Urban Planning* (2010, 97:4), pp. 273–82.

7 Where one study has found a significant link between body-/self-image and endurance sport (B.D. Kirkcaldy, R.J. Shephard and R.G. Siefen, 'The Relationship Between Physical Activity and Self-Image and Problem Behaviour Among Adolescents', *Social Psychiatry and Psychiatric Epidemiology* [2002, 37:11], pp. 544–50), another has suggested that it was good for all groups barring younger women, who reported more negative relationships between levels of exercise and satisfaction with body image and self-esteem (Marika Tiggemann and Samantha Williamson,

'The Effect of Exercise on Body Satisfaction and Self-Esteem as a Function of Gender and Age', *Sex Roles* [July 2000, 43:1–2], pp. 119–27.) *See also* Daniel Longman et al., 'Can Persistence Hunting Signal Male Quality? A Test Considering Digit Ratio in Endurance Athletes', *PLOS* (8 April 2015, 10).

8   Elizabeth Hinton and Steven Taylor, 'Does Placebo Response Mediate Runner's High?', *Perceptual and Motor Skills* (1986, 62:3), pp. 789–90.

9   Rod Dishman and Patrick J. O'Connor, 'Lessons in Exercise Neurobiology: The Case of Endorphins', *Mental and Physical Activity* (2009, 2), pp. 4–9. *See* p. 8.

10 John Ratey and Eric Hagerman, *Spark! How Exercise Will Improve the Performance of Your Brain* (London: Quercus, 2009), p. 5.

11 Gina Kolata, *Ultimate Fitness: The Quest for Truth about Health and Exercise* (London: Picador, 2004). *See* 'Is There a Runner's High?', pp. 175–202.

12 Quoted in Gina Kolata, 'Runner's High? Endorphins? Fiction, Some Scientists Say', *New York Times* (21 May 2002), www.nytimes.com/2002/05/21/health/runner-s-high-endorphins-fiction-some-scientists-say.html?pagewanted=all&src=pm.

13 This is from an interview that Davis gave at the Australasian Podiatry Conference in 2011. The interview can be found at https://www.youtube.com/watch?v=JZmvg8OsJTc. These specific comments can be found at 9.20 mins.

14 Thomas Hardy, *Under the Greenwood Tree,* ed. Tim Dolin (London: Penguin, 1998), p. 7.

15 Grinde's review article is particularly helpful in outlining the potential and spread of discords in contemporary culture. *See* Bjørn Grinde, 'Can the Concept of Discords Help Us Find the Causes of Mental Diseases?', *Medical Hypotheses* (2009, 73), pp. 106–9. *See also* W. Irons, 'Adaptively Relevant Environments Versus the Environment of Evolutionary Adaptedness', *Evolutionary Anthropology* (1998, 6), pp. 194–204; C. Crawford and D. Krebs, *Handbook of*

Evolutionary Psychology: Ideas, Issues and Applications (New York: Laurence Erlbaum Associates, 1997); A. Lundberg, *The Environment and Mental Health: A Guide for Clinicians* (New Jersey: LEA, 1998).

16 Discords are not always 'bad'. Breathable waterproof clothing, hot-water bottles, in–out sewage systems, all provide comfort, convenience or life-saving hygiene. Many aspects of modern life, though, may be discordant without our being aware of them.

17 Plato, *Phaedrus,* in *Plato in Twelve Volumes, Vol. 9,* translated by Harold N. Fowler (London: William Heinemann, 1925), section 275a.

18 Elizabeth L. Eisenstein, *The Printing Press as an Agent of Change: Communications and Cultural Transformations in Early Modern Europe* (Cambridge: Cambridge University Press, 1979). Gessner's *Bibliotheca Universalis* (in four volumes, 1545–9) was the first bibliography of all books from the first century of the printing press.

19 *See, for example*, Laura Marcus, *The Tenth Muse: Writing About Cinema in the Modernist Period* (Oxford: Oxford University Press, 2007), pp. 168–9, 208, 273.

20 'The popularity of this new pastime among children has increased rapidly . . . This new invader of the privacy of the home has brought many a disturbing influence in its wake. Parents have become aware of a puzzling change in the behaviour patterns of their children. They are bewildered by a host of new problems, and find themselves unprepared, frightened, resentful, helpless. They cannot lock out this intruder because it has gained an invincible hold of their children.' Azriel L. Eisenberg, *Children and Radio Programs* (New York: Columbia University Press, 1936).

21 *See, for example*, Wilbur Lang Schramm, Lawrence Z. Freedman et al., *Television in the Lives of Our Children, with a Psychiatrist's Comment on the Effects of Television by Lawrence Z. Freedman* (Stanford: Stanford University Press, 1961): 'It brought the world to everyone's living

room, but most particularly it gave children an earlier look at far places and adult behaviour. It became the greatest and loudest salesman of goods, and sent children clamouring to their parents for box tops. It created heroes and villains, fads, fashions, and stereotypes, and nowhere so successfully, apparently, as with the pliable minds of children.'

22 *See,* Rob Cowen, *Common Ground* (London: Hutchinson, 2015): Michael Symmons Roberts and Paul Farley, *Edgelands: Journeys into England's True Wilderness* (London: Cape, 2011).

23 Scarlett Thomas, 'Nowhere to Run: Did My Fitness Addiction Make Me Ill?', *Guardian* (7 March 2015), www.theguardian.com/lifeandstyle/2015/mar/07/fitness-addiction-ill-scarlett-thomas.

24 *See* Vincenzo Di Marzo, Maurizio Bifulco and Luciano De Petrocellis, 'The Endocannabinoid System and Its Therapeutic Exploitation', *Nature Reviews Drug Discovery* (September 2004, 3), pp. 771–84; and P.B. Sparling, A. Giuffrida, D. Piomelli, L. Rosskopf and A. Dietrich, 'Exercise Activates the Endocannabinoid System', *NeuroReport* (2003, 14:17), pp. 2209–11.

25 D.S. Raichlen et al., 'Wired to Run: Exercise-Induced Endocannabinoid Signaling in Humans and Cursorial Mammals with Implications for the "Runner's High"', *Journal of Experimental Biology* (2012, 215), pp. 1331–6.

26 Trials have been done that focus specifically on hippocampal neurogenesis and running, but only in mice. O. Lazarov et al., 'Environmental Enrichment Reduces Abeta Levels and Amyloid Deposition in Transgenic Mice', *Cell* (2005, 120:5), pp. 701–13; and H. van Praag et al., 'Exercise Enhances Learning and Hippocampal Neurogenesis in Aged Mice', *Journal of Neuroscience* (September 2005, 25:38), pp. 8680–5.

27 Ratey and Hagerman, *Spark!*, p. 19.

28 BDNF helps with neurogenesis, but it has also been shown to assist dendridogenesis and synaptogensis.

29 *See* A Dietrich, 'Transient Hypofrontality as a Mechanism for the Psychological Effects of Exercise', *Psychiatry Research* (November 2006, 29:145, 1), pp. 79–83. 'Building on the fundamental principle that processing in the brain is competitive and the fact that the brain has finite metabolic resources, the transient hypofrontality hypothesis suggests that during exercise the extensive neural activation required to run motor patterns, assimilate sensory inputs, and coordinate autonomic regulation results in a concomitant transient decrease of neural activity in brain structures, such as the prefrontal cortex, that are not pertinent to performing the exercise. An exercise-induced state of frontal hypofunction can provide a coherent account of the influences of exercise on emotion and cognition.'

30 John Ruskin, *Modern Painters, Volume One*, in Ruskin, *The Works of John Ruskin*, eds Edward Tyas Cook and Alexander Wedderburn, 39 vols (London: George Allen, 1903–12), vol. 3, p. 494.

31 'Our Rising Ad Dosage: It's Not as Oppressive as Some Think', *Media Matters* (15 February 2007). Mmm . . . 600 to 625 seems pretty bad to me – consider the source.

32 Owen Wilson, 'Shopper's Eye View of Ads that Pass Us By', *Guardian* (19 November 2005).

33 They were so naughty. At dinner time, Bonnie, wily and streetwise, would run to the door, barking at an imagined potential burglar, bringing the other, more stupid one, Jez, running, barking louder and longer than Bonnie who had since run back to finish Jez's dinner for her. When out with Jez, if you didn't throw a ball for her quickly enough, she wouldn't bother barking at you, she would just jump and give you a full body-slam. Another time, Aylla came home from work to discover that while she was away, they had somehow got into the kitchen cupboards, got a tin of tomatoes off the shelf, opened it, then run all around the house leaving the white walls and furnishings splattered arterial red, like a horrific scene from *CSI*.

34 R.S. Ulrich, R.F. Simons et al., 'Stress Recovery During Exposure to Natural and Urban Environments', *Journal of Environmental Psychology* (1991, 11), pp. 201–30. And, C.-Y Chang and P.-K. Chen, 'Human Responses to Window Views and Indoor Plants in the Workplace', *Horticultural Science* (2005, 40), pp. 1354–9.

35 R. Kaplan and S. Kaplan, *The Experience of Nature: A Psychological Perspective* (Cambridge: Cambridge University Press, 1989).

36 J. Pretty et al., 'Green Exercise: The Benefits of Activities in Green Places', *Biologist* (2006, 53), pp. 143–8; J. Barton and J. Pretty, 'What is the Best Dose of Nature and Green Exercise for Improving Mental Health? A Multi-Study Analysis', *Environmental Science and Technology* (2010, 44:10), pp. 3947–55; M.D. Velarde, G. Fry and M. Tveit, 'Health Effects of Viewing Landscapes – Landscape Types in Environmental Psychology', *Urban Forestry and Urban Greening* (2007, 6), pp. 199–212. In this last analysis, it was argued that natural environments have consistently enriching health benefits, whereas urban landscapes have the opposite effect.

37 T. Takano et al., 'Urban Residential Environments and Senior Citizens' Longevity in Megacity Areas: The Importance of Walkable Green Spaces', *Journal of Epidemiology and Community Health* (2002, 56), pp. 913–8.

38 Bjørn Grinde and Grete G. Patil, 'Biophilia: Does Visual Contact with Nature Impact on Health and Well-Being?', *International Journal of Environmental Research and Public Health* (2009, 6:9), pp. 2332–43.

39 Richard Louv, *Last Child in the Woods: Saving Our Children from Nature-Deficit Disorder* (London: Atlantic, 2010).

40 For a substantial meta-analysis of these findings see J. Thompson Coon et al., 'Does Participating in Physical Activity in Outdoor Natural Environments Have a Greater Effect on Physical and Mental Wellbeing than Physical Activity Indoors? A Systematic Review', *Journal of Environmental Science and Technology* (2011, 45),

pp. 1761–72. *See also* R.P. Yeung, 'The Acute Effects of Exercise on Mood State', *Journal of Psychosomatic Research* (1996, 40:2), pp. 123–41.

41 This last fact is frequently misunderstood – the trials report the beneficial effects of being in natural environments, not whether individuals consciously like being in them.

42 Marc G. Berman, John Jonides and Stephen Kaplan, 'The Cognitive Benefits of Interacting with Nature', *Psychological Science* (2008, 19:12), pp. 1207–12.

43 *See* Stephen Kaplan, 'The Restorative Benefits of Nature: Toward an Integrative Framework', *Journal of Environmental Psychology* (1995, 16), pp. 169–82. Kaplan proposed that the experience of natural environments mitigated stress while also preventing it. *See also* S. Kaplan, 'The Urban Forest as a Source of Psychological Well-being', in G.A. Bradley, ed., *Urban Forest Landscapes: Integrating Multidisciplinary Perspectives* (Seattle: University of Washington Press, 1995); S. Kaplan and J.F Talbot, 'Psychological Benefits of a Wilderness Experience', in I. Altman & J.F. Wohlwill, eds, *Behavior and the Natural Environment* (New York: Plenum, 1983), pp. 163–203; Rachel Kaplan, 'The Role of Nature in the Context of the Workplace', *Landscape and Urban Planning* (1993, 26:1), pp. 193–201; Rachel Kaplan, 'The Nature of the View from Home: Psychological Benefits', *Environment and Behavior* (2001, 33), pp. 507–42; Stephen Kaplan, 'Meditation, Restoration, and the Management of Mental Fatigue', *Environment and Behavior* (2001, 33), pp. 480–506; Kaplan and Kaplan, *The Experience of Nature*; Kalevi M. Korpela et al., 'Restorative Experience and Self-Regulation in Favorite Places', *Environment and Behavior* (2001, 33), pp. 572–89.

44 This idea had been mooted in an earlier study: R. Berto, 'Exposure to Restorative Environments Helps Restore Attentional Capacity', *Journal of Environmental Psychology* (2005, 25), pp. 249–59.

45 *See, for example*, Frances E. Kuo and Andrea Faber Taylor, 'A Potential Natural Treatment for Attention-Deficit/

Hyperactivity Disorder: Evidence From a National Study', *American Journal of Public Health* (September 2004, 94:9), pp. 1580–6.

46 A number of recent studies show that an increased cadence can have a positive impact on injury rates in runners. The ideal is thought to be around 180 steps per minute, so if you want to benefit from this sort of training without going to a clinic, just load some 90bpm music onto your MP3 player and step in time to the music. You don't need to run faster, just at a higher turnover. There is lots of music out there for you to keep pace with. My favourites are: 'Lose Yourself', Eminem; 'Our Number's Oracle', Puressence; 'Still Ill', The Smiths; 'Waiting for My Real Life to Begin', Colin Hay; 'Bodysnatchers', Radiohead; 'Whole Lotta Love', Led Zeppelin; 'I'm on Fire', Bruce Springsteen; 'Northern Sky', Nick Drake; 'Protection', Massive Attack; 'Angel', Kirsty MacColl.

47 Jason Duvall, 'Enhancing the Benefits of Outdoor Walking with Cognitive Engagement Strategies', *Journal of Environmental Psychology* (2008, 31), pp. 27–35.

48 Adam Akers, Jo Barton, Rachel Cossey, Patrick Gainsford, Murray Griffin and Dominic Micklewright, 'Visual Color Perception in Green Exercise: Positive Effects on Mood and Perceived Exertion', *Environmental Science and Technology* (2012, 46), pp. 8661–6.

49 *See* F.E. Kuo, 'The Role of Arboriculture in a Healthy Social Ecology', *Journal of Arboriculture* (2003, 29:3), pp. 148–55.

50 *See* F.E. Kuo and W.C. Sullivan, 'Environment and Crime in the Inner City: Does Vegetation Reduce Crime?', *Environment and Behavior* (2001, 33/3), pp. 343–367.

51 Ibid.

52 Agnes E. van den Berg et al., 'Green Space as a Buffer Between Stressful Life Events and Health', *Social Science and Medicine* (April 2010, 70:8), pp. 1203–10.

53 The first is viewing nature, as through a window or in a painting – *see* E.O. Moore, 'A Prison Environment's Effect on Health Care Service Demands', *Journal of Environmental*

Systems, (1981, 11), pp. 17–34; R. S. Ulrich, 'View Through a Window May Influence Recovery from Surgery', *Science* (1984, 224), pp. 420–21; C.M. Tennessen, & B. Cimprich, 'Views to Nature: Effects on Attention', *Journal of Environmental Psychology*, (1995, 15), pp. 77–85; P. Leather, M. Pyrgas, D. Beale, and C. Lawrence, 'Windows in the Workplace', *Environment and Behaviour*, (1998, 30), pp. 739–63; S. Kaplan, 'Meditation, Restoration, and the Management of Mental Fatigue', *Environment and Behaviour*, (2001, 33), pp. 480–506; and G.B. Diette, N. Lechtzin, E. Haponik, A. Devrotes, and H. R. Rubin 'Distraction Therapy with Nature Sights and Sounds Reduces Pain During Flexible Bronchoscopy: a Complementary Approach to Routine Analgesia' *Chest*, (2003, 123), pp. 941–8.

The second is being in the presence of nearby nature, which may be incidental to some other activity, such as walking or cycling to work, reading on a garden seat or talking to friends in a park – *see* Clare Cooper-Marcus and Marni Barnes, eds, *Healing Gardens: Therapeutic Benefits and Design Recommendations* (New York: Wiley, 1999); especially, R.S. Ulrich, 'Effects of Gardens on Health Outcomes: Theory and Research' in *ibid.*; S. Whitehouse, J.W. Varni, M. Seid, C. Cooper Marcus, M.J. Ensberg, J.R. Jacobs et al., 'Evaluating a Children's Hospital Garden Environment: Utilization and consumer satisfaction', *Journal of Environmental Psychology*, (2001, 21:3), pp. 301–14.

The third is active participation and involvement with nature, such as gardening or farming, trekking or camping, cross-country running or horse-riding – *see* Betty B. Rossman & Joseph Ulehla, 'Psychological Reward Values Associated with Wilderness Use: a Functional-Reinforcement Approach', *Environment and Behaviour*, (1977, 9:1), pp. 41-66; T. Hartig, M. Mang, and G.W. Evans, 'Restorative Effects of Natural Environment Experiences', *Environment and Behaviour*, (1991, 23), pp. 3–26; T. Hartig, G.W. Evans, L.D. Jamner, D.S. Davis,

T. Gärling, 'Tracking Restoration in Natural and Urban Field Settings', *Journal of Environmental Psychology* (2003, 23), pp. 109–123; L.M. Fredrickson, and D.H. Anderson, 'A Qualitative Exploration of the Wilderness Experience as a Source of Spiritual Inspiration', *Journal of Environmental Psychology,* (1999, 19), pp. 21–39; H. Frumkin, 'Beyond Toxicity: Human Health and the Natural Environment', *American Journal of Preventative Medicine* (2001, 20:3), pp. 234-40; K. Williams and D. Harvey, 'Transcendent Experience in Forest Environments', *Journal of Environmental Psychology*, (2001: 21), pp. 240–60; T. Herzog, H.C. Chen, J.S. Primeau, 'Perception of the Restorative Potential of Natural and Other Settings', *Journal of Environmental Psychology* (2002, 2), pp. 295–306; and Jules Pretty et al., 'The Mental and Physical Health Outcomes of Green Exercise', *International Journal of Environmental Health Research* (2005, 15:5), pp. 319–37.

54 *See also* J. Pretty, 'How Nature Contributes to Mental and Physical Health', *Spirituality and Health International* (2004, 5:2), pp. 68–78.

55 Leo Tolstoy, *Anna Karenina*, trans. Richard Pevear (London: Penguin, 2000), pp. 226, 252.

56 One of the ways in which directed attention and exercise have been theorised is through 'transient hypofrontality'. This process posits a pathway linking exercise with attention restoration. Prefrontal-cortex (PFC) activation is associated with processes of directed attention. Exercise promotes transient hypofrontality and decreases in prefrontal-cortex activity which occur in conjunction with increased motor-cortex activity, facilitating prefrontal-cortex restoration. During exercise, this decreased prefrontal-cortex activity may be detrimental to cognitive performance. However, following prolonged opportunity for prefrontal-cortex restoration, transient hypofrontality improves post-exercise executive functioning and cognitive performance. On transient hypofrontality *see* A. Dietrich, 'Functional Neuroanatomy of Altered States of Consciousness: The

Transient Hypofrontality Hypothesis', *Consciousness and Cognition* (2003, 12), pp. 231–56; and 'Transient Hypofrontality as a Mechanism for the Psychological Effects of Exercise', *Psychiatry Research* (2006, 145), pp. 79–83. On PFC activation and directed attention *see* K.R. Daffner, L. Scinto et al., 'The Central Role of the Prefrontal Cortex in Directing Attention to Novel Events', *Brain* (2000, 123), pp. 927–39; M.T. Gailliot and R.F. Baumeister, 'The Physiology of Willpower: Linking Blood Glucose to Self-Control', *Personality and Social Psychology Review* (2007, 11), pp. 303–27; M. Milham, M. Banich et al., 'The Relative Involvement of Anterior Ingulate and Prefrontal Cortex in Attentional Control Depends on Nature of Conflict', *Cognitive Brain Research* (2001, 12), pp. 467–73; and E.K. Miller and J.D. Cohen, 'An Integrative Theory of Prefrontal Cortex Function', *Annual Review of Neuroscience* (2001, 24), pp. 167–202. On decreased PFC activity as detrimental to cognitive performance *see* V. Labelle, L. Bosquet et al., 'Decline in Executive Control During Acute Bouts of Exercise as a Function of Exercise Intensity and Fitness Level', *Brain and Cognition*, (2013, 81). On improved functioning post-exercise *see* H. Yanagisawa, I. Dan et al., 'Acute Moderate Exercise Elicits Increased Dorsolateral Prefrontal Activation and Improves Cognitive Performance with Stroop Test', *Neuroimage* (2010, 50), pp. 1702–10; and K. Byun, K. Hyodo et al., 'Positive Effect of Acute Mild Exercise on Executive Function via Arousal-Related Prefrontal Activations: An fNIRS Study', *NeuroImage* (2014, 98), pp. 336–45.

57 As Mike Rogerson explained to me, higher cognitive function is impaired during intense exercise because it shifts the blood flow away from the frontal cortex and into the motor cortex which needs to increase its work rate to instruct your movements accurately. There is research suggesting that substrates move away from the amygdala, in the same way that they move away from the frontal cortex (prefrontal cortex). This is one (of many) of the mechanisms

that have been suggested to explain why negative mood is alleviated by exercise – because lower amygdala activity means that it is not telling you to be scared or depressed. *See* Arne Dietrich and Phillip B. Sparling, 'Endurance Exercise Sselectively Impairs Prefrontal-Dependent Cognition', *Brain and Cognition* (55, 2004), pp. 516–24.

Chapter 4

1 Thomas Hardy, *Far from the Madding Crowd*, eds Rosemarie Morgan and Shannon Russell (London: Penguin, 2003), p. 308.
2 Thomas Hardy, *The Mayor of Casterbridge*, ed. Dale Kramer (Oxford: Oxford University Press, 1987), p. 86.
3 Hardy, *Far from the Madding Crowd,* p. 215.
4 William Shakespeare, *Othello*, I.iii.208.
5 John Keats, 'Lines Written in the Highlands After a Visit to Burns's Country', in *The Complete Poems* (London: Penguin, 1988), p. 266.
6 Francis Pryor, *Britain bc: Life in Britain and Ireland Before the Romans* (London: HarperCollins, 2003).
7 Daniel Lieberman, *The History of the Human Body* (London: Allen Lane, 2013), pp. 151, 196.
8 Hardy, *The Mayor of Casterbridge*, p. 63.
9 Thomas Hardy; *The Life and Work of Thomas Hardy*, ed. Michael Millgate (London: Macmillan, 1984), p. 33.
10 It features in Hardy's wonderfully creepy story 'The Withered Arm', in his *Wessex Tales* from 1888.
11 *See* Francis Pryor, *The Making of the English Landscape: How We Have Transformed the Land, from Prehistory to Today* (London: Allen Lane, 2010), pp. 133–7.
12 Bertrand Russell, 'In Praise of Idleness', in *In Praise of Idleness and Other Essays* (London: Routledge, 2010), p1
13 Ibid., 12
14 A good history of these debates may be found in 'Why Crunch Mode Doesn't Work: Six Lessons', www.igda.org/?page=crunchsixlessons.

15 *See* 'Pootling', in Richard Mabey, *A Brush with Nature: Reflections on the Natural World* (London: BBC Books, 2010), pp. 34–40.

16 Ironically, Darwin never actually used this term. It belongs to one of his supporters, Herbert Spencer.

17 *The Epic of Gilgamesh*, trans. Andrew George (Harmondsworth: Penguin, 1999).

18 Chaucer, 'The Nun's Priest's Tale', in *The Riverside Chaucer* (Oxford: Oxford University Press, 1988), pp. 252–61.

19 Human territoriality in public spaces is fascinating and not in the least predictable or straightforward. Public space is shared space, but we are not very good at sharing it. I was at an academic talk recently and a man was in front of me, one seat to the right. Directly in front of me was his bag, which he had placed on the chair. At one point during the talk, I leaned forward slightly. After a few moments he took his bag away and placed it on the other side of him. I had not invaded his space, but his bag's. We were in a church.

20 This is the opening to chapter VI, 'The Judges', in Leo Tolstoy, *Resurrection*, trans. Louise Maude (Oxford: Oxford University Press, 1994), p. 20.

21 *A Canterbury Tale*, dir. Michael Powell and Emeric Pressburger, 1944.

22 George Meredith, 'The Lark Ascending', in *Selected Poems* (London: Constable, 1903), ll. 2–3.

Chapter 5

1 'Art, considered as the expression of any people as a whole, is the response they make in various mediums to the impact that the totality of their experience makes upon them, and there is no sort of experience that works so constantly and subtly upon man as his regional environment . . . It is the thing always before his eye, always at his ear, always underfoot. Slowly or sharply it forces upon him behaviour patterns such as earliest become the habit of his blood.' From

Mary Hunter Austin, 'Regionalism in American Fiction', *The English Journal* (February 1932, 21), pp. 97–107.

2 Farouk Al-Rawi and Andrew George, 'Back to the Cedar Forest: The Beginning and End of Tablet V of the Standard Babylonian Epic of Gilgameš', *Journal of Cuneiform Studies* (2014, 66), pp. 69–90.

3 Sigmund Freud, 'Introductory Lectures on Psycho-Analysis; a Course of Twenty-Eight Lectures Delivered at the University of Vienna', trans. Joan Riviere (London: George Allen and Unwin, 1922), pp. 311–2.

4 E.M. Forster, 'George Crabbe: The Poet and the Man', *The Listener* (29 May 1941).

5 Simeon Brough, 'Narcissi', in *Narcissi and Other Poems* (Hastings, 1872).

6 *See* Fred Pearce, 'The Legacy', *Granta – What Have We Done* (2015, 133), p. 92.

7 Richard Jefferies, *After London, or Wild England* (London: Cassell, 1885).

8 John Ruskin, 'The Lamp of Memory', in *The Seven Lamps of Wisdom* (London: Smith Elder, 1849).

9 Anton Checkhov, 'Lights', in *The Tales of Checkhov, Volume 13 – Love and Other Stories*, trans. Constance Garnett (New York: Macmillan, 1923), p. 28.

10 Ted Hughes, 'The Environmental Revolution', in *Winter Pollen: Occasional Prose* (London: Faber & Faber, 1994), pp. 128–35.

11 *See* Raymond Williams, *Keywords: A Vocabulary of Culture and Society* (London: Collins, 1976), p. 184.

12 'Economic Costs of Physical Inactivity', British Heart Foundation report: www.bhfactive.org.uk/userfiles/Documents/eonomiccosts.pdf.

13 'At Least Five a Week: Evidence on the Impact of Physical Activity and its Relationship to Health', a report from the Chief Medical Officer, 29 April 2004, http://webarchive.nationalarchives.gov.uk/+/dh.gov.uk/en/publicationsandstatistics/publications/publicationspolicyandguidance/dh_4080994.

14 If you search IMDB for Miriam Margoyles it comes up with the subtitle 'Actress, Babe'. (She provided the voice of Babe in the movie of that name.)

15 The solution seems not dissimilar to warning people to stay indoors because of harmful pollution levels. As I write, the BBC this morning broadcast a pollution alert, 'In areas experiencing very high levels of air pollution, adults and children with lung problems, adults with heart problems and older people are advised to avoid strenuous activity. People are also advised to reduce physical exertion, particularly outside, and asthma sufferers may need to use their reliever inhaler more often': www.bbc.co.uk/news/uk-32233922.

16 John Manwood, *A Treatise and Discourse of the Lawes of the Forrest Wherin Is Declared Not Onely those Lawes, as They Are Now in Force, but also the Originall and Beginning of Forrestes* (London, 1598).

17 D. Rojas-Rueda et al., 'The Health Risks and Benefits of Cycling in Urban Environments Compared with Car Use: Health Impact Assessment Study', *British Medical Journal* (August 2011): 'Compared with car users the estimated annual change in mortality of the Barcelona residents using a cycling programme (n=181 982) was 0.03 deaths from road traffic incidents and 0.13 deaths from air pollution. As a result of physical activity, 12.46 deaths were avoided (benefit:risk ratio 77). The annual number of deaths avoided was 12.28. As a result of journeys by Bicing, annual carbon-dioxide emissions were reduced by an estimated 9 062 344 kg. – Conclusion: Public bicycle sharing initiatives such as Bicing in Barcelona have greater benefits than risks to health and reduce carbon dioxide emissions.'

18 Qing Li et al., 'Effect of Forest Bathing Trips on Human Immune Function', *Environmental Health and Preventive Medicine* (2010, 15:1), pp. 9–17.

19 B.J. Park et al., 'The Physiological Effects of *Shinrin-yoku* (Taking in the Forest Atmosphere or Forest Bathing): Evidence from Field Experiments in 24 Forests Across

Japan', *Environment Health and Preventative Medicine* (2010, 15), pp. 18–26.

20 Qing Li et al., 'Acute Effects of Walking in Forest Environments on Cardiovascular and Metabolic Parameters', *European Journal of Applied Physiology* (2011, 111), pp. 2845–53.

21 E. Morita et al., 'A Before and After Comparison of the Effects of Forest Walking on the Sleep of a Community-Based Sample of People with Sleep Complaints', *BioPsychoSocial Medicine* (2011, 5:13).

22 *See* Novalis (Georg Philipp Friedrich von Hardenberg), 'Die Lehrlinge zu Sais', in *Novalis Schriften*, vol. 1, eds Paul Kluckhohn and Richard Samuel (Stuttgart: Kohlhammer, 1960), pp. 79–110, especially p. 105.

23 Leo Tolstoy, *Anna Karenina*, trans. Louise and Aylmer Maude (Oxford: Oxford University Press, 1999), p. 979.

24 G.J. Walker and R. Chapman, 'Thinking Like a Park: The Effects of Sense of Place, Perspective-taking, and Empathy on Pro-environmental Intentions', *Journal of Park and Recreation Administration* (2003, 21:4), pp. 71–86.

25 Jaime Berenguer, 'The Effect of Empathy in Proenvironmental Attitudes and Behaviours', *Environment and Behavior* (March 2007, 39:2), pp. 269–83. *See also* Jaime Berenguer, 'The Effect of Empathy in Environmental Moral Reasoning', *Environment and Behavior* (January 2010, 42:1), pp. 110–34.

26 John Marzlruff interview for *Discovery News*: news. discovery.com/animals/zoo-animals/angry-crows-memory-life-threatening-behavior-1106281.htm.

27 J.M. Zelenski and E.K. Nisbet, 'Happiness and Feeling Connected: The Distinct Role of Nature Relatedness', *Environment and Behavior* (January 2014, 46:1), pp. 3–23.

28 E.K. Nisbet and J.M. Zelenski, 'Underestimating Nearby Nature: Affective Forecasting Errors Obscure the Happy Path to Sustainability', *Psychological Science* (September 2011, 22:9), pp. 1101–6. Studies have also tested whether

being in natural environments make us nicer people. In a trial later called 'Green Altruism', the investigators wanted to measure the willingness of the subjects to help out a stranger who had done something as inconsequential as dropping a glove. The result was that the passers-by were more willing to help if they had previously been immersed in a natural environment. Nicolas Guéguen and Jordy Stefan, '"Green Altruism": Short Immersion in Natural Green Environments and Helping Behavior', *Environment and Behavior* (1 July 2014).

29 Recent studies have begun to focus on the fostering of empathy in our little ones. *See* Diane M. McKnight, 'Overcoming "Ecophobia": Fostering Environmental Empathy Through Narrative in Children's Science Literature', *Frontiers in Ecology and the Environment* (2010, 8:6), e10–e15.

30 Netta Weinstein et al., 'Can Nature Make Us More Caring? Effects of Immersion in Nature on Intrinsic Aspirations and Generosity', *Personality and Social Psychology Bulletin* (October 2009, 35:10), pp. 1315–29.

31 *The Runners*, Banyak Films, 2013, http://vimeo.com/87169386.

32 I seem to remember the author Haruki Murakami expressing a similar sentiment in *What I Talk About When I Talk About Running*. He fell out of love with the marathon because his awareness of his times impacted negatively on his experience of the runs themselves.

33 Gaétan Chevalier, the director of the Earthing Institute, works in the department of Developmental and Cell Biology at the University of California.

34 This is a review article of some of the studies to date. Gaétan Chevalier et al., 'Earthing: Health Implications of Reconnecting the Human Body to the Earth's Surface Electrons', *Journal of Environmental and Public Health* (2012, 3): 'The research done to date supports the concept that grounding or earthing the human body may be an essential element in the health equation along with

sunshine, clean air and water, nutritious food, and physical activity.'

Chapter 6

1   'Letter to Mathilde Wurm', Rosa Luxemburg, *The Rosa Luxemburg Reader*, eds Peter Hudis and Kevin Anderson (New York: Monthly Review, 2004), p. 389–90.

2   I now know from experience that exercise alone is not an effective way to lose weight. When I trained for the London Marathon, I would frequently run over 40 miles a week (about two day's worth of calorie intake) and I did not lose a pound. Research has shown that our metabolisms are not as flexible as we might think, and that when we exercise, we compensate with both rest and food. It is still much healthier to be fitter, but don't put on your running shoes if you want to lose weight, do it because you want to run. This is what Terence Wilkin, Professor of Endocrinology and Metabolism, had to say in a review article from 2004: 'Physical activity is effective only for as long as it lasts, and is less efficient in achieving weight loss than calorie reduction. Some 70–75 per cent of energy expenditure is obligatory in the form of resting energy requirements, so that a doubling of physical activity does not double energy expenditure. Halving food intake will necessarily halve calorie intake, and portion size is possibly the most important modifiable factor in the management of obesity.' Terence J. Wilkin and Linda D. Voss, 'Metabolic Syndrome: Maladaptation to a Modern World', *Journal of the Royal Society of Medicine* (November 2004, 97:11), pp. 511–20.

3   Much research has been carried out on the problem of gym attendance. *See* C. Pentecost and A. Taket, 'Understanding Exercise Uptake and Adherence for People with Chronic Conditions: A New Model Demonstrating the Importance of Exercise Identity, Benefits of Attending and Support', *Health Education Research* (2011, 26:5), pp. 908–22;

and Roberta Sassatelli, 'Fitness Gyms and the Local Organization of Experience', *Sociological Research Online* (1999, 4:3); and Nate McCaughtry et al., 'The Ecology of the Gym: Reconceptualized and Extended', *Quest* (2008, 60:2), pp. 268–89.

4   Pailoor Subramanya and Shirley Telles, 'Changes in Midlatency Auditory Evoked Potentials following Two Yoga-Based Relaxation Techniques', *Clinical EEG and Neuroscience* (July 2009, 40:3), pp. 190–5; and Sara W. Lazar et al., 'Functional Brain Mapping of the Relaxation Response and Meditation', *NeuroReport* (15 May 2000, 11:7), pp. 1581–5.

5   Cesare Beccaria, *An Essay on Crimes and Punishments, Translated from the Italian; with a Commentary, Attributed to Mons. de Voltaire* (Dublin: John Exshaw, 1767).

6   John Howard, William Blackstone and William Eden, 'Penitentiary Act: Act of Parliament to Explain and Amend the Laws Relating to the Transportation, Imprisonment, and Other Punishment, of Certain Offenders, Authorising Building of Two Penitentiaries' (held at London Metropolitan Archives, City of London) (London, 1779).

7   'Penitentiary Act', p. 551.

8   Ibid., 558.

9   Ibid., 552.

10 Michel Foucault, *Discipline and Punish: The Birth of the Prison*, trans. Alan Sheridan (Harmondsworth: Penguin, 1977), p. 16.

11 *See Gentleman's Magazine* (9 July 1822). I am not the first to show a philosophical interest in treadmill running. Douglas R. Hochstetler thinks about it in terms of William James's and Henry David Thoreau's work, focussing on the lack of concentration induced by the activity. *See* Douglas R. Hochstetler, 'Can We Experience Significance on a Treadmill?', in *Running and Philosophy: A Marathon for the Mind*, ed. Michael W. Austin (Oxford: Blackwell, 2007).

12 *The Monthly Magazine and British Register* (2 November 1796), p. 799.

13 Ibid.

14 Jean-Jacques Rousseau, *Discourse on Inequality*, in *The Basic Political Writings*, 2nd ed., trans. Donald A. Cress (Cambridge: Hackett, 2011), p. 48.

15 Anthony Trollope, *The Eustace Diamonds* (Oxford: Oxford University Press, 2011), p. 525.

16 H. Montgomery Hyde and Sir Travers Humphreys, *The Trials of Oscar Wilde: Regina (Wilde) v. Queensbury: Regina v. Wilde and Taylor* (London: William Hodge & Co., 1948), p. 339.

17 Oscar Wilde, 'The Soul of Man under Socialism', *Fortnightly Review* (1891, 290), p. 303.

18 Richard Ellmann, *Oscar Wilde* (New York: Knopf, 1988), pp. 495–506.

19 Frank Harris and Alfred Lord Douglas, *Oscar Wilde, His Life and Confessions: Including the Hitherto Unpublished Full and Final Confession by Lord Alfred Douglas and My Memories of Oscar Wilde by Bernard Shaw* (New York: Garden City, 1930), pp. 232–3, 235.

20 Oscar Wilde, *Oscar Wilde: The Major Works*, ed. Isobel Murray (Oxford: Oxford University Press, 2000), p. 554, ll. 223–8.

21 P.G. Wodehouse, *Something Fresh* (London: Arrow, 2010), p. 10.

22 They have co-authored an article (currently in review): 'Indoor Versus Outdoor Running: Understanding How Recreational Exercise Comes to Inhabit Environments Through the Detail of Practitioner Talk'.

23 In an online survey of 1,600 participants in 2012, the Nuffield Health charity found that those who earn £20k or over spend three times the amount of time in the gym than those on lower incomes. www.nuffieldhealth.com/fitness-and-wellbeing/news/exercise-good-your-salary-survey-reveals.

24 Longnian Lina, Remus Osana and Joe Z. Tsien, 'Organizing Principles of Real-time Memory Encoding: Neural Clique Assemblies and Universal Neural Codes', *Trends in Neurosciences* (2006, 29:1), pp. 48–57.

25 Walter Pater, *Studies in the History of the Renaissance*, ed. Matthew Beaumont (Oxford: Oxford University Press, 2010), p. 120.

26 *See* Alex Huryn and John Hobbie, *Land of Extremes: A Natural History of the Arctic North Slope of Alaska* (Fairbanks: University of Alaska Press, 2012), p. 58.

27 George Orwell, 'Pleasure Spots', *Tribune* (11 January 1946), reprinted in *In Front of Your Nose: The Collected Essays, Journalism and Letters of George Orwell, Volume 4, 1945–1950*, ed. Sonia Orwell and Ian Angus (London: Secker, 1968).

28 Charles Dickens, *Bleak House* (Oxford: Oxford University Press, 1996), p. 235 (and throughout).

29 'Domicilium', in Thomas Hardy, *Thomas Hardy: The Complete Poems*, ed. James Gibson (Basingstoke: Palgrave, 2001), p. 3.

30 Cholera was rife in the capital, but it is said that it was only because of the peculiar heat at the time, and the situation of the Houses of Parliament within smelling range right on the Thames, that the legislation was passed by government to fund a completely new sewage system for the capital – one on which it still relies. *See* Stephen Halliday, *The Great Stink of London: Sir Joseph Bazalgette and the Cleansing of the Victorian Metropolis* (Stroud: Sutton, 2001).

31 *See* Evelyn Hardy and Robert Gittings, *Some Recollections of Emma Hardy* (Oxford: Oxford University Press, 1980).

32 This was Emma Gifford's own figure, meaning that nine miles was the distance between her and her closest neighbours of an equivalent class, not including the more local farm hands and labourers.

33 'Poems of 1912–3', in Hardy, *Thomas Hardy: The Complete Poems*.

34 'Green Slates', in Hardy, *Thomas Hardy: The Complete Poems*, p. 3.

35 Thomas Hardy, *A Pair of Blue Eyes*, ed. Pamela Dalziel (London: Penguin, 1998), p. 215.

36 In her autobiographical recollections, Emma said: 'Scarcely any author and his wife could have had a much more romantic meeting with its unusual circumstances in bringing them together from two different though neighbouring counties such to this one at this very remote spot, with beautiful sea-coast, and the wild Atlantic Ocean rolling in with its magnificent waves and spray.' Quoted by Thomas Hardy, in *The Life and Work of Thomas Hardy*, ed. Michael Millgate (London: Macmillan, 1989), p. 71.

37 'Wessex Heights', in Hardy, *Thomas Hardy: The Complete Poems*, pp. 319–20, ll. 1–4, 13–16.

38 Simeon Brough, *Narcissi & Other Poems* (Hastings: Brough, 1882), p. 11.

39 'Wessex Heights', in Hardy, *Thomas Hardy: The Complete Poems*, p. 320, ll. 29–32.

Chapter 7

1 Edwin A. Abbott, *Flatland* (London, 1884).

2 *See* Jon Cook, *Hazlitt in Love* (London: Short Books, 2007); Duncan Wu, *William Hazlitt: The First Modern Man* (Oxford: Oxford University Press, 2008); and A.C. Grayling, *The Quarrel of the Age: The Life and Times of William Hazlitt* (London: Weidenfeld & Nicolson, 2000).

3 The essay was first published in January 1822, but later appeared in the second volume of his *Table-Talk* essays later that year. *See* William Hazlitt, *Table-Talk; or, Original Essays on Men and Manners* (London: Henry Colburn, 1824).

4 Anon., *Liber Amoris: or, The New Pygmalion* (London: John Hunt, 1823).

5 There are efforts in the UK to change the law for greater access. Don't get excited, though; it is not for us. It is to permit fracking companies the freedom to run pipes and diagonal bore holes under private land to permit access to and transportation of shale gas, without having to pay the landowner for the privilege.

6   Elizabeth Gaskell, *Mary Barton: A Tale of Manchester Life* (London: Penguin, 2009).

7   The 1953 case of Crewdson and Gregory tells of their sustaining injury from their legs up to their head by a gun blast. The gamekeeper said that he had mistakenly loaded the gun with a 12-bore cartridge instead of a blank and was acquitted. *See* Tom Stephenson and Ann Holt, *Forbidden Land: The Struggle for Access to Mountain and Moorland; with a Personal Memoir by Mike Harding* (Manchester: Manchester University Press, 1989), pp. 90–2.

8   Matthew Hollis, *Now All Roads Lead to France: The Last Years of Edward Thomas* (London: Faber & Faber, 2011).

9   Major Tufton Beamish, member for Lewes, 31 March 1949: 'It was quite obvious to me that 95 per cent of those . . . who wished to abolish these snorts were townsmen who probably did not know the difference between a badger and a fox or, at any rate, not the difference between their smells.' His greatest concern was that his friends that enjoyed, hunting, shooting and fishing could continue to do so in peace, without the darned rabble ruining it for everyone. The debate can be read in full on Hansard: hansard. millbanksystems.com/commons/1949/mar/31/national-parks-and-access-to-the.

10   'Privatisation of UK Woodlands is Happening by the Backdoor', *Guardian*: www.theguardian.com/environment/blog/2015/feb/17/privatisation-uk-woodlands-happening-by-backdoor. 'Despite its wildlife, landscape and wider social value, the Forestry Commission believes that Fineshade wood is the right place to plonk down 70 luxury holiday cabins, extra roads, and a sewage treatment plant.'

11   John Clare, 'Trespass', in *The Poems of John Clare*, 2 vols, ed. J.W. Tibble (London: J.M. Dent, 1935), vol. II, p. 373.

12   Iain Sinclair, *London Orbital: A Walk around the M25* (London: Granta, 2002); *London Orbital*, dir. Christopher Petit, Iain Sinclair, Keith Griffiths, released 31 August 2002.

13 Henry David Thoreau, *The Portable Thoreau*, ed. Jeffrey S. Cramer (London: Penguin, 2012), p. 560.

14 The Situationist International movement was a loose collection of anti-authoritarian Marxists and avant-garde writers, artists and thinkers, most prominent in Paris in the 1960s.

15 Guy Debord, 'Introduction to a Critique of Urban Geography', in *Situationist International: Anthology*, ed. Ken Knabb (Berkeley: Bureau of Public Secrets, 1981), p. 8.

16 George Orwell, 'Pleasure Spots', *Tribune* (11 January 1946), reprinted in *In Front of Your Nose: The Collected Essays, Journalism and Letters of George Orwell, Volume 4, 1945–1950*, ed. Sonia Orwell and Ian Angus (London: Secker, 1968).

17 George Orwell, *The Complete Works of George Orwell: Down and Out in Paris and London*, ed. Peter Davison (London: Secker, 1986); Ernest Hemingway, *A Moveable Feast* (London: Jonathan Cape, 1964).

18 Martin Heidegger, *Nietzsche I (1936–39)*, ed. Brigitte Schillbach (Frankfurt: Klostermann, 1996), p. 99.

Chapter 8

1 William Golding, *The Inheritors* (London: Faber & Faber, 1955), p. 1.

2 *See* Book 10 of Plato, *Republic*, ed. & trans. C.J. Rowe (London: Penguin, 2012).

3 Cory Doctorow has already used similar terminology in describing his efforts to achieve focus and concentration while writing at his desk. Cory Doctorow, 'Writing in the Age of Distraction', *Locus* (January 2009).

4 *See* Peter Hampson Ditchfield, *English Villages* (London: Methuen, 1901), p. 33.

5 Alastair Dunn, *The Great Rising of 1381: The Peasants' Revolt and England's Failed Revolution* (Stroud: Tempus, 2002), *see* p. 78; and Jonathan Sumption, *Divided Houses: The Hundred Years War III* (London: Faber & Faber, 2009).

6 Alison Weir, *Lancaster and York: The Wars of the Roses* (London: Jonathan Cape, 1995); Edward Vallance, *A Radical History of Britain* (London: Abacus, 2009); I.M.W. Harvey, *Jack Cade's Rebellion of 1450* (Oxford: Oxford University Press, 1991).

7 Ann Wroe, *The Perfect Prince: The Mystery of Perkin Warbeck and His Quest for the Throne of England* (New York: Random House, 2004), pp. 307–11.

8 I looked at the photo again just recently, and although I wasn't fat, I was surprised how much heavier I was on my 40-mile week. This is common among marathon trainees: so much cortisol is released into the system by the stress of the training. Without the adequate recovery times of a normal training schedule, the hormone tells the body to store abdominal fat.

9 *The Stones of Venice II*, in John Ruskin, *The Works of John Ruskin*, eds Edward Tyas Cook and Alexander Wedderburn, 39 vols (London: George Allen, 1903–12), vol. 10, p. 193.

10 John Ruskin, *Pre-Raphaelitism*, pamphlet, 1851.

11 One of the odd things about this period of industrialisation was that it led to a north–south divide in wages in the middle of the nineteenth century. Because of the rise of the factories in the north, wages climbed too – leaving the south of England poorer as a result.

12 *The Stones of Venice II*, in Ruskin, *The Works of John Ruskin*, vol. 10, p. 161.

13 John Ruskin, *Seven Lamps of Architecture* (London: George Allen, 1903), p. 218.

14 *See* Charles Nicholl, *Leonardo da Vinci: The Flights of the Mind* (London: Penguin, 2005), pp. 121–2.

15 These comments were made in a miscellaneous collection of da Vinci's papers (*Codex Atlanticus*, held at the Biblioteca Ambrosiana in Milan) and have been transcribed elsewhere in various editions of his notebooks. *See* Leonardo da Vinci, *Notebooks of Leonardo da Vinci*, eds Irma A. Richter and Thereza Wells (Oxford: Oxford University Press, 2008), p. 267.

16 'Richard Hawley: "At night, invisible roller skates come out of my shoes and propel me towards the pub"', *Guardian* (22 October 2015).

Epilogue

1 'The number of people taking part in athletics weekly has risen from 1.4 million in 2005-06 to over 2.3 million today.' *See* www.sportengland.org/research/who-plays-sport/by-sport/.

2 *See Coronary Heart Disease Statistics* (London: British Heart Foundation, 2012), https://www.bhf.org.uk/~/media/files/publications/research/2012_chd_statistics_compendium.pdf.

3 *See* 'Healthy Life Expectancy: Key Points' (Scottish Public Health Observatory), www.scotpho.org.uk/population-dynamics/healthy-life-expectancy/key-points.

4 *See* 'Deprivation and Health: A Report by the National Public Health Service for Wales', www2.nphs.wales.nhs.uk:8080/hiatdocs.nsf/c944d98bdfffc71880257005004 3d5cd/2eaebe01733430f8802576ea004bc063/$FILE/Deprivationreport10Dec04.pdf.

ACKNOWLEDGEMENTS

Writing a book is the most satisfying way of accruing debts that, unlike the financial kind, are both a joy to remember and easy to repay. Arts Council England kindly helped to fund some of the research in the latter stages of the book, as did the University of Kent – and I'm especially grateful to my colleagues who granted me study leave to complete the manuscript (and to David Herd and Peter Brown, in particular); as well to the editors of *Critical Survey* for permission to use part of 'Running Wilde: Landscape, the Body, and the History of the Treadmill', 24:3, in chapter 6. I am indebted to the staff of the London Library for their help in tracking down some of the source materials, and to the magus Kev Carvosso, and all at Back on Track in Catford, for keeping me on the road.

Gathering material for this book, I was on many occasions the recipient of the generosity of the artists, academics and researchers in fields other than mine that patiently gave their time and advice so that I might get up to speed in their disciplines, among them: the unbelievably impressive Irene Davis, Robert Morrison and Hannah Rice at Spaulding, Daniel Lieberman at Harvard, Jason Duvall and Avik Basu at Michigan, Mike Rogerson and John Wooller at Essex, Alan Latham and Russell Hitchings at UCL, Simon Cook at Royal Hollway, Véronique Chance at Anglia Ruskin, Ryan Fong and Eleanor Adkins; most read parts of the manuscript, but any errors remain my own. Rod Edmond, Amy Sackville, Catherine Brereton and Jennie Batchelor all had the patience to read the first draft of the manuscript in its entirety; Carolyn Burdett, Ariane Mildenberg and Holly Furneaux kindly shared their thoughts on sections.

Several people helped me from the very beginning of this book. Scarlett Thomas is an inspiration and she remains the single most enjoyable person to compete with in the world (I bet my acknowledgements are better than yours), and I thank her for enthusiasm and guidance. Lynne Truss has been a great friend and also gave lots of helpful advice as well as the occasional room to write in. I am grateful to Josephine Greywoode and Judith Murray for looking at the bigger picture earlier in the process.

Very special thanks to my agent, Jane Graham-Maw at GMC (non-fiction supremo!) for all the help and encouragement; to my editors at Ebury: Andrew Goodfellow for championing the book, and especially Anna Mrowiec who has been a doughty pleasure to work with and has seen everything through to completion with assured expertise. I have David Surman to thank for his sublime skill as an illustrator, and the wonderful Will Atkins for his keen eye.

I have Johanna Reid to thank for many things, among them, with Margaret Cantwell, their shared knowledge of their brother, Jim Hogan. Thanks to Siân Prime for being as great a friend as she is a capable supporter and advisor. And over the years, Erika, Adam, Ralph and Liberty Sinclair, Rebecca, Mike, Lloyd, Elliot and Scarlet Fairhurst, John, Lauren and Natasha Reid, Huw Bevan, Nicola Ibba, Aylla MacPhail and Sandra Cryan, have all encouraged me along the paths. Some students have followed me along those paths, too, especially Alice Bryant, Lev Green, Hannah Preece, Emily Rowe, Courtney Salvey and Molly Shrimpton; I'm grateful to all. Last, or first, among these is Adam O'Farrell for his enduring kindness and enthusiasm (and, not least, those hundreds of glasses of water that were at the ready when I tumbled in from a run). For these, and the numerous other kindnesses over the years, thank you.

If you would like to see pictures of some of the places where I ran – often from the day that the run described took place – or if you'd just like to say hello, please come and find me at www.psychojography.com or on Twitter @vybarr.